IMPERIAL BYZANTINE PORTRAITS

IMPERIAL BYZANTINE PORTRAITS

A Verbal and Graphic Gallery

Constance Head

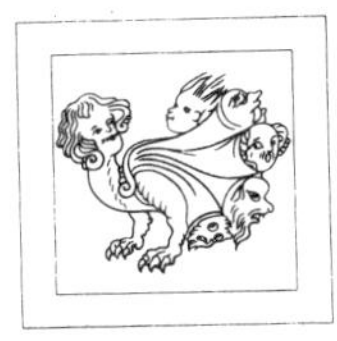

CARATZAS BROTHERS, PUBLISHERS
NEW ROCHELLE, NEW YORK
1982

Acknowledgment is made for permissions given by the following institutions to reproduce works in their collections: Musei Capitolini, Rome; The Louvre, Bibliothèque Nationale, Paris; The American Numismatic Society, New York; Real Academia de la Historia, Biblioteca Nacional, Madrid; Ny Carlsberg Glyptotek, Copenhagen; Museo Nazionale del Bargello, Florence; The British Museum, London; Dumbarton Oaks, Washington, D.C.; Marcian Library, Venice; Biblioteca Apostolica Vaticana; Biblioteca Estense, Modena, Österreichische Nationalbibliothek, Vienna; Bayerische Staatsbibliothek, Munich; Landesbibliothek, Stuttgart. Acknowledgment is made to Walter de Gruyter & Co. for permission to reproduce illustrations from the 1933 edition of Delbrueck's *Spätantike Kaiserporträts*, and to Hirmer Fotoarchiv, Munich; Fotografia Calvaresi, Barletta; and Bildarchiv Foto, Marburg for permission to reproduce photographs.

Library of Congress Number 82-072211

ISBN 0-89241-084-1

Published by

Caratzas Publishing Co. Inc.
Distributed by
Caratzas Brothers, Publishers
Box 210 (481 Main Street)
New Rochelle, New York 10802 (U.S.A)

Contents

Preface

At the outset, it is essential to clarify what this volume sets out to do: as the subtitle indicates, it presents "a verbal and graphic gallery" of the Byzantine emperors. The book is a survey, designed to deepen the reader's acquaintance with the eighty-eight reigning sovereigns of Byzantium through a fusion of political history and iconography. Above all, my objective in this work is to present the emperors as individual human beings, not simply as figures in pictures nor as the faceless, characterless names and numbers they sometimes become in political narratives.

Imperial Byzantine Portraits claims no definitive status. Although for some of the emperors, several notable portraits exist, the prohibitive expenses of printing have necessitated choosing (in almost every instance) only one likeness per ruler. Interested readers will find in the notes, suggested readings, and bibliography information on the location of other portraits. The annotated bibliography also contains a survey of important works in the field of Byzantine imperial iconography. Since the early efforts of S. Lampros to collect "all" the imperial portraits he could discover in his *Leukoma ton Byzantinon Autokratoron* (Album of the Byzantine Emperors), several notable studies have appeared dealing specifically with the theme of imperial iconography from the standpoint of art history. André Grabar's *L'Empereur dans l'art byzantin*, presenting a topical rather than chronological approach, remains the classic in the field. Much more recent, and certain to prove of immense value for the whole study of portraiture in Byzantine art is the monograph by Ioannis Spatharakis, *The Portrait in Byzantine Illuminated Manuscripts*.

Throughout the Empire's long existence, depiction of the emperor was a frequent subject of artistic endeavor, and although much has undoubtedly been lost, contemporary portraits of many of the Byzantine sovereigns still exist. Most of the earliest Byzantine emperors are commemorated by statues; later, when sculpture in the round ceased to be produced in the Byzantine world, mosaic work and ivory carving provide excellent likenesses of some of the emperors. Many others are depicted in manuscript miniatures, ranging in character from the elegant portraits of Nikephoros Botaneiates in a devotional volume designed for his own use to the crude but lively illustrations of Skylitzes' *Chronicle*, relating Byzantine history in a long series of story-telling pictures.

But while there is a wealth of iconographic material for a number of the Byzantine rulers, for certain others the only available likeness is a coin portrait, and through much of Byzantine history, the monarch's image on the coins is so stylized as to provide no clue to his actual appearance. Other issues, however, present vivid glimpses of the rulers depicted, for instance the coins of the fat, round-faced Leontios, the long-bearded Constans, or the sword-wielding Isaac Komnenos.

Although I have made free use of numismatic likenesses of the emperors, as needed, there is no intention in the present volume to dwell in detail on this area of Byzantine art. Several very excellent modern works (including those of Whitting, Wroth, Hendy, and the lavish *Dumbarton Oaks Catalogues*) treat the subject of Byzantine numismatic iconography in detail, and interested readers can find a wealth of material in the volumes listed in the bibliography.

Whenever possible in the following series of Byzantine imperial portraits, a contemporary likeness has been chosen; when such is not available some later work of Byzantine art is provided (and even, in a few instances, works from the post-Byzantine period). Effort is made, too, in the accompanying text to quote source writers who give physical descriptions of the emperors. Though in some eras of history, such descriptions are entirely lacking, many Byzantine chroniclers and historians, true to the classical tradition, attempted to supply vivid word-portraits of their sovereigns. Through comparison of these with the graphic likenesses, and through the accompanying biographical summaries, it is our object to show the Byzantine emperors as eighty-eight distinctive individuals, each of whose life and personality made its impact on the great and long-lived empire of a thousand years.

With the rapid proliferation of books and monographs in many languages in recent years, bibliographies can no longer hope to be exhaustive. The selected bibliography at the end of the present volume consists of several parts. First is a listing of the major primary sources consulted and cited in the notes. Then follows an annotated survey of particularly helpful secondary studies in the specialized fields of imperial iconography and numismatics, and the following section directs the reader to general narrative works that cover large blocks of Byzantine political history. The notes and suggested readings at the end of each imperial biography are designed to provide additional bibliographical guidance. While preference is given to works in English, some important studies in other languages have also been cited.

Byzantium—the Roman Empire of the East—is still an unfamiliar land to many readers of history. There through the thousand years that historians have come to call the Middle Ages, the heritage of classical Greece and Rome lived on. There for eleven centuries ruled an unbroken line of emperors, fascinating individuals about whom a wealth of information is preserved, yet who, all too often, are mere names on a list even to persons genuinely interested in the medieval world.

The eighty-eight emperors of Byzantium present a sundry gallery, from uneducated peasants to princes born-in-the-purple, from powerful warriors to peaceable stay-at-homes. There are a few who reached the throne in childhood and others who did not attain power until their old age. There are saints and profligates; men of learning and those who scorned culture. There is the long-lived Basil II whose reign spanned half a century, and the tragic Stavrakios whose entire reign consisted of a few weeks of death-bed agony., There are the women: the cruel 'Emperor' Irene, frivolous 'Little Mother' Zoe, the aged nun Theodora Porphyrogenita, and the crafty widow Eudokia Makrembolitissa. A diverse assembly were these wearers of the Byzantine crown, yet alike in one thing: the belief cherished by Byzantines through the centuries that each emperor was chosen for rulership by the Hand of God. Imperial birth was never an absolute prerequisite for the throne, for even though a family might reign for several generations, it was still felt by the Byzantines that God could select His chosen one from any walk of life. Thus, if He willed to give the crown to an illiterate peasant or a small town tax-collector or a champion wrestler (and all these things actually happened), there was no Byzantine who would have denied that these events reflected the mysterious workings of the divine plan.

And yet what God gave, He might take away from one who proved unworthy. Most of the emperors were hard-working, dedicated statesmen, who understood their office as a sacred charge. Those who failed in this respect usually did not last long, for to the Byzantine, the Hand of God well might move through revolution.

Then finally came a time when Byzantium was no more, when the last of the emperors, Constantine XI, gave his life for his people and the imperial city passed into the hands of the Turks. May 29, 1453—the end of the empire is a date easily pinpointed.

It is considerably more difficult to determine the point at which Byzantine history begins. The Byzantines themselves saw their empire as the continuator of ancient Rome. They would always speak of themselves as 'Romans'; Constantinople was the 'New Rome', and the emperors who ruled there were the heirs not only of Constantine the Great and Theodosius, but of Caesar Augustus.

These ties with ancient Rome notwithstanding, it is true none the less that it was the fourth Christian century—a century of vast upheaval and change, of the fading of antiquity and the beginning of the Middle Ages—that witnessed the origin of several of the most crucial elements of Byzantinism. It was then that Christianity, for three hundred years a forbidden sect, was transformed into a prop for the imperial throne. Recognized by a series of imperial converts beginning with the first Constantine, Christianity became, before the fourth century was over, the only lawful religion.

The relocation of the Roman imperial capital in the east in A.D. 330 is equally significant for the beginnings of the Byzantine world. The small town of Byzantium, renamed Constantinople and promoted to supreme rank by its founder, would always be the hub of Byzantine civilization, the 'city of all cities', seemingly secure and well defended behind its mighty walls, glittering with the prosperity engendered by vast trade that poured into its markets from all over the known world.

It is understandable, then, why the roll of the Byzantine rulers usually begins with Constantine the Great, the first Christian emperor and mover of the capital. Without the City and the Faith, Byzantine history is unthinkable.

CONSTANTINE I, THE GREAT
306-337

Visionary or crafty schemer, enlightened despot or heavy-handed tyrant, Constantine the Great is among the most significant men in world history. His decisions unalterably affected the course of Western civilization, yet he left only a few traces of his genuine personality behind a mass of pious legend and folklore.

Born on February 17, probably in the year 274, Flavius Valerius Constantine was the son of Helena, an innkeeper's daughter, and Constantius Chlorus, a Roman officer. Although his birthplace, Naissus in Illyria (present-day Nish, Yugoslavia) is well attested, medieval legends frequently depicted him as a native of Britain and fancifully transformed his mother Helena into a British princess, daughter of 'old King Cole'.

After his parents were divorced, Constantine, then a young man in his teens, was sent to the court of Diocletian, the Roman emperor of the East, as a hostage for his father's loyalty to the crown. Later, when Diocletian abdicated and Constantius Chlorus reigned briefly as Emperor of the West, Constantine escaped to join him. Chlorus died while on campaign in Britain in 306. Although, according to Diocletian's long-range plans, the imperial succession was not supposed to be hereditary, the troops who had fought for Chlorus acclaimed his son Constantine as emperor.

In the next years, Constantine faced and defeated several other claimants to the throne. Most significant was his victory over his brother-in-law and rival, Emperor Maxentius, at Milvian Bridge near Rome in 312. Shortly before this encounter, Constantine claimed to have had a vision in which the God of the Christians promised him assistance. Constantine's forces marched into battle under the sign of the Chi-Rho ☧ , a symbol derived from the first two letters of the name of Christ in Greek. Though he was not baptized until many years later, Constantine began to look with favor upon the Christian Church, granting not only religious freedom but extensive favors, tax exemptions, gifts of land, and generally preferential treatment. One of his notable achievements was sponsorship of the building of the original St. Peter's Basilica on the Vatican Hill; his wife Fausta donated her Lateran Palace to become the residence of the Bishop of Rome.

Constantine spent most of his long reign in the western provinces and in Rome. In 324, he defeated another brother-in-law, Licinius, who governed the East, and thus united the whole empire under his rule. His sponsorship of the great ecumenical Council of Nicaea in 325 is a milestone in church history. While it failed in its objective of eliminating heresy, the Council's effort to resolve the theological differences between Arian and Athanasian Christians

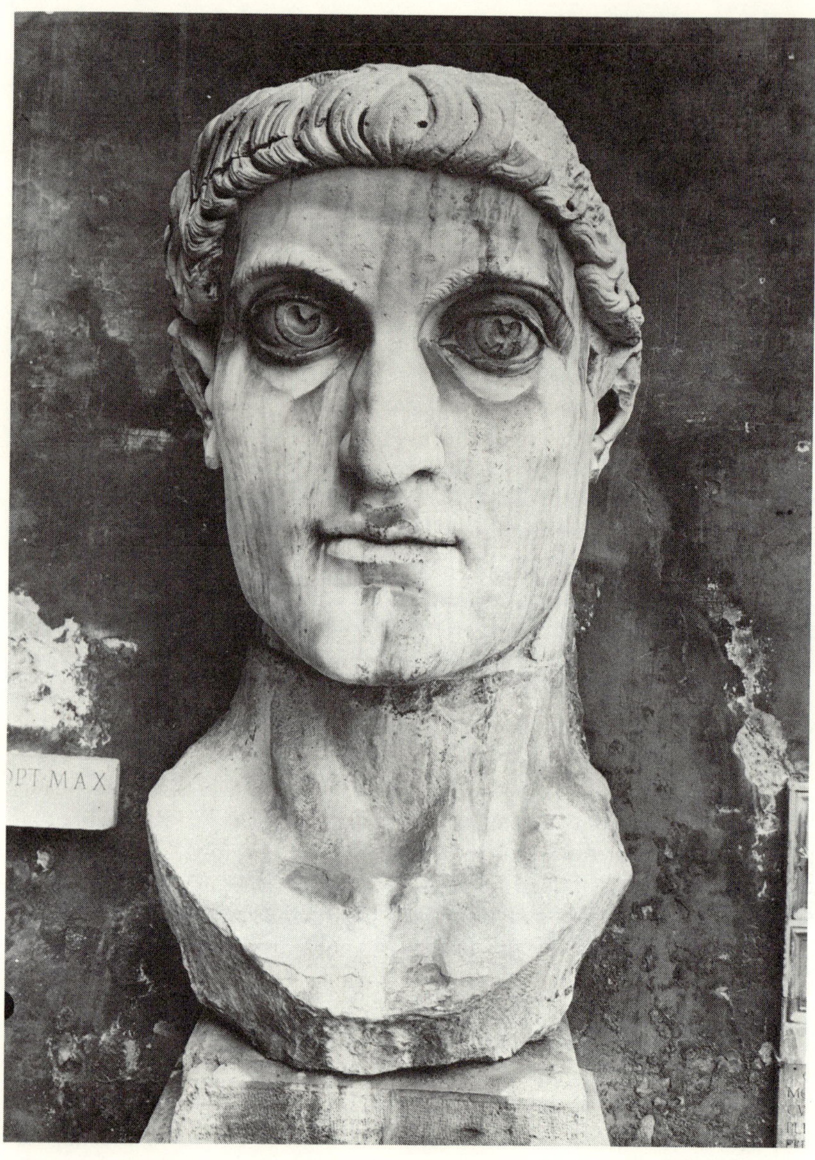

Constantine I, marble head. Palazzo dei Conservatori, Rome.

set the precedent for imperial intervention in ecclesiastical affairs, a prerogative which the later Byzantine emperors never gave up.

Several years later, Constantine carried out his plans for building the new capital city in the East that would bear his name. Geographically, Constantinople was ideally situated; surrounded on three sides by water, it was at the crossroads of East-West commerce and easy to defend in times of war. Dedicated as the New Rome on May 11, 330, Constantinople was the emperor's principal residence until his death seven years later.

Constantine's personal life was marred by tragedies, chief among them the mysterious deaths of his wife Fausta and his oldest son Crispus. Crispus was Constantine's son by an early liaison with a woman called Minervina, and apparently was much hated by his step-mother Fausta. It seems that she contrived false charges against Crispus, and that Constantine, believing them, ordered his son's execution. Later, discovering Fausta's treachery, he killed her, too, reportedly by scalding her in her bath. Details of the whole sordid matter remain most uncertain, as Constantine was determined to erase Fausta from history, and it was not until well after his death that historians dared to report anything about her.

In spite of these unseemly blots on the record of the first Christian emperor, Constantine was generally a humane ruler, and most authorities hold that his enthusiasm for Christianity was motivated by genuine religious feeling. Ignoring his inclinations toward Arian Christianity in his later years, Eastern Orthodoxy reveres him as a saint. His mother Helena, who is famed for her great pilgrimage to the Holy Land in her old age and her reputed discovery of numerous relics, is sainted both by the Orthodox East and the Latin West.

Constantine accepted baptism on his deathbed from the hands of an Arian Christian bishop. Presumably, he died happy, believing all his sins were washed away.

Coin portraits of Constantine usually depict him in profile with his gaze directed upward, as if anticipating another heavenly vision. Several excellent sculptured likenesses of Constantine also exist; perhaps best known is the colossal head now located at the Palazzo dei Conservatori in Rome. The written sources are less satisfactory, since Constantine's contemporaries give only vague and idealized descriptions of his appearance. For instance, his close friend, Bishop Eusebius of Caesarea, recalled that when Constantine was young, "No one was comparable to him for grace and beauty of person, or height of stature," and at the age of about sixty, "he still possessed a sound and vigorous body, free from all blemish and of more than youthful vivacity."[1] More details appear in the much later chronicle compilation of Cedrenus, who writes: "The Great Constantine was of medium height, with broad shoulders and a thick neck. His skin was ruddy; his hair neither thick nor curly; his beard sparse, his nose somewhat crooked, his eyes lion-like, and his countenance most serene."[2]

---

[1]Eusebius, *Vita Constantini*, I.19 and IV.53. (Anon. Bagster, pp. 20 and 218.)

[2]Cedrenus (Bonn), I, 472–473.

CONSTANTIUS II
337-361

The second of the three sons of Constantine and Fausta, Constantius II (who turned out to be his father's favorite), was named for his grandfather, Chlorus, who is counted as Constantius I. Born August 7, 317, the second Constantius was not quite twenty years old when his father died and he succeeded to the throne of the eastern Empire, including Constantinople. The western provinces were assigned to his two brothers, Constantine II and Constans I, who were also granted the imperial title.

Among the first acts of Emperor Constantius was the massacre of most of his close male relatives (except his two brothers, who were far away). Although some sources allege that the army acted spontaneously, without official orders for these slayings, it is more likely that it was a deliberate step by young Constantius designed to eliminate rival claimants for the throne.

In the area of religion, Constantius aligned himself with Christianity of the Arian sect, the group that believed that Jesus Christ is of similar substance, but not the same, as God the Father. Though the Council of Nicaea had pronounced Arianism heretical, it still had numerous adherents. Like Constantine before him, Constantius devoted a great deal of time to the religious squabbles of the rival Christian sects, and seemed to delight in theological argument. Orthodox (Athanasian) Christians were sometimes persecuted during his reign, and pagans found it wise not to be too outspoken in their loyalty to the old gods.

Throughout Constantius's long reign, the empire was torn by incursions of barbarian tribes along the northern frontiers and by war with the strong Persian kingdom to the east. Although he sometimes led his troops in person, the emperor preferred to remain in the security of his palace and to write up 'official' reports of his forces' victories, claiming that he had been present personally on the field and had played a crucial role in his enemies' defeat.[1]

Constantius apparently got along well enough with both his brothers, and avoided taking part in their quarrels with each other. Since both of them died young and neither had sons, Constantius, from 350 until his death, was emperor of the entire Roman world. In his later years, he spent much of his time in the West, in his palace in Milan.

Rival claimants to his throne continued to appear sporadically throughout his reign, but Constantius was always successful in quashing the various rebels who sought to replace him. The intrigues of his court are depicted in somber tones by the contemporary historian Ammianus Marcellinus; the emperor, it seems, was entirely too dependent on the counsel of certain court eunuchs and other unsavory characters. On the other hand, he was famed for his deep

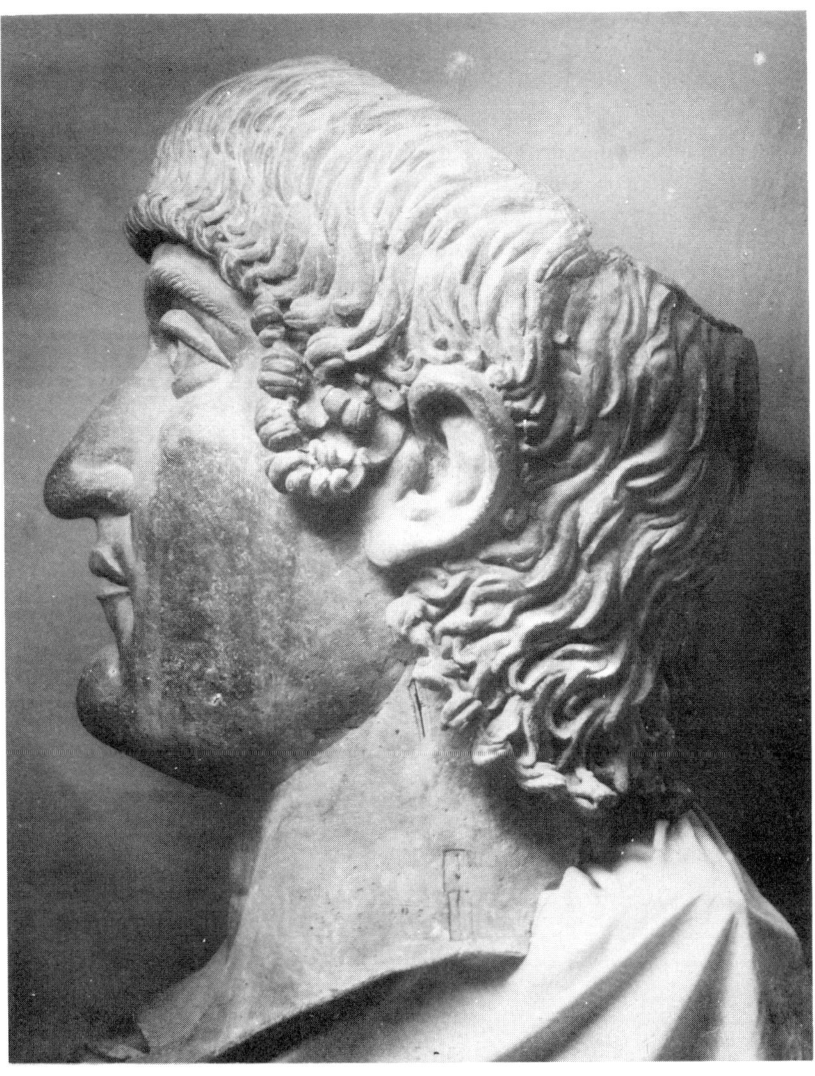

Constantius, bronze head. Palazzo dei Conservatori, Rome.

devotion and loyalty to his second wife, the beautiful Eusebia of Macedon, who exerted considerable good influence upon her difficult husband.

Neither his first wife Galla (who died very young) nor her successor Eusebia presented Constantius with an heir. Troubled by the uncertainties of the succession, he finally appointed one of his few surviving kinsmen, his cousin Gallus, as Caesar, only to discover that Gallus was cruel and unstable, totally unfit to rule. The young man was executed, and Julian, Gallus' half-brother, was appointed Caesar in his place. He would eventually be Constantius' successor, for though Constantius fathered a posthumous daughter by his third wife, Faustina of Antioch, she was never considered a candidate for the succession.

According to Ammianus Marcellinus, Constantius was much admired for his conspicuous self-control during public appearances. He could ride through throngs of his subjects looking neither right nor left, as immobile as a statue. Ammianus remarks, too, that he never spat in public—a revealing commentary on the times, since this was considered a sign of unusually elegant manners.[2] Ammianus also provides an interesting description of Constantius' physique: "He was rather dark, with bulging eyes, and sharp-sighted; his hair was soft and his regularly shaven cheeks were neat and shining; from the meeting of neck and shoulders to the groin he was unusually long, but his legs were very short and bowed, for which reason he was good at running and leaping."[3] Cedrenus adds that he was "golden-haired."[4] The bronze head preserved in the Palazzo dei Conservatori, with its unflattering rendering of his prominent hooked nose, is probably a reliable portrait and originally may have been part of a full statue. Another likeness of Constantius, clad in full armor and mounted on horseback, may be found on a silver plate, presently housed in the Hermitage in Leningrad.[5] Also of interest to art historians is a much later copy of the "Calendar of 354," containing a manuscript portrait of Constantius, seated in splendor and clad in the full consular regalia.[6]

---

[1]Ammianus Marcellinus, XVI.12.69-70 (Rolfe, II, 301-303).

[2]Amm. Marc., XXI.16.7 (Rolfe, II, 177).

[3]Amm. Marc., XXI.16.19 (Rolfe, II, 185).

[4]Cedrenus (Bonn), I, 520-521.

[5]For a full color print of this item, see André Grabar, *The Golden Age of Justinian* (New York, 1967), p. 302.

[6]See E. Condurachi, "L'origine et l'evolution du loros impérial," *Arta şi Arheologia* 11-12 (1935-36), 37.

JULIAN
361-363

Flavius Claudius Julianus, better known as Julian, was the son of a half-brother of Constantine the Great and was the first child of the imperial family born in the new capital city of Constantinople. His mother died when he was an infant. When he was six he lost his father also in Emperor Constantius' massacre of possible rivals for the throne. Although Julian and his half-brother

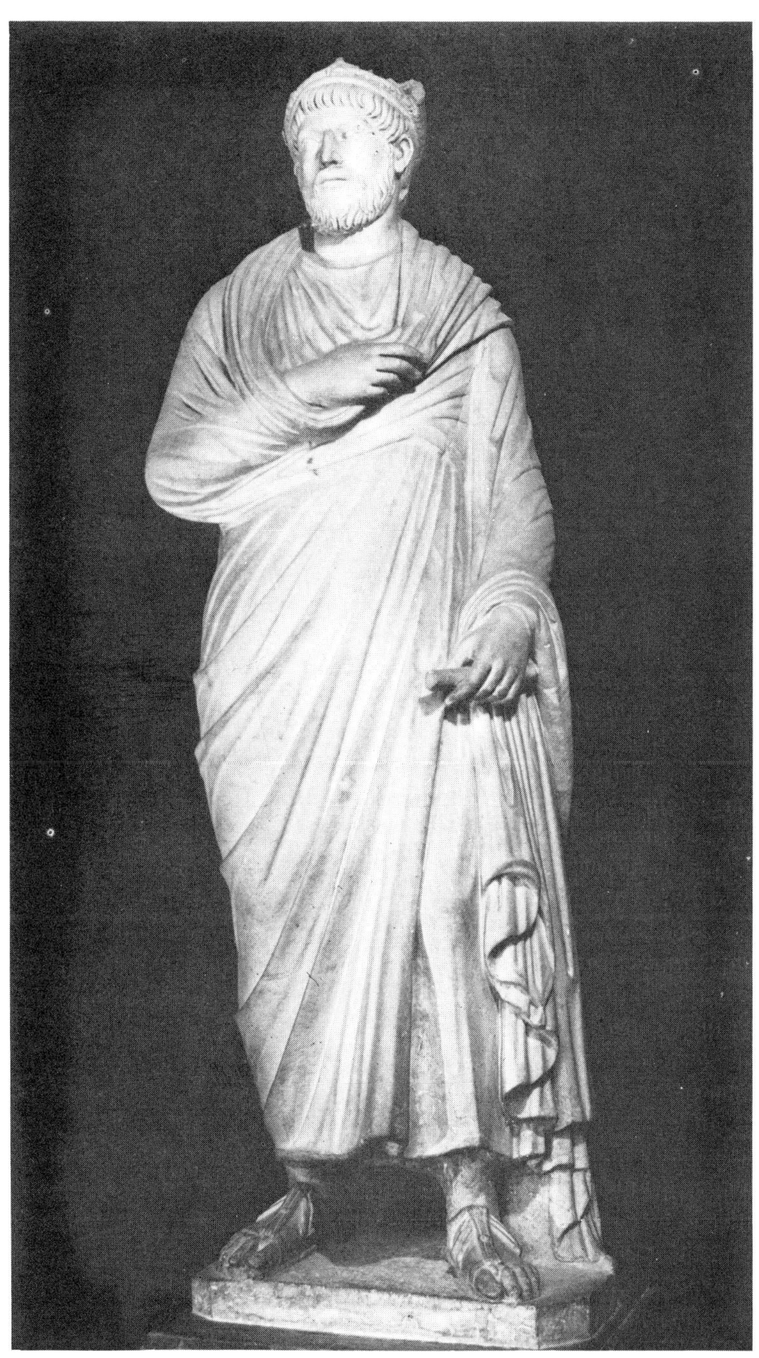

Julian, marble statue. The Louvre.

Gallus were spared from execution because of their youth, their childhood was haunted by insecurity, and for several years they were held in custody in the remote fortress of Macellum in Cappadocia. It is almost certain that Julian's intense dislike of Christianity—the religion of Constantius—grew out of these early experiences.

Young Julian proved to be a brilliant student. But although he became an expert on the content of the Christian scriptures, his real love was the classical literature and philosophy of ancient Greece. To the gods and heroes of antiquity he gave the loyalty he could not give to Christianity.

As Julian grew to manhood, Constantius allowed him to travel to various cities of the empire to continue his education, and at some point in his teens, he was secretly initiated into the cult of Helios-Mithra. Later, he studied for a while in Athens. Although the style of the times dictated that men be clean-shaven, Julian grew a 'philosopher's beard', a fashion he continued to follow as emperor some years later.

Julian's studies were interrupted very suddenly when he was twenty-three and his cousin Constantius decided to make him Caesar of Gaul. Since he had no military training, many (including Julian himself) suspected that Constantius gave him this assignment hoping it would result in his death. Ironically, Julian turned out to be a splendid military man with a gift for strategy and organization that soon won him the intense admiration of his troops. His abilities as a civil administrator, including his granting of substantial tax reductions, also endeared him to the Gallic provincials. Through his years in Gaul, he continued to conform outwardly to the Christian faith (Arian variety), though his close associates knew he was secretly a devout worshipper of the old gods.

At length, incensed over unreasonable orders from Constantius for their transfer to the East, Julian's troops declared him emperor in his cousin's place in A.D. 360. Civil war would have inevitably resulted had not Constantius died before Julian's forces completed the long march from Gaul to Constantinople.

Now as undisputed successor to the empire, Julian announced to the world his intention of restoring the 'Old Religion'. Though he would never have admitted it, his paganism actually borrowed much from Christianity, for he insisted on a high moral code and encouraged charity and benevolence in the name of his gods. Though some of his subjects applauded his ideas, most were astonished by the behavior of this unconventional emperor who liked to write books and make speeches on philosophy. Devout Christians (both Arian and Orthodox) called him 'the Apostate', and despised him heartily when he cancelled all of his recent predecessors' favors to the Church. Incidentally, Julian never seems to have been impressed by the theological differences between Arianism and Orthodoxy, but disliked both varieties of Christianity with equal intensity. His personal philosophy was a curious mixture of superstition, logic, and an ardent belief that all the gods were manifestations of the Unknowable One. Persons of practically all religions, he felt, with the exception of 'stubborn' Christians, could get along together with just a bit of effort. While he was most reluctant to persecute, not wanting to give Christians their longed-for opportunity for martyrdom, a few rabble-rousers who demonstrated too vigorously were apprehended.

Even among Julian's admirers, there were many who deplored his lack of imperial splendor. Unlike the 'living statue' Constantius, Julian cared very little for court etiquette, and disregarded it as much as possible. In physique, he was short and stocky, his clothes were often ill-fitting, and his fingers usually stained with ink from his endless literary endeavors.[1] Intensely moral, even ascetic, in his personal life, he scorned worldly pleasures. His wife, Helena (who was Constantius' sister and was considerably older than Julian) died in Gaul shortly after he claimed the crown. He did not remarry, but chose to bind himself by a vow of celibacy.

Julian's reign lasted less than two years. In 363, he led his army into Persia on a campaign which proved disastrous. In the course of their retreat, Julian was fatally wounded in a skirmish against the Persians. But the weapon that inflicted the blow was reportedly a Roman spear, and many believed, then and now, that the thirty-one-year-old emperor was slain by one of his own men.

Because a great number of his own letters, speeches, and treatises have survived through the ages, Julian is one of the best known of the emperors. He leaves behind him the unforgettable impression of an intense young man: sincere, intelligent, basically kind and decent, deeply committed to his ideals, yet out of harmony with the world in which he lived.

The portrait statue of Julian now located in the Louvre in Paris depicts the emperor clad in the robes of the high priest of paganism, a role he cherished among the most important of his imperial duties.[2] Ammianus Marcellinus, who served in Julian's army both in Gaul and in Persia, presents a vivid description of the emperor's appearance: "His hair lay smooth as if it had been combed, his beard was shaggy and trimmed so as to end in a point, his eyes were fine and full of fire, an indication of the acuteness of his mind. His eyebrows were handsome, his nose very straight, his mouth somewhat large with a pendulous lower lip. His neck was bent, his shoulders large and broad. From top to toe he was a man of straight, well-proportioned bodily frame."[3] Cedrenus adds that Julian's hair was black, a detail found in none of the earlier sources.[4]

---

[1]For Julian's unflattering description of himself see his "Misopogon," (Wright), II, 423-427.

[2]A. Piganiol, "La couronne de Julien César," *Byzantion* 13 (1938), 245.

[3]Amm. Marc., XXV.4.22 (Rolfe, II, 513-515).

[4]Cedrenus (Bonn), I, 531.

JOVIAN
363-364

In spite of his pagan name (which indicates one dedicated to Jove), the emperor Jovian was a Christian, probably of the Orthodox variety. It is more likely that he received his name because his father was commander of the Jovian Legion than from any sign of allegiance to the old gods.

Selected emperor by the army immediately after Julian's death, Jovian was in his early thirties and had served with distinction as an army officer for some years. He was so tall that he seemed almost comical in the imperial robe hastily borrowed from Julian's wardrobe for his first appearance as emperor. Because he was very good-natured, cheerful, and somewhat lacking in imperial dignity, many doubted his prospects of being an effective ruler. Ammianus Marcellinus, who knew him well, particularly regretted his love of "wine and women" and his tendency to jest with his friends in public. But, the historian added, had he reigned longer, he might have eventually proved an excellent ruler since he was basically of a kindly nature.[1]

Jovian's first duty was to secure the withdrawal of his forces from enemy territory and to negotiate a peace with Persia. Eager to end the hostilities he agreed to a generous surrender of frontier territory to the Persians, a move which seemed unnecessarily humiliating to many of his subjects.

Jovian never reached Constantinople. While still on his way toward the imperial capital, he stopped in the town of Dadastana, and there, one morning, he was found dead in his bedroom. Since he had not been ill, some suspected foul play; others suggested that he died of acute indigestion brought on by one of his lavish banquets; but the most likely explanation is that his death was caused by noxious fumes from the charcoal stove near his bed.

Jovian and his wife Charito had a little son, Varronianus, but he was too young to be considered a suitable candidate for emperorship, since the army demanded a ruler who could provide personal leadership.

Other than his emphasis on the fact that Jovian was considerably taller than Julian, Ammianus gives relatively few details of this emperor's appearance. "His eyes were grey," the historian recalls. "He walked with a dignified bearing; his expression was very cheerful."[2] Because his reign was so short—only eight months—apparently the only contemporary portraits of Jovian are to be found on medals and coins.

---

[1] Amm. Marc., XXV.10.15 (Rolfe, II, 563).

[2] Amm. Marc., XXV.5.6 and 10.14 (Rolfe, II, 521 and 563).

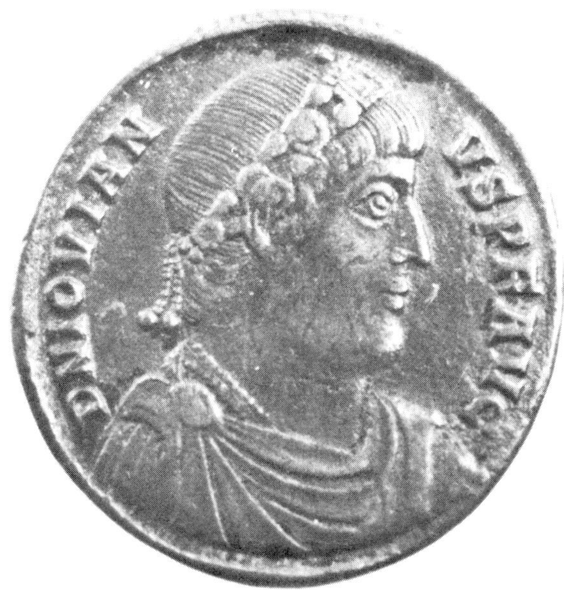

Jovian, coin of his reign. American Numismatic Society.

VALENS
364-378

When Jovian died, the army selected as his successor a prominent young general, Valentinian. Immediately the new emperor was pressured to select a co-emperor from among his associates: the Roman world was simply too large for one-man rule. Valentinian promised to act on this advice and after some days he announced his choice to his officers (almost every one of whom hoped to be chosen). He had selected, he said, the man whom he knew the best and whom he had known for the longest time: his brother, Valens.[1]

Since Valentinian I took charge of the Western Roman Empire and Valens the East, it is the latter who is listed among the Byzantine sovereigns. Because he was an Arian Christian, Valens was very unpopular with his Orthodox subjects. Nor does the pagan historian Ammianus Marcellinus have much good to report of him. He was extremely superstitious and ignorant; "he had an uncultivated mind . . . ," so much so that many men of learning found it prudent to destroy or conceal their personal libraries, for Valens tended to think that books were full of dangerous magic. To Valens' credit Ammianus

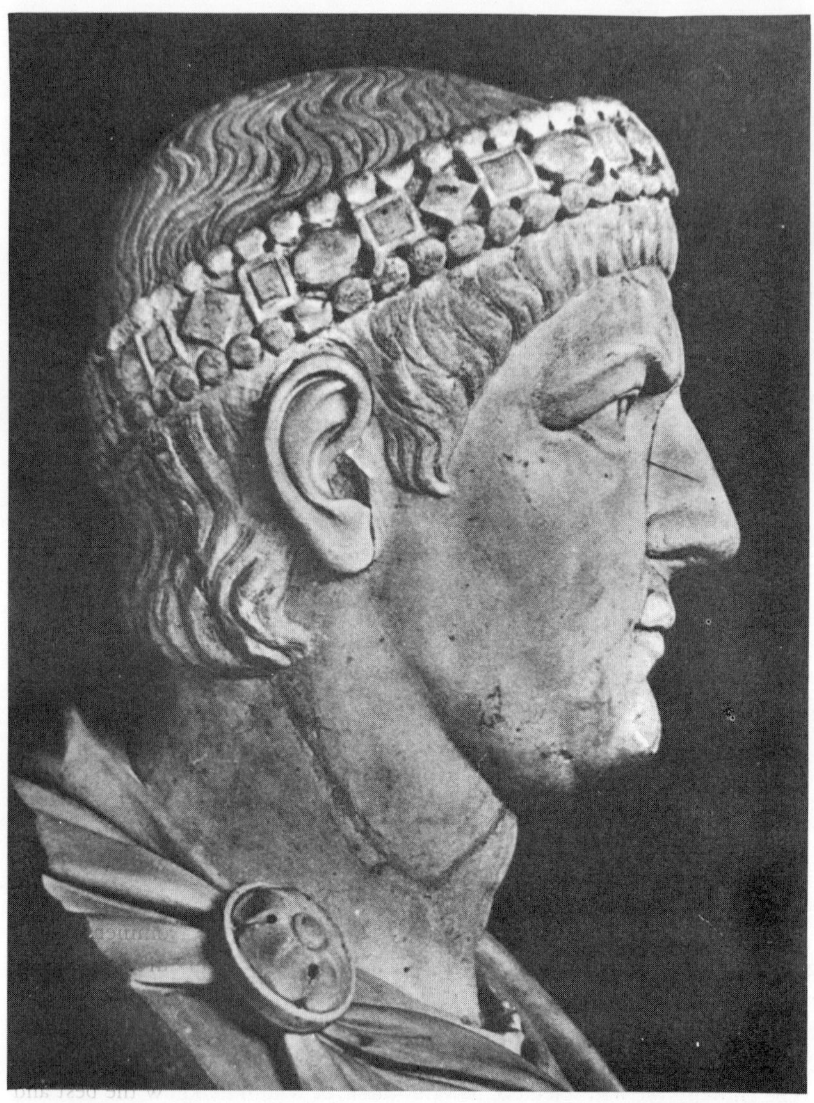

Valens, marble head. Uffizi, Florence (Photograph from Delbrueck Spätantike Kaiserporträts).

notes that he was conscientious in his governing of the provinces, and even though he was very harsh toward the nobles, the average citizen prospered under his rule.[1] Although the emperor and his wife Albia Domnica spent more time in Antioch than in Constantinople, the capital city received one major benefit during his reign, the famous Aqueduct of Valens, which continued in use throughout Byzantine history and is still standing today.

Valens faced a serious crisis when he agreed to let the Visigoths migrate as a body across the Danube and settle in imperial territory. This was the first time that an entire tribe of Germanic barbarians had entered the empire as settlers, though there were already thousands of individual barbarians in the Roman world. If the emperor and his agents had lived up to their promises to supply the Visigoths with food and other necessities, all might have been well, but the east Roman state failed to keep its word. The Visigoths had to plunder the countryside, and the city mob in Constantinople jeered at Valens for doing nothing to stop them.

Valens would have been wiser to wait for military aid from the western Empire, but, sensitive to the widespread criticism of his inactivity, he marched out with a small army to quell the disturbances. At the subsequent battle of Adrianople in August, 378, the Visigoths won a devastating victory. Realizing that the battle was lost, Valens fled from the field and took refuge in a peasant's house. The triumphant Visigoths in their mopping up operations burned everything for miles around, including the building where the emperor lay in hiding.[2] His body was never recovered, and among the tombs of the Byzantine emperors in the Church of the Holy Apostles in Constantinople, there was no memorial to Valens.

Ammianus Marcellinus, who had seen Valens face to face, preserves some interesting data on his personal appearance. "His complexion was dark, the pupil of one of his eyes was dimmed but in such a way as not to be noticed at a distance; his body was well-knit, his height neither above nor below the average; he was knock-kneed and somewhat pot-bellied."[3] Portraits of Valens are very scarce, probably due to Orthodox destruction after the much hated Arian emperor was killed. Fragments of one such ruined bust, pieced together again, are found in the Uffizi in Florence and provide probably the best existing likeness.

Since Valens left no surviving sons, the vacant throne was filled, months later, by an appointee nominated by the emperor Gratian of the West.

---

[1]Amm. Marc., XXVI.4.1-3 (Rolfe, II, 585-587).

[2]Amm. Marc., XXXI.13.14-16 (Rolfe, III, 479-481).

[3]Amm. Marc., XXXI.14.7 (Rolfe, III, 487).

THEODOSIUS I, THE SPANIARD
379-395

Theodosius was born to an aristocratic military family in the Roman province of Spain. For obscure reasons, although he was only in his mid-thirties, he was living in retirement on his estate there when summoned by the western emperor Gratian to fill the vacant throne in Constantinople.

Theodosius was fervently Orthodox, but like many Christians of the fourth century he planned to postpone his baptism until his deathbed. Always in delicate health, he suffered a severe illness early in his reign and was baptized, only to recover.[1] These circumstances seem to have made a profound impression upon him, and he was determined to prove that he was, as his name indicates, 'Given-by-God' to rule the Empire.

Unfortunately, like many Christians of the time, Theodosius' devotion to Orthodoxy carried with it a vigorous spirit of intolerance toward any other religion, be it paganism or another Christian sect. Before the end of his reign, Theodosius was responsible for legislation making Orthodox Christianity compulsory. Religious freedom perished, though it is reported that some worshippers of the old gods chose martyrdom rather than submission to baptism.

On the more constructive side, Theodosius worked for a peaceful settlement with the Visigoths, who had cost Valens his throne. According to the original plan, they were settled on imperial lands as allies of the Roman state.

Some of the most serious troubles of Theodosius' reign were caused by rival claimants to the throne. In a battle against Eugenius, one of these usurpers, the story is told that Theodosius sprang from his horse, fell to his knees, and began praying for divine assistance, whereupon a sudden storm arose blowing thick clouds of dust straight into the faces of the enemy, thus ensuring their defeat.

From the tenth-century Byzantine chronicler Leo Grammaticus, who apparently utilized earlier sources no longer extant, come these details on Theodosius' personal appearance: "He was handsome and well proportioned of body, rosy-faced, with blond hair, and a thin, aquiline nose."[2] Theodosius' famous silver *missorium*, a large ceremonial plate depicting the emperor with his court, presents an excellent likeness of the frail, hollow-cheeked emperor, clad in his ceremonial robes. The *chlamys* (cloak) fastened on his right shoulder by a jewelled *fibula* (brooch) would long be featured as an important item in the imperial wardrobe.

The *missorium* was unearthed in nineteenth-century Spain. Found intact, it was broken by the two men who discovered it, so that each could take his share. Both pieces were recovered and the *missorium* is today housed in the Royal Academy of History in Madrid. Though the men who broke it could not have

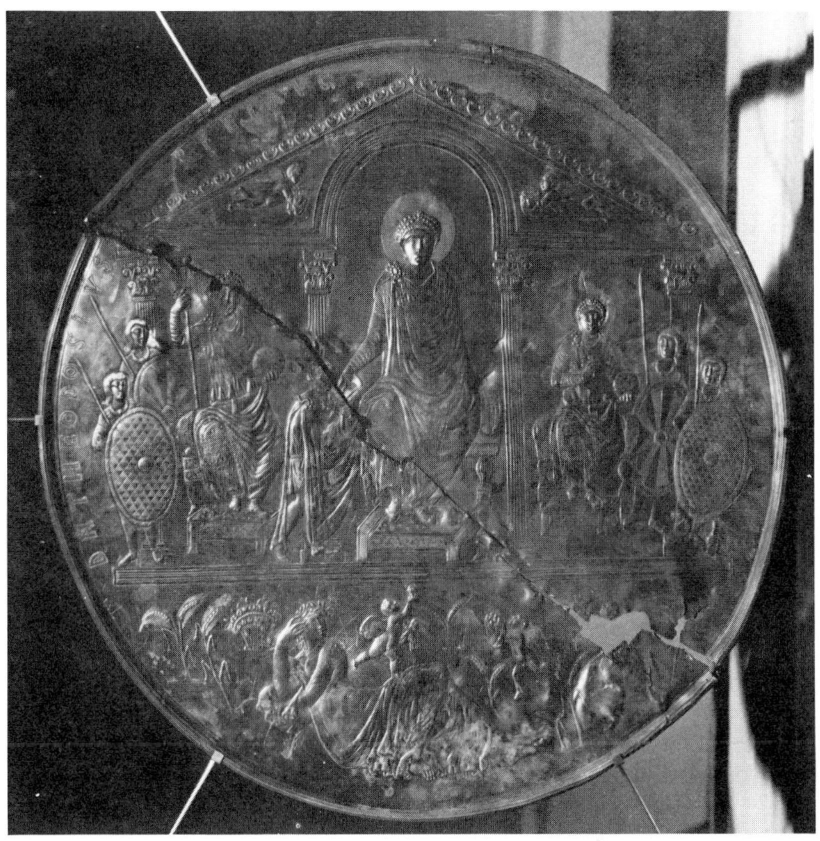

Theodosius I, silver missorium. Academia de la Historia, Madrid.

dreamed it, the irreparable crack in Theodosius' plate is in a sense symbolic of one of the most important facts of his reign: the permanent split of the Roman Empire into its eastern and western divisions. Toward the end of his reign, Theodosius was emperor of both East and West, but in his will he provided for the redivision of the empire between the two sons borne him by his first wife, Aelia Flaccilla: Arcadius and Honorius. With his death in 395, this arrangement went into effect, and Theodosius the Spaniard was the last man ever to rule the entire Roman Empire from the Atlantic coast to the borders of Persia.

[1]Thomas Hodgkin, *The Dynasty of Theodosius* (1899, reprint New York, 1971), pp. 108-109.

[2]Leo Grammaticus (Bonn), p. 101.

ARCADIUS
395-408

Neither of Theodosius' sons inherited their father's ability as a statesman. They were in fact both rather slow, though the elder son, Arcadius, who at seventeen suceeded to the throne in Constantinople, seemed positively brilliant compared to his younger brother Honorius, who received the western provinces. There was no brotherly love lost between the two young emperors, and off and on through their respective reigns they were actually at war with each other.

In spite of his youth, Arcadius was lacking in energy. His laziness made him a pliable tool in the hands of his conniving advisors and, later, of his wife, Eudoxia the Frank. Arcadius selected Eudoxia as his bride when he saw her portrait.[1] Though she was of barbarian descent (her father Bauto was a Frankish chieftain who had become a Roman officer), the family was thoroughly Romanized. Eudoxia, crafty yet charming, and far more ambitious than her weak husband, was destined to be a storm-center throughout her years as empress. The fiery and very popular Patriarch of Constantinople, John Chrysostom, preached openly against her excessive luxuries, until, on more than one occasion, she reciprocated by having him banished. The struggles of these two powerful personalities occupy a great deal of the attention of historians of the time.

Eudoxia presented Arcadius with a large family of daughters and one little son, named Theodosius for his grandfather and proclaimed co-emperor when still a child. There is a delightful contemporary description of Arcadius' pride at the baptism of his heir: "his face cheerful and more radiant than the purple robe he was wearing."[2] It was a rare occasion indeed when Arcadius appeared in public; his extreme lethargy indicates that he must have suffered from some undiagnosed disease, as does his early death at the age of thirty. In sum, though Arcadius' reign witnessed great events in church and state, the emperor himself was scarcely a part of them.

A marble portrait head, found in Istanbul in recent times, is generally believed to represent Arcadius. On his head he wears the imperial diadem, a crown of the sort used by the emperors at least since Diocletian; it was probably made of heavy fabric adorned with pearls and other jewels and tied in the back with jewelled pendants. While the sculptor has portrayed his subject as a handsome if somewhat vapid young man, the chronicle tradition remembers him as unattractive. Cedrenus writes: "Arcadius was in body almost deformed; he was very dark-skinned and in stature very small."[3]

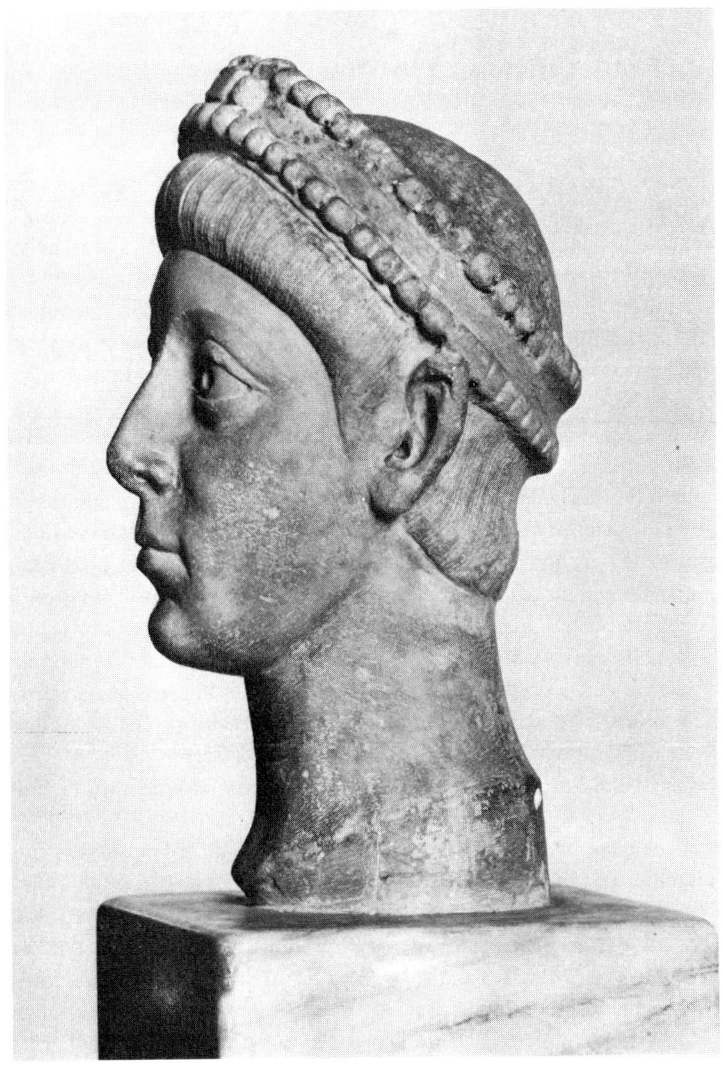

Arcadius, marble head. Archaeological Museum, Istanbul (Photograph: Hirmer, Munich).

[1]J.B. Bury, *A History of the Later Roman Empire*, 2 vols. (reprint New York, 1958), I, 109.

[2]Porphyrius of Gaza as quoted by Bury, *A History of the Later Roman Empire*, I, 146.

[3]Cedrenus (Bonn), I, 574.

THEODOSIUS II, THE CALLIGRAPHER
408-450

The long reign of Theodosius II is marked by the rapid rise of the barbarian threat both in the Byzantine Empire of the East and in the West where close relatives of Theodosius reigned. When the Huns under Attila threatened Constantinople, the ministers of Theodosius secured their withdrawal by paying heavy tribute; Germanic invaders were regularly dealt with in the same way. Thus, the Byzantine Empire was able to weather the storm of the most serious barbarian invasions, while the West, economically poorer, suffered far greater hardships at the invaders' hands.

Completely unmilitary in his habits, the emperor Theodosius II took almost no personal role in the defense of his empire. 'Little Theodosius' was seven when he succeeded his father Arcadius. He grew up frail and scholarly, more interested in his hobby of copying manuscripts than in affairs of state. His beautiful handwriting earned him the epithet 'the Calligrapher', but even as a grown man he was more often spoken of as 'Little Theodosius'. "He grew to no great size," reports a historian of the time, "because he was shut up in the palace."[1] "His eyes were black and sharp sighted," adds Leo Grammaticus, "his nose thin and straight, his hair honey-blond."[2] In spite of his very long reign, there are almost no extant portaits of Theodosius II; the best is the marble head (somewhat restored) housed in the Louvre.

Basically kind-hearted but easily swayed by those around him, Theodosius II gladly allowed his older sister Pulcheria extensive powers in the state. At the age of fifteen she had herself proclaimed empress and for years was the real power behind her brother's throne.[3]

Theodosius' wife was Athenaïs Eudokia, the beautiful and learned daughter of an Athenian professor. In later centuries, Byzantine chroniclers often repeated the folktales that clustered around the name of this romantic figure. Athenaïs, it was said, first attracted the emperor's notice when she came to Constantinople to plead a lawsuit before the empress Pulcheria. The shy young emperor was watching from behind a curtain and, seeing Athenaïs, decreed she was the only girl in the world for him.[4] There was no rule that the emperor had to marry a princess or even a noblewoman. Athenaïs and Theodosius were married, and for years seemed unusually well suited to each other. The University of Constantinople, established under their patronage, was probably as much her project as it was his. Though they had no sons who survived infancy, they were the parents of a daughter Licinia, who eventually married the western emperor, Valentinian III.

Then, after many years of matrimony, Theodosius and Athenaïs quarrelled bitterly. According to a folktale, the emperor's jealousy was

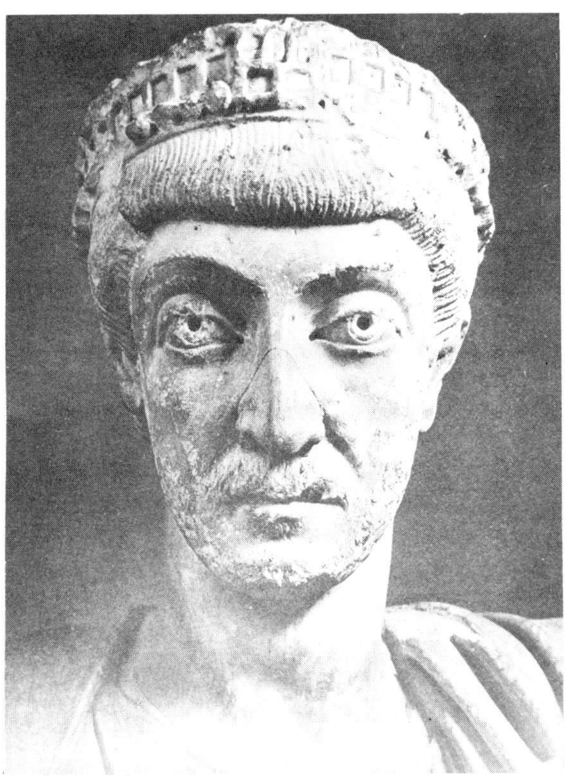

Theodosius II, marble head. The Louvre (Photograph from Delbrueck Spätantike Kaiserporträts).

aroused when his wife sent an apple to a sick friend, Paulinus, and then lied about having done so. While the details may be legendary, the imperial pair were permanently separated, and Athenaïs spent her last years in Jerusalem, engaged in works of Christian charity.

'Little Theodosius' was in his late forties when he died as the result of injuries sustained when he fell off his horse. His closest relative was his sister Pulcheria, who had never married. Although a woman could not reign alone, the future course of Byzantine history was at that moment in her hands.

---

[1]Joannes Antiochenus, fr. 193, as quoted by C.D. Gordon, *The Age of Attila* (Ann Arbor, 1966), p. 27.

[2]Leo Grammaticus (Bonn), p. 107; Cedrenus (Bonn), I, 587.

[3]Bury, *LRE*, I, 214. It is interesting to note that in Byzantium the title of Augusta (Empress) was not restricted to the emperor's wife and/or mother.

[4]Charles Diehl, *Byzantine Empresses*, trans. Harold Bell and Theresa de Kerpely (New York, 1963), pp. 22–43, retells in detail the chronicle traditions of Athenaïs.

MARCIAN
450–457

Pulcheria, aged fifty-one, selected as her consort the retired general Marcian and personally conducted his coronation ceremony.[1] Although theirs was a marriage in name only, for Pulcheria insisted on remaining true to her girlhood vow of celibacy, the emperor and empress seem to have been most compatible in matters of state policy. In spite of the fact that Pulcheria's choice was prompted by Aspar the Alan, a powerful Germanic military chief who hoped to become the power behind the throne, Marcian proved to be an independent-minded emperor. Among his first official acts was his decision to stop subsidy payments to Attila the Hun. This policy did not prove the disaster that many Byzantines had feared, for the Huns stepped up their attacks on the West, and Byzantium gained a much-needed breathing space. Marcian was able to reduce taxes, a policy that insured his widespread popularity.

Marcian shared Pulcheria's intense interest in theology, and the Ecumenical Council of Chalcedon was conducted under their sponsorship. This action was widely applauded by their Orthodox subjects, and for centuries thereafter, Marcian and Pulcheria would be commemorated as saints on the Orthodox calendar.

Because he was a popular emperor and one who had come to the throne late in life, many stories were circulated to attempt to prove that even as a young man Marcian was divinely destined for future greatness. One chronicler reports that when young Marcian was on his way to the town of Philippolis to enlist in the army, he spied a body lying beside the road. Apparently believing that the unfortunate man might be still alive, he stopped to see if he might render aid; when he discovered he was too late, he lingered beside the corpse to offer prayers for the dead. Some passers-by saw him, reported the incident, and Marcian was arrested and charged with murder. The circumstantial evidence plainly pointed to his guilt, and he would have been executed had not the actual murderer been apprehended and made to confess soon thereafter.[2]

Having survived this brush with death, Marcian continued on his way to Philippolis, where he enlisted in the army. Instead of enrolling him at the lowest rank, the recruiting officers immediately offered him the place on the military roster belonging to a soldier who had recently died, but this favor was contingent upon Marcian's accepting the name of the dead soldier—Augustus. He willingly agreed and was enrolled as Marcian Augustus, a name which later seemed a clear omen of his rise to the imperial dignity, since Augustus was a title regularly accorded to the emperor.[3]

Marcian survived his empress, Pulcheria, by several years. Later Byzantine historians would look back to their reign as a golden age of peace and

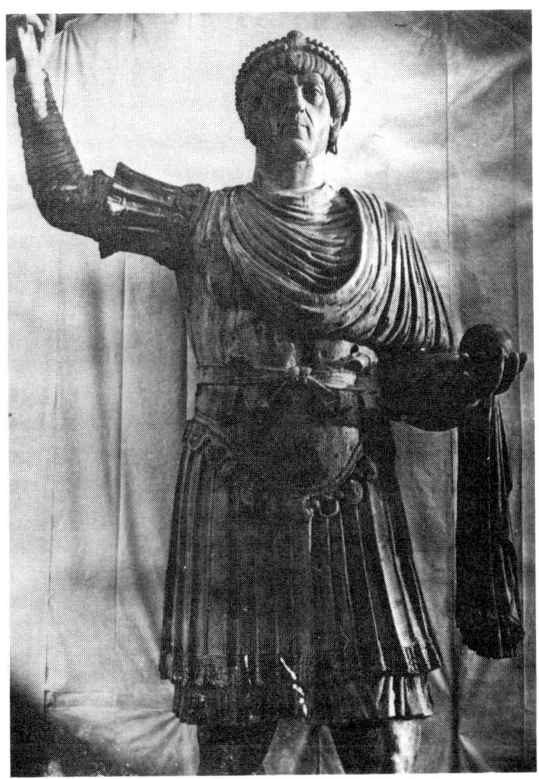

The Emperor of Barletta: presumed portrait of Marcian. Barletta, Italy (Fotografia Calvaresi).

Orthodoxy, a calm before terrible storms to come. Ironically, though they praise him highly, no details of Marcian's appearance are preserved other than the fact that his face was florid.[4]

The colossal bronze statue of an emperor located in Barletta, Italy, has been variously identified, but there is strong evidence for believing it depicts the emperor Marcian.[5] Clad in military costume, the figure also wears the diadem adorned with short jewelled pendants (*pendilia*) on each side, ornaments which would be a regular feature of the Byzantine crown for centuries to come.

---

[1]Bury, *History of the Later Roman Empire*, I, 236.

[2]Evagrius, *Ecclesiastical History*, II, 1.

[3]*Ibid.*

[4]Leo Grammaticus (Bonn), p. 111; Cedrenus (Bonn), I, 603.

[5]Richard Delbrueck, *Spätantike Kaiserporträts* (Berlin, 1933), p. 219; Wolfgang Fritz Volbach, *Early Christian Art*, trans. Christopher Ligota (New York, n.d.), p. 325.

LEO I
457-474

Like Marcian, Leo I was an army officer and a protege of Aspar the Alan, who, at Marcian's death, secured the throne for him. Leo and his empress, Verina, were of humble origin. One rumor (probably legend) reports that they once worked in a butcher shop in Constantinople.

Whatever his background, Leo proved less amenable to Aspar's advice than Aspar had anticipated. Thinking to offset the undue power of the Germanic element in the army and at the court, the emperor recruited a large number of Isaurian tribesmen from Asia Minor to serve as his bodyguard and married his elder daughter, Ariadne, to their chieftain, Tarasikodissa Zeno.

For some years thereafter, the Byzantine court was the scene of intense rivalry and distrust between the Germans and the Isaurians. The historian Candidus reports how, on one occasion, Aspar grabbed Leo by the cloak and admonished him, "Emperor, it is not right that the man wearing this cloak should lie!"

"Nor is it right that he should be restrained and driven like a slave!" Leo answered, indicating clearly his growing dislike for the man who had gained him his throne.[1]

Eventually Zeno and his Isaurians contrived to slay Aspar and other leading Germanic officers at the court. This massacre undoubtedly contributed to the future shaping of Byzantine history; had Aspar and others like him remained in positions of authority, the eastern Empire might well have broken up into separate Germanic kingdoms, just as the western Empire was doing at this same time.

Although Leo was scarcely a popular emperor, he was a conscientious one, and there are several anecdotes illustrative of a more peaceable side of his nature. Once he ordered a special gift of money to be given to a noted philosopher, and, when one of his officials protested, saying that the money was needed for the army, Leo replied, "May it happen in my time that the pay of the soldiers is handed over to teachers."[2]

Leo is also remembered for having stated, "The Emperor should distribute pity to those on whom he looks, just as the sun distributes warmth to those on whom it shines."[3] He adopted a novel method for keeping in touch with popular opinion: when his sister set up a statue of him in front of her house, people began to deposit statements of their grievances at the statue's feet, and Leo sent an official to collect these written pleas every day.

Because he had no sons, Leo contemplated designating his son-in-law Zeno as his heir, but this proposal met with so much opposition that he decided instead, shortly before his death, to name his young grandson, Leo II, Zeno and Ariadne's child, as co-emperor.

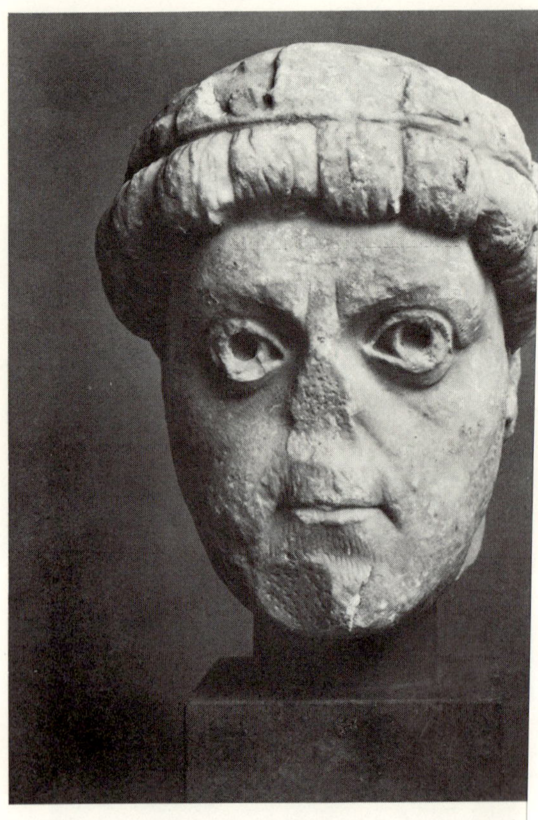

Leo I. Ny Carlsberg Glyptotek, Copenhagen.

The portraits of Leo I found on his coins depict him a
sometimes clean-shaven, and noticeably roundfaced; but
period are stylized, it is impossible to gain from them a c
emperor's appearance. A sadly damaged portrait head, n
hagen, has been identified as Leo I, largely on the basis
blance to the emperor's plump, round-cheeked daughter
utilized by Leo Grammaticus, however, complicates t
report: "Leo [I] was very thin in body, beardless, and v

[1]Zonaras, XIV.1 as quoted by Gordon, *Age of Attila*, p. 131.

[2]Malchus, fragment 2a, quoted by Gordon, *Age of Attila*, p. 131.

[3]Bury, *History of the Later Roman Empire*, I, 321.

[4]Vagn Poulsen,
Byzantion 25-27 (19

[5]Leo Grammatic
(Bonn), I, 607.

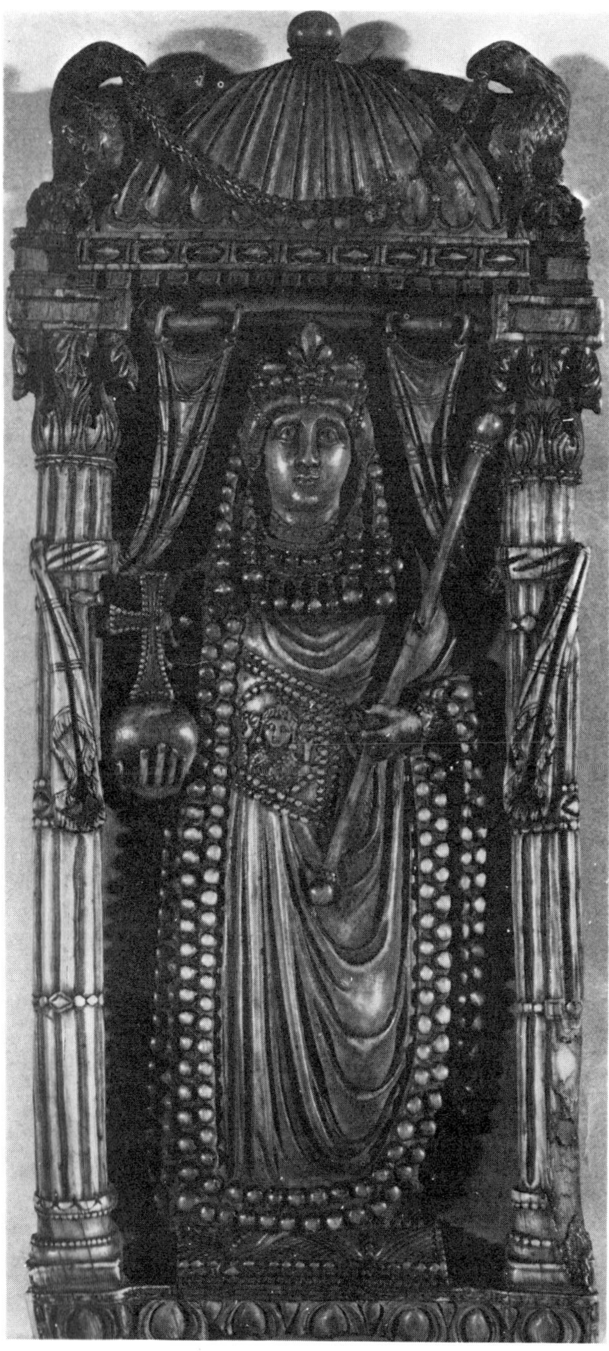

Leo II, portrait on the cloak of Ariadne: leaf of ivory diptych. Bargello, Florence.

LEO II
474

Leo II, the only son of Zeno and Ariadne, was about six or seven years old when his grandfather Leo I died. Although he was a frail child, his right to the succession was unquestioned. It was, however, evident that the real power in the state was in the hands of his father, Zeno the Isaurian, and not many weeks had passed before a ceremony was held at which the boy monarch placed an imperial crown on his father's head and designated him co-emperor.

A few months later, Leo died of some childhood disease, and Zeno the Isaurian reigned alone—the only instance in Byzantine history where a father succeeded his own son as emperor.

Leo II's coins provide a most unsatisfactory portrait of the boy emperor, depicting him as a full-grown man clad in armor. On the other hand, a detail from an ivory diptych furnishes what is probably a near contemporary portrait of young Leo II: the diptych leaf depicts Ariadne, and the portrait of her little son is embroidered on her *chlamys* according to the fashion of the time.[1] In this representation, Leo is clad in a *loros*—a long ceremonial scarf—and holds the *mappa* (a red napkin), symbols of the consular office.

---

[1]Robert Browning, *Justinian and Theodora* (New York, 1971), p. 31.

ZENO THE ISAURIAN
474-491

Zeno's real name was Tarasikodissa; he changed it to the more pronounceable Zeno, in memory of an earlier Isaurian hero, when he married the princess Ariadne, daughter of Leo I.

Zeno's enemies—and he had many—have practically nothing good to report of him except that he was a very fast runner. "Bushy haired and ill-formed, Zeno was in aspect just as the Greeks depicted Pan, goat-footed and hairy legged, black skinned, absurd in stature," reports the chronicle tradition in Leo Grammaticus' source.[1] Elsewhere it alleged that he was such a coward that he did not even like to look at a picture of a battle.[2] This charge of

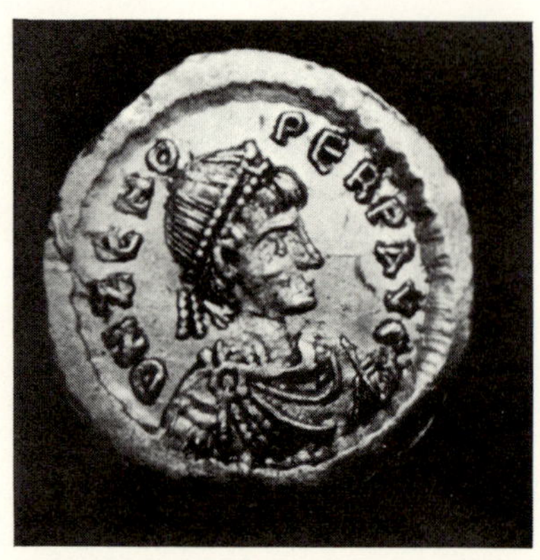

Zeno, coin of his reign. American Numismatic Society.

cowardice seems most unfair, for although Zeno avoided personal command of his army whenever possible, he could fight when he had to and the numerous uprisings against him through his reign meant that he had to fight a great deal.

Perhaps Zeno's bitterest enemy was his mother-in-law, Verina. It was she who sparked the coup d'etat in 475 that sent Zeno and Ariadne scurrying out of Constantinople disguised as ordinary citizens in an old farm wagon. For about a year, Zeno remained in his native Isaurian mountains recruiting forces for his return to the capital, while the pretender Basiliscus, Verina's brother, held court in Constantinople. It is reported that during this time Zeno frequently cried openly, despairing of ever retaining his crown, but in 476 he returned to his capital. The unfortunate Basiliscus was whisked off to prison, where reportedly he starved to death.[3]

Though Basiliscus had posed the most serious threat to Zeno's throne, there were other attempted coups later in his reign, at least one more of which was prompted by Verina. Zeno finally compelled his troublesome mother-in-law to retire to a convent.

While Zeno reigned in Constantinople, the last of the western Roman emperors, Romulus Augustulus, was dethroned in Italy by the barbarian chieftain Odovacer. Zeno had too many problems closer to home to attempt intervention in the West. He simply recognized the *status quo* by conferring upon Odovacer the title of Patrician of the Empire. A few years later, he induced the Ostrogoths, under their great leader Theodoric, to invade Odovacer's realm, with the promise that if the Ostrogoths conquered Italy they could have it—subject to imperial authority.

In the realm of theology, Zeno was an adherent of the Monophysite doctrine, a variety of Christianity considered heretical by the Orthodox. His famous edict, the *Henotikon*, was an attempt to resolve the religious controversies tearing the empire: all Christians should acknowledge as sufficient the theological pronouncements of the first two ecumenical councils, and for the rest, they should agree to disagree. Practically no one appreciated Zeno's ideas on this subject, and the *Henotikon* caused widespread protest.

A later Byzantine legend reports that one evening when Zeno fell into a drunken stupor at a banquet, Ariadne had him carried out and buried alive.[4] Though this story was recopied by many Byzantine chroniclers, it is without basis in fact.

Among the coins of Zeno are some which bear a profile portrait. The unflattering line of his sharp jutting chin suggests that this is possibly a hint at an authentic likeness of the Isaurian emperor of Byzantium.

---

[1]Leo Grammaticus (Bonn), p. 117; Cedrenus (Bonn), I, 615.

[2]John Lydus as quoted by Bury, *History of the Later Roman Empire*, I, 390, n.2.

[3]J. B. Bury, *History of the Later Roman Empire from Arcadius to Irene*, Vol. I (London, 1889), p. 252.

[4]Philip Grierson, "The Tombs and Obits of the Byzantine Emperors," *Dumbarton Oaks Papers*, 16 (1962), 44 and n. 59.

ANASTASIUS I
491-518

When Zeno died, the Byzantine Senate requested the empress Ariadne to select his successor and—in order to retain her position as empress—to marry him. Her choice, whom she described as "endowed with every virtue," as perfect as a man can possibly be, came as a surprise to many.[1] Anastasius was over sixty years old, a former palace doorkeeper who had risen to a responsible post in the imperial treasury. "He was very large in stature, shorthaired, gracious in manner, round faced; the hair of his head and his beard were turning grey. His right eye was a light blue, while the left was black, nevertheless his eyes were most attractive. He frequently shaved his beard," reports the chronicler Malalas.[2]

As it turned out, Anastasius' greatest abilities were in the realm of finances. The people of Constantinople scoffed when he held a sale to auction off the late emperor Zeno's clothes (which were too small for him to wear); but this was merely the first of many economy measures he introduced. Many of the court hangers-on, especially Isaurians, found their lucrative but unproductive jobs abolished, and while they grumbled, the majority of Byzantines admired Anastasius' tax cuts and declared that the old doorkeeper was turning out to be a good emperor after all.

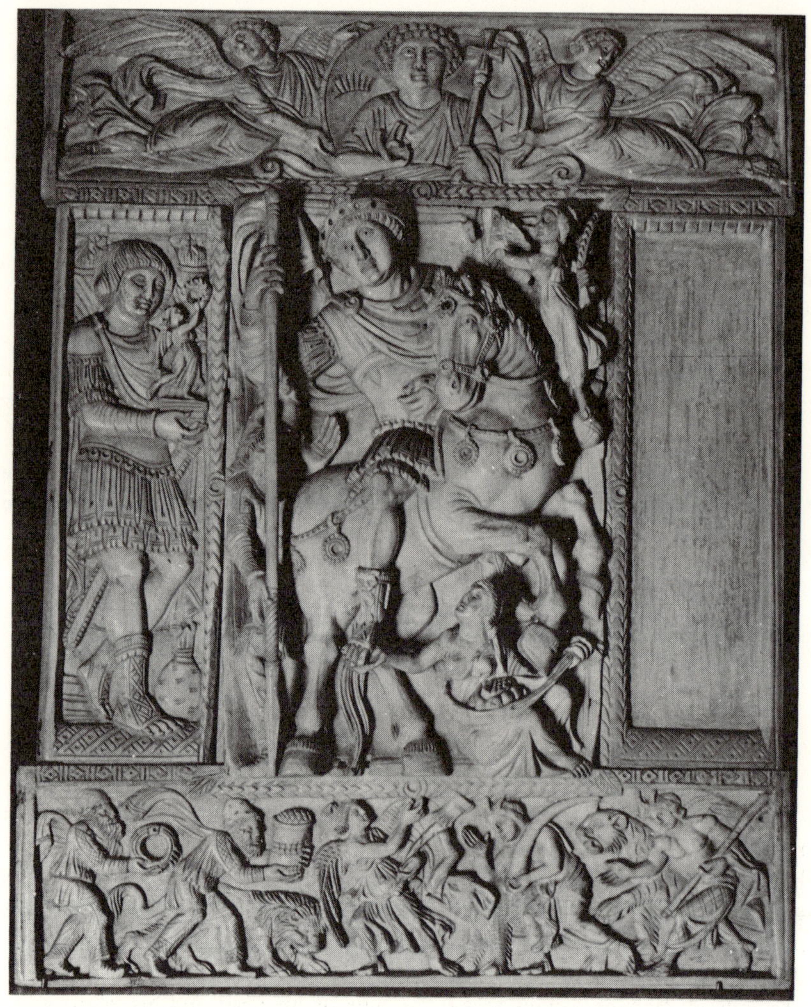

The Barberini Ivory: diptych leaf, presumed portrait of Anastasius I. The Louvre.

Unfortunately from the Orthodox point of view, Anastasius was, like Zeno, a Monophysite. As a younger man, before his succession to the throne, he had been in the habit of taking a folding chair into the Church of Hagia Sophia; when curious persons gathered round (as they were sure to do, since Byzantines ordinarily stood up in church), Anastasius would preach sermonettes on Monophysite doctrines.[3] Though he promised on becoming emperor to abide by the Orthodox faith, his Monophysite inclinations were too strongly ingrained in him, and controversy on theology continued unabated.

Both Ariadne and Anastasius lived to ripe old age, Anastasius surviving her by about a year. He died suddenly on the night of a great storm, reportedly struck by lightning, which was declared by some to have been a sign of divine disapproval of his Monophysitism.[4] If so, the bolt from Heaven was long in coming, since he reached the age of eighty-eight, the greatest age of any Byzantine emperor.

The emperor depicted on a diptych leaf known as the "Barberini Ivory" is usually identified as Anastasius. While the military costume he wears might seem inappropriate for the thoroughly civilian emperor, who never led his forces in person, such garb was no doubt worn on certain ceremonial occasions.

---

[1]Bury, *History of the Later Roman Empire*, I, 429-430.

[2]Joannes Malalas, Bk. XVI (Bonn), p. 392.

[3]Bury, *History of the Later Roman Empire*, I, 431.

[4]Browning, *Justinian and Theodora*, p. 31; see also Grierson, "Tombs and Obits," p. 45.

JUSTIN I
518-527

Anastasius died without naming an heir, though he had probably intended to designate one of this three nephews as his successor. The actual course of events following his sudden death, however, produced one of the most unlikely of all emperors, old Justin, a peasant-born soldier and former swineherd, who had risen to the rank of commander of a troop of the palace guards. In the confusion just after Anastasius' death, a scheming nobleman gave Justin a large sum of money to distribute among his troops in order to induce them to cheer for a certain Theocritus for emperor. Justin distributed the gold but remained silent as to where it came from. His troops immediately began to acclaim him as emperor, and before any effective opposition could be organized, Justin's accession became an accomplished fact.[1]

By birth an Illyrian peasant, the tall, good-looking Justin had come to Constantinople as a youth seeking his fortune, carrying his only worldly goods, a sack of dry biscuits. He volunteered for service in the palace guard, and over the years, though he apparently never had much formal education, he had had a distinguished military career.

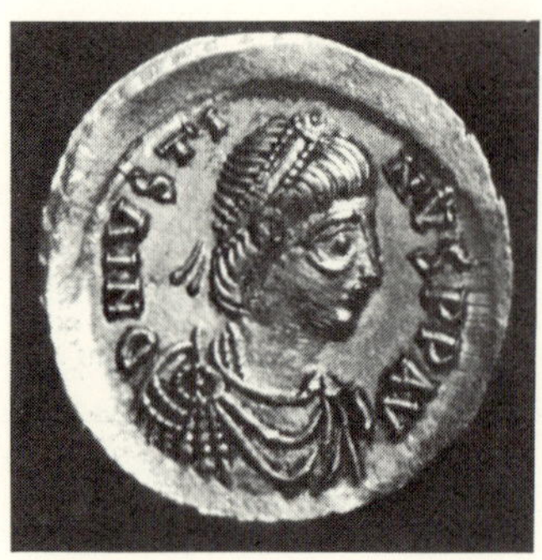

Justin I, coin of his reign. American Numismatic Society.

Justin was in his late sixties when he became emperor. In spite of his unlikely background, he was widely admired by his subjects for his religious Orthodoxy. On the other hand, the Byzantines did not hesitate to make fun of old Justin's lack of education, declaring that he could only sign his name on state documents with the aid of a stencil plate—a charge that may or may not be true.[2] In any event, Justin was not lacking in intelligence. He chose excellent advisors, particularly his nephew (and adopted son), Justinian.

Justin's empress was Lupicina-Euphemia, a former prisoner-of-war and camp cook whom he had purchased as a slave and then legally married, many years before his accession to the throne. In her unanticipated role as empress, old Euphemia was noted mainly for her conspicuous piety. Justin also brought his aged mother, who must have been about ninety, from her home village to live in the splendor of the Byzantine court.

An old leg wound which had not healed properly made Justin something of an invalid throughout his reign, and was finally the cause of his death when it became gangrenous. Shortly before he died, he designated his adopted son Justinian as his co-emperor and heir.

Like most Byzantine emperors, old Justin was an enthusiastic patron of the arts. One source tells of a series of murals he commissioned, depicting his rise from swineherd to sovereign.[3] Unfortunately neither these nor any other portraits of Justin survive, beyond the highly stylized image on his coins, and the reader is left to imagine him as he is described by the historian Malalas: "He was above medium height, well-built, with curly hair, completely grey, a well-made nose, and a rosy, handsome face."[4]

---

[1]A. A. Vasiliev, *Justin the First* (Cambridge, Mass., 1950), p. 81 ff.

[2]Procopius, *Secret History*, ch. VI (Atwater, p. 33).

[3]Vasiliev, *Justin the First*, p. 89.

[4]Malalas, Bk. XVII (Bonn), p. 410.

JUSTINIAN I
527-565

Among the best known of all Byzantine sovereigns is Justinian I, whose long reign marks a period of brilliant achievement for the empire. The codification of Roman law under his direction has assured him of historical immortality. This great work, carried out by a committee of learned jurists and scholars, spread its influence far beyond the Byzantine world, as it was adopted by most of the developing nations of western Europe later in the Middle Ages. An equally enduring monument of Justinian's reign is the great church of Hagia (or Sancta) Sophia, rebuilt under his sponsorship after the destruction of the original building in the Nika Riots of 532. Hagia Sophia represents Byzantine architecture at its finest. The huge building was constructed in the amazingly short period of five years; its breathtaking beauty inspired the praises of Byzantines and visitors down through the centuries.

Justinian's interest in building did not stop with Hagia Sophia. Throughout his empire, numerous churches, public buildings and fortifications were constructed at the emperor's command. In Ravenna, Italy, in the Church of San Vitale, Justinian and his empress Theodora are depicted in mosaic portraits that are among the finest surviving examples of this art form in which the Byzantines so excelled.

The likenesses of the imperial pair in Ravenna are a reminder of Justinian's program of reconquest of the West. Though he never went to war personally, it was his plan to bring the lost western provinces of the Roman world back under imperial sway. His generals, particularly the famous, intensely loyal Belisarius, met with considerable success in the early years of the reconquest program, and the Kingdom of the Vandals in North Africa was restored to the empire. The Kingdom of the Ostrogoths in Italy offered more resistance, and only after years of hard fighting was Italy successfully brought under Byzantine rule. A small part of Spain was also reconquered. While these territorial gains look impressive on the map, the Byzantines were not able to hold them as long as Justinian had hoped, and in the years following his death, much of the West fell again to new waves of barbarian invaders.

Justinian's wife, Theodora, who played a very active part in his governing of the empire, was one of the most colorful of the Byzantine empresses. Daughter of a Hippodrome bear-keeper, she became an actress as a young girl, and, before she met Justinian, she was a famous—and notorious—courtesan. Justinian was able to marry her only after he persuaded his uncle, Emperor Justin I, to alter the law forbidding marriage between an aristocrat and a stage performer.[1] In spite of her past, Theodora proved a loyal and devoted wife.

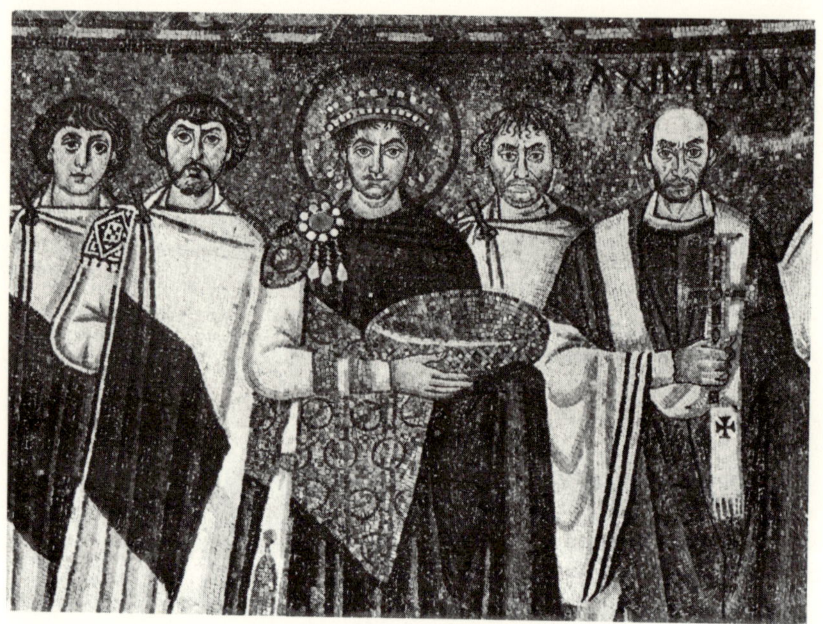

Justinian I, mosaic panel. San Vitale, Ravenna (Photograph: Hirmer, Munich).

Contemporaries found her far more difficult to deal with than the relatively good-natured Justinian, and they stood in fear of her implacable wrath and subtle intrigues.

The Ravenna mosaic only vaguely suggests the dark, delicate beauty who captivated Justinian's heart, for by the time her portrait was made, the empress was in her late forties and slowly dying of cancer. Justinian's likeness depicts the sturdy, peasant-born emperor, with wavy black hair and deep brown eyes, while Malalas provides a detailed written description. Justinian was "short of stature, broad chested, with a well-made nose, fair skin, curly hair, a round face, handsome, but going slightly bald, with a florid countenance, and hair and beard turning grey."[2] Procopius, in his *Secret History*, a work bitterly hostile to Justinian, adds: "In physique he [Justinian] was neither tall nor short but of average height; not thin, but moderately plump; his face was round, and not bad looking, for he had good color, even when he fasted for two days."[3]

The Ravenna mosaics are among the best visual sources for early Byzantine imperial costume. Justinian is clad in a purple *chlamys*, ornamented with a *tablion* panel of figured material. His crown—probably of enamel and pearls—displays four small *pendilia*, while on his feet are the red shoes which were among the most conspicuous tokens of Byzantine emperorship.

Although he was considerably her senior, Justinian outlived Theodora by seventeen years. He never remarried, and as he grew older he devoted increasingly more time to theological study. He remained healthy far into his old age, though he often fasted for several days at a time and slept so little that rumors were circulated describing him as unable to sleep at all. He was still seeking a universal Christian creed that would have united the Orthodox and the Monophysites, when he died at the age of eighty-three, leaving as his heir his nephew, Justin II.

---

[1]Browning, *Justinian and Theodora*, pp. 68-69.
[2]Malalas, Bk. XVIII (Bonn), p. 425.
[3]Procopius, *Secret History*, ch. VIII (Atwater, p. 41).

JUSTIN II
565-578

Thousands of Byzantines who could remember no emperor but the long-lived Justinian rejoiced at the accession of his nephew Justin, a peaceable, seemingly mild-mannered bureaucrat who promised to reduce government spending. "He was conspicuous in outward appearance," reports Leo Grammaticus, "broad shouldered and well-formed, a blue-eyed blond."[1] The reign of Justin II, however, ushers in one of the darkest periods of Byzantine history. His refusal to meet subsidy payments to the Avars meant that this fierce tribe plundered the Balkan area, while the Germanic Lombards invaded Italy and seized for themselves much of the hard-won territory there.

Justin also refused payments to Byzantium's powerful eastern neighbor, Persia. War broke out on the eastern front, and when the bad news of repeated Byzantine losses was conveyed to the emperor, he suffered a complete mental collapse.

His illness made Justin violent; in fits of insanity he would attack and bite his courtiers. His wife, Sophia, found he was happiest when his servants pulled him through the halls of the palace in a little cart, accompanied by the court musicians.[2] Though he occasionally had a lucid spell, he was obviously unable to govern, and the empress Sophia, who was Theodora's niece and like her a crafty politician, assumed the regency.

Since Justin and Sophia had no surviving sons, the empress was vitally concerned in arranging for an orderly succession to the throne. She selected as an 'adopted son' the handsome young commander of the palace guards, Tiberius, and persuaded Justin, during a lucid period, to make the adoption

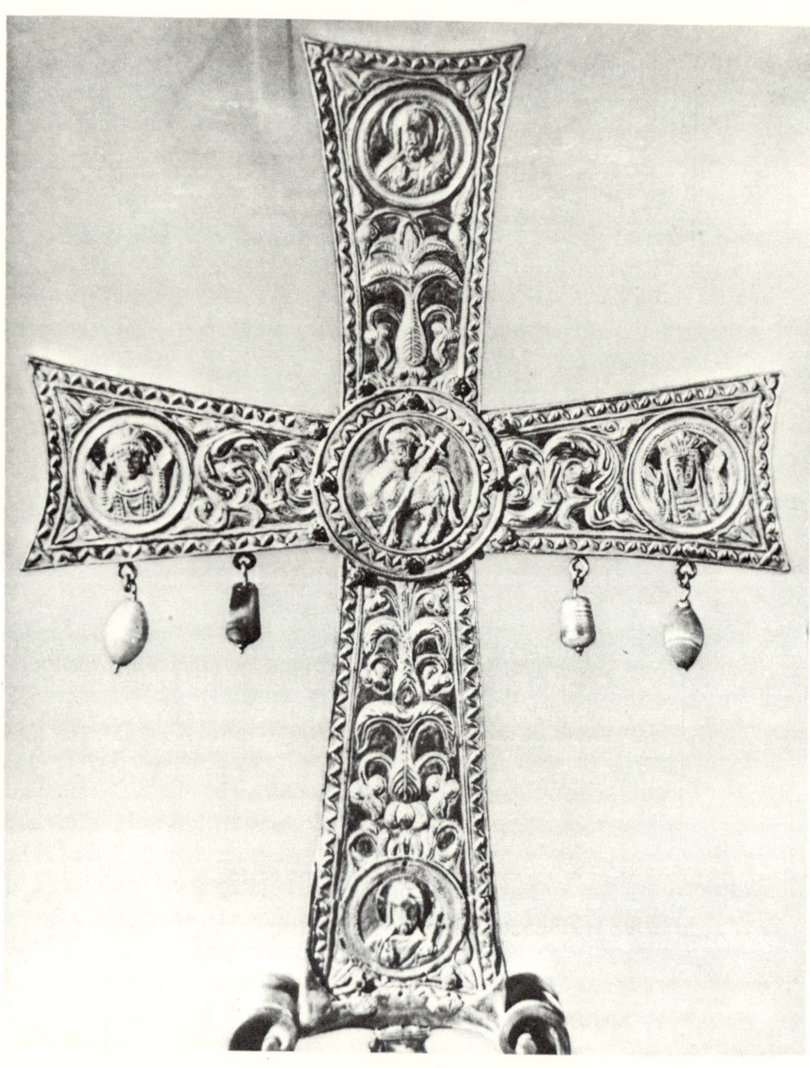

Justin II: gold reliquary cross with medallion portraits of Justin II (left) and his empress Sophia (right). Vatican.

official. Tiberius henceforth assisted Sophia in the regency, though the aloof young throne-heir and his aging adoptive 'mother' did not work well together.

Among the oldest treasures in the Vatican is the famous jewelled cross presented to the Pope as a gift from Justin and Sophia. On the reverse side of the cross are gold medallion portraits of the emperor (left) and the empress (right), their hands lifted in the *orant* position, the typical Byzantine posture for prayer.

---

[1]Leo Grammaticus (Bonn), p. 132; Cedrenus (Bonn), I, 680.

[2]Barker, *Justinian and the Later Roman Empire* (Madison, Wis., 1966), p. 218.

TIBERIUS CONSTANTINE
578-582

The stylized portraits on his coins provide the only contemporary likenesses of the emperor Tiberius Constantine. For a more accurate idea of this emperor's appearance one must rely on descriptions from Byzantine historians. Leo Grammaticus relates: "He was well proportioned in body, with a firm chest, beautiful eyes somewhat blue, blond in the hair of his head and beard, fair skinned, with a fresh, vigorous face; and he was good and magnanimous, even to excess."[1] Perhaps the brevity of his term as emperor enhanced Tiberius' favorable reputation. In any event, his reign was, like that of his predecessor, marked by the ongoing struggle with the Persians and the Avars.

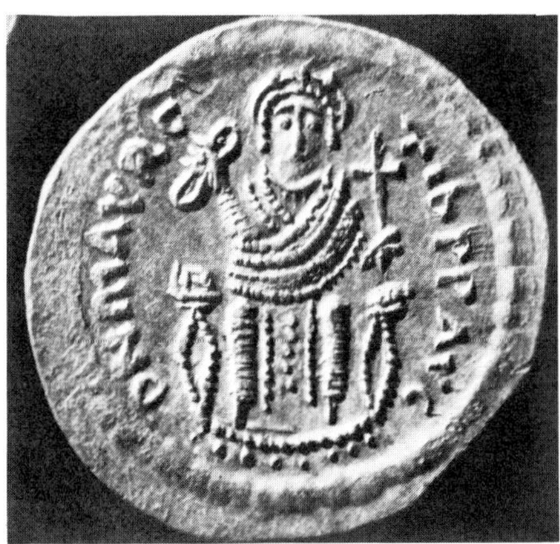

Tiberius Constantine, coin of his reign. American Numismatic Society.

Tiberius bestowed upon himself the additional name Constantine, in token of the first Christian emperor. His wife was called Ino. When she was proclaimed Empress, the crowds in the Hippodrome shouted that she should have a more Christian name, and by popular demand it was changed to Anastasia.[2]

Tiberius Constantine was greatly assisted in his military campaigns by a brilliant Cappadocian general, Maurice, who eventually received the promise of the emperor's young daughter Constantina for his wife. When Tiberius died, after a lingering illness which was probably tuberculosis, Maurice and his bride Constantina succeeded to the throne.

---

[1] Leo Grammaticus (Bonn), p. 137; Cedrenus (Bonn), I, 688.

[2] J. B. Bury, *History of the Later Roman Empire from Arcadius to Irene*, Vol. II, p. 79.

MAURICE TIBERIUS
582-602

It has well been commented that if only there existed better portraits of the emperor Maurice, this great sovereign might be as famed in world history as Justinian I. Throughout the Middle Ages he was certainly remembered. The subject of many legends, he even appears in Chaucer's *Canterbury Tales*, in the "Man of Law's Tale," as the infant cast adrift with his mother in a rudderless boat. There is no historical foundation for this legend, nor for the other, no less fantastic, stories told of Maurice by the Byzantines themselves.

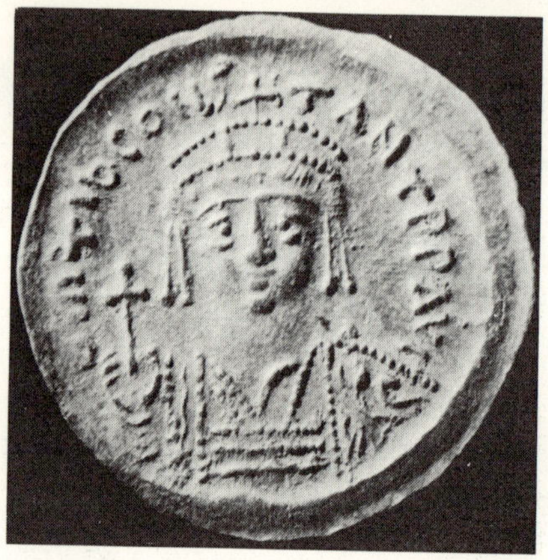

Maurice Tiberius, coin of his reign. American Numismatic Society.

Maurice (more correctly Mavrikios) was by birth a Cappadocian who rose to prominence in the army and won the hand of the princess Constantina. As emperor, he assumed the additional name of Tiberius in memory of his predecessor and father-in-law. In due time, Maurice and Constantina were the parents of nine children 'born in the purple'. This large family, after almost two centuries of emperors without sons, seemed to promise the establishment of a long-lived dynasty.

Less favorable was the situation in the Balkans, where Avars and Slavs continued their incursions, and in Italy, overrun by the Lombards. To cope more effectively with frontier defenses, Maurice organized the exarchate of Ravenna: Byzantine Italy was placed under the authority of an exarch, a governor who combined civil and military powers. A similar official was installed in Carthage in North Africa. These governmental reforms of Maurice helped lay the basis for the system of *Themes*—the Byzantine military provinces that developed more fully in the seventh and eighth centuries and that proved a vital factor in saving the empire from collapse.[1]

Although Maurice was a great administrator, he was unpopular with his troops. He had been a successful general before his accession to the throne, but as emperor he refused to lead his forces in person, and the generals he selected were not of the best. Determined to enforce rigid economy in military spending, Maurice ordered in 602 that the troops campaigning against the Avars north of the Danube should remain there throughout the winter, instead of returning to home bases as was the usual custom. Moreover, they were informed that no rations would be sent them; they were to live off the land.

These unreasonable orders sparked a revolution. Maurice, in his strongly walled capital might yet have saved his throne, but the city militia, the *Demes* of the Blues and the Greens, also turned against him and joined forces with the rebels. Maurice, Constantina, and their children fled, while the rebel leader Phokas entered the city and was acclaimed as emperor. Soon thereafter, Maurice and his sons were captured. Phokas compelled him to watch the execution of his sons, including the youngest, a mere infant, before he was himself beheaded.[2] The first Byzantine emperor to lose his throne and his life by revolution, Maurice reportedly met his death with truly imperial courage.

Coins provide the only surviving contemporary portraits of Maurice. These are so stylized that it is difficult to distinguish his likeness from that of his predecessor, Tiberius Constantine. The chronicle tradition as found in Leo Grammaticus has, however, considerable detail. "Maurice was of medium height, robust, with fair skin, a round face, reddish-gold hair beginning to go bald, and without any beard since he shaved it off as is the custom of the Romans."[3]

---

[1]George Ostrogorsky, *History of the Byzantine State*. 2nd English ed., trans. Joan M. Hussey (Oxford, 1968), p. 80.

[2]A. N. Stratos, *Byzantium in the Seventh Century*, trans. Marc Ogilvie-Grant, Vol. I (Amsterdam, 1968), p. 52.

[3]Leo Grammaticus (Bonn), p. 139; Cedrenus (Bonn), I, 691.

PHOKAS
602-610

Phokas was a tyrant, cruel and capricious, of whom little good can be said. Even his physical appearance was repellent; it was commonly said that he was as hideous as the fabled monster Medusa whose glance turned people into stone.[1] "Phokas was of medium height," says Leo Grammaticus, "but ill

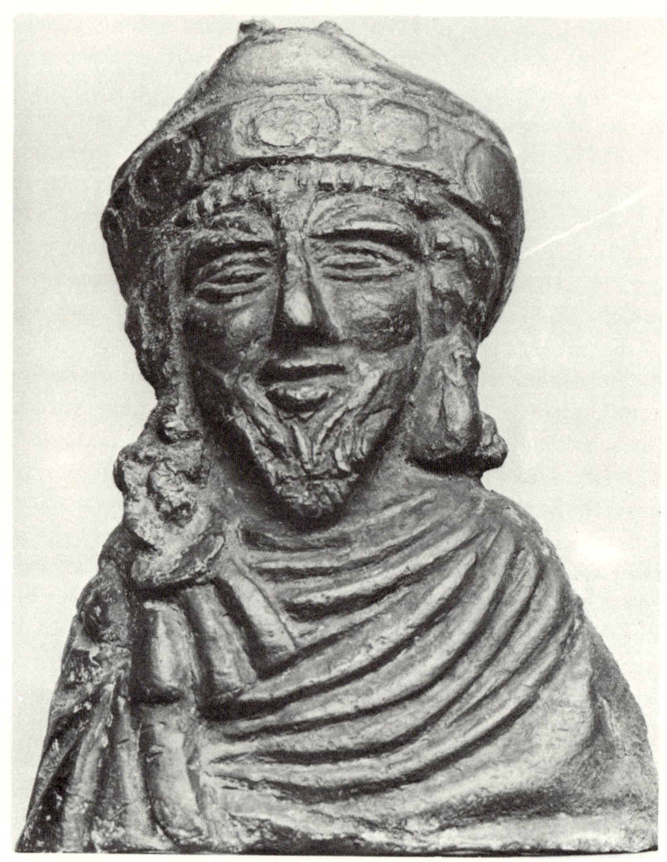

Phokas, steelyard weight. British Museum.

formed, with a swollen face, red hair, and eyebrows which grew together. His beard was clipped off and on his cheek he had a scar which darkened whenever he was angry."[2] This was all too often, as Phokas' temper was even uglier than his appearance. Lacking background for imperial responsibility (he was a non-commissioned officer when he seized the throne), he tended to be suspicious of everyone and disposed of presumed enemies with ruthless energy. His heavy drinking and carousing with the wives of his courtiers did not improve his reputation. Of his wife and empress, Leontia, practically nothing is known except that public opinion deemed her "as bad as Phokas."[3]

As emperor, Phokas was a conspicuous failure. The Persians, posing as avengers of his predecessor Maurice, invaded the empire, wreaking havoc through the eastern provinces and reaching almost to Constantinople itself, while Phokas, fearful of conspirators in his midst, indulged in a round of executions of real and imagined enemies. It was widely remarked that it was difficult to say which was doing more harm to the state: "the Persians without or the emperor within."[4]

Strangely enough, in spite of all this, Phokas remained in the good graces of the saintly and benevolent pope, Gregory the Great. The Column of Phokas, erected in the emperor's honor in the Roman Forum, is still standing, and is often called the "last monument of classical antiquity."

Phokas lost his throne as the result of a revolution launched by Herakleios, the son of the exarch of Carthage. If he had ruled badly, Phokas at least knew how to die with dignity. Brought aboard the ship of his victorious opponent, Phokas addressed his last words to Herakleios: "Are you sure that you will be able to do any better?" He was then beheaded and his remains publicly burned—to the general rejoicing of the people of Constantinople.

Byzantine historians who firmly believed the emperor to be chosen by God were puzzled as to how to explain Phokas' tenure of the throne. At last they concluded that he must have been sent to punish the empire for its sins, for God could not have found one any worse.

A steelyard weight in the form of an imperial bust provides a contemporary portrait of Phokas. In spite of the chronicler's remark that his beard was clipped off, this item and the image on his coins agree in depicting Phokas with a prominent pointed beard, grown probably to conceal at least partially the disfiguring scar on his face. He was the first emperor in many years to favor a beard, and ironically enough, set a precedent for beards that would last until the end of the empire nine centuries later.

---

[1]Bury, *Later Roman Empire from Arcadius to Irene*, II, 197.

[2]Leo Grammaticus (Bonn), p. 143; Cedrenus (Bonn), I, 708.

[3]Hugh Goodacre, *A Handbook of the Coinage of the Byzantine Empire* (London, 1957), p. 89.

[4]Stratos, *Byzantium in the Seventh Century*, I, 69.

[5]John of Antioch as quoted by Stratos, *Byzantium in the Seventh Century*, I, 90.

HERAKLEIOS OF CARTHAGE
610-641

"Herakleios was of average height, robust, with a broad chest, beautiful blue eyes, golden hair, fair complexion, and a wide, thick beard," reports Leo Grammaticus;[1] he seemed, in fact, ideally cast for his role as a heaven-sent deliverer to rescue the empire from the heavy hand of Phokas.

Herakleios' father was the exarch of Carthage, and it was he who financed the naval expedition against Constantinople that gained his son the throne. The state that Herakleios took over in 610 was on the verge of extinction, and like the mythical hero Herakles (Hercules) for whom he was named, the new emperor was called upon to perform seemingly superhuman labors to relieve the desperate situation. Through the first few years of his reign, the Persian crisis grew progressively worse. Byzantine forces were repeatedly defeated, and Palestine and Syria fell into enemy hands. Jerusalem was captured after only a short siege, and the Persians carried off the True Cross, one of the most revered of holy relics. They then moved on to attack Egypt, while elsewhere in the empire, Avars, Slavs, and Lombards continued their inroads.

At the low point, in about 620, Herakleios, who was always moody and easily moved to tears, wept openly and declared he was going back to Carthage, but the patriarch Sergios promised him the use of the extensive wealth of the Church if only he would agree to remain as emperor.[2] Encouraged, Herakleios determined to undertake new efforts. He decided, contrary to the usual custom, to lead his forces in person, and, supported by the resources supplied by the patriarch, the Byzantines launched an offensive to regain the provinces occupied by the Persians. Recruits were enlisted in return for grants of land, a system that proved very successful and that continued in use for several centuries thereafter. During the next few years, the Persians were pushed back. After Jerusalem was retaken, Herakleios entered the city in triumph to restore the True Cross to its place, an occasion that would be long remembered among the most glorious in Byzantine history.

Wherever he went, Herakleios was accompanied by his loyal wife, Martina. Several of the ten children that she bore him were born in military outposts on the far borders of the empire. While the majority of Byzantines—soldiers and civilians alike—seemingly adored Herakleios, his marriage was unpopular because Martina was his niece as well as his wife. Many believed the union incestuous and the imperial children illegitimate; the blame for all this was placed upon the empress, though most unfairly so.

By the early 630s, the Byzantine world under Herakleios apparently stood at the gateway to a new golden age. Not only was the Persian foe subdued, but the Avars had suffered a crushing defeat, and many of the Slavs were being peaceably settled on government land grants. The emperor stood on good terms with all the major powers from the Kingdom of the Franks in the west to India in the east.

When new trouble arose, it came from an area where it was least expected. Out of the Arabian desert burst warriors inflamed by Islam, the new religion established by the prophet Muhammed only a few years earlier. Byzantium's eastern provinces, drained by the long war with Persia and full of strife among rival sects of Christians, were easy prey for the Muslim conquerors. Syria and Palestine were lost again—this time forever.

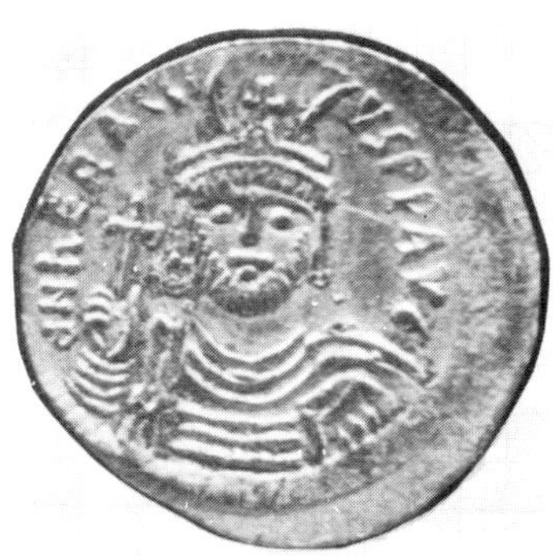
Herakleios of Carthage, coin of his reign. American Numismatic Society.

The emperor Herakleios, old and ill, was so disheartened by this wave of disasters that he seemed unable to provide decisive leadership. His lifelong phobias grew worse; he was so afraid of water that on one occasion he lingered for months on the coast of the Bosphoros opposite Constantinople, finally agreeing to cross over a bridge of boats heavily camoflauged with shrubbery.[3] For several years longer, the emperor lingered in his palace, torn by intense mental and physical agony, attended by his faithful Martina, while the empire he had worked so hard to rebuild continued to disintegrate before the forces of Islam.

Herakleios' coins provide what is probably a good likeness of this emperor. On early issues his beard is short; in his old age, his beard, which the sources tell us turned from gold to snowy white, is very long. Except for the coins, there are apparently no surviving contemporary portraits of Herakleios.[4]

---

[1]Leo Grammaticus (Bonn), p. 147.

[2]Stratos, *Byzantium in the Seventh Century*, I, 126-127.

[3]A. N. Stratos, *Byzantium in the Seventh Century*, Vol. II, trans. Harry T. Hionides (Amsterdam, 1972), p. 139.

[4]A manuscript miniature of Job and his daughters is sometimes interpreted as a portrait of Herakleios and the women of his family. For details see Joannis Spatharakis, *The Portrait in Byzantine Illuminated Manuscripts* (Leiden, 1976), pp. 16-20.

HERAKLEIOS-CONSTANTINE
641

Herakleios of Carthage had his first-born son christened Herakleios ho neos Konstantinos—Herakleios the new Constantine. This confusing name is shortened in various ways by subsequent historians, and the short-lived, frail emperor appears variously as Herakleios II, Constantine II, or even Constan-

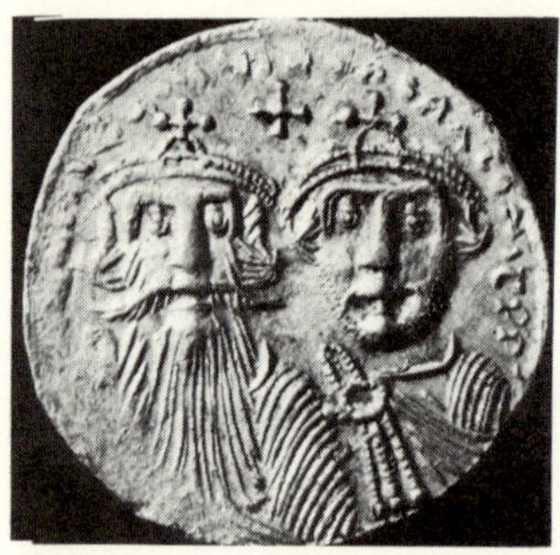

Herakleios with his son Herakleios-Constantine, coin of their joint reign. American Numismatic Society.

tine III. Probably it is best to call him Herakleios-Constantine, since he used both names officially himself.

Herakleios-Constantine's mother was not Martina, but Fabia-Eudokia, a Carthaginian girl whom Herakleios married immediately after his accession to the throne. Fabia died very young. Her son seemingly inherited something of her physical weakness, for although he was not quite thirty when he succeeded to his father's throne, he was already dying of a malady that was most likely tuberculosis. "He was weak of body," writes Leo Grammaticus, "and grew weaker every day."[1]

Herakleios-Constantine had been co-emperor for some years before his father's death, and during that time, before he was so incapacitated by illness, he gave promise of being a capable and dedicated ruler. It was he who directed affairs of state in the capital during the long years that his father was absent on military campaigns.

In Herakleios' old age, the emperor, pressured by Martina and probably realizing, too, that his eldest son's poor health rendered it unlikely that he would reign long, decreed in his will that the throne should be shared by Herakleios-Constantine and Martina's young son, Heraklonas. Both were to look to Martina for political guidance, an unrealistic provision, almost sure to lead to trouble.

As it turned out, Herakleios-Constantine outlived his father by only three months. While his death was clearly the result of his long illness, Martina's numerous enemies alleged that she had poisoned him.[2] The empire, torn by Muslim invaders, was on the verge of dire internal upheavals as well.

Something of the insecurity of the times is seen in the fact that the chronicle sources represented in the later writings of Leo Grammaticus, Cedrenus, and others, cease at this point to provide any physical description of the emperor; the only contemporary portraits of Herakleios-Constantine are those of the young co-emperor beside his father Herakleios, on the coins of their joint reign.

---

[1]Leo Grammaticus (Bonn), p. 156.

[2]Stratos, *Byzantium in the Seventh Century*, II, 183.

Herakleonas, his father Herakleios and his half-brother Herakleios-Constantine, coin of their joint reign. American Numismatic Society.

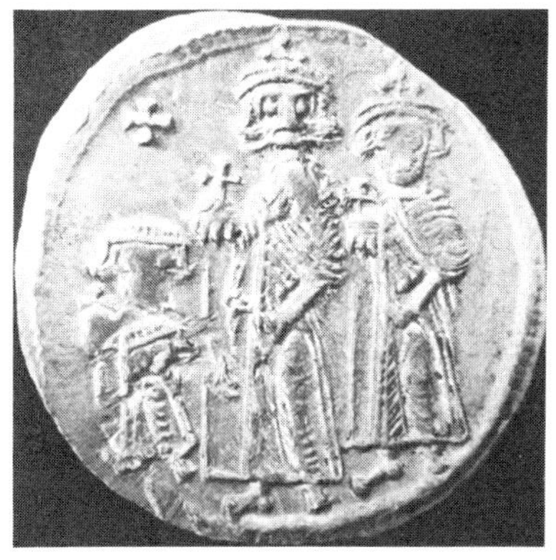

HERAKLEIOS II (called Heraklonas)
641

Heraklonas is a nickname meaning little Herakleios. Since Herakleios of Carthage bestowed his own name on more than one of his sons, this young emperor was generally called Heraklonas to distinguish him from others in the family.

Though several of Martina's other children were physically afflicted, Heraklonas seems to have been a normal, healthy boy. He was fifteen at the time of his father's death. When his half-brother, Herakleios-Constantine, died three months later, Heraklonas became sole emperor. The persons who opposed Martina were eager to bring about his downfall and, hoping to avert this, Heraklonas agreed to accept his young nephew, Constans, Herakleios-Constantine's son, as his co-emperor.

It was a useless effort. Within a few months, the enemies of Martina, led by prominent members of the Byzantine Senate, took her and her son into custody. Contrary to the usual rule sparing women from punishment by mutilation, Martina was subjected to *glossotomia*: her tongue was cut out. The sentence inflicted upon young Heraklonas was *rhinokopia*, mutilation of the nose. Mother and son were then whisked away to the island of Rhodes where they completely disappear from history.[1]

The only portraits of Heraklonas are those where he appears as a small boy on the coins of his joint reign with father and half-brother. The written sources give no hint as to his appearance.

---

[1]Stratos, *Byzantium in the Seventh Century*, II, 205.

CONSTANTINE III (also known as Constans II)
641-668

It is difficult to imagine the emperor Constans as ever being young, for the coin-portraits from his later years depict him with what is probably the longest beard in the entire series of Byzantine emperors. Actually, Constans was a boy of eleven when he succeeded to the throne. At that time, he changed his baptismal name of Herakleios to Constantine. The people apparently always called him by the nickname Constans (little Constantine), and it is by that name that he is usually listed among the Byzantine sovereigns.[1]

Although he was not personally to blame for the deposition and mutilation of his young uncle Heraklonas and the empress Martina, Constans grew up stern and hard, and it seems probable that the grim set of circumstances that secured him his throne made a deep impression on his character.

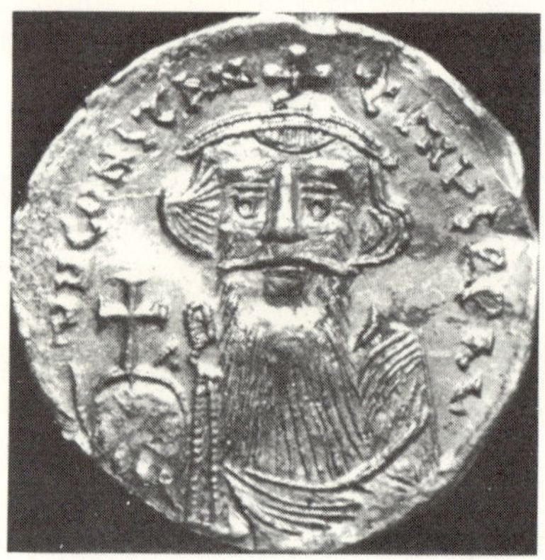

Constantine III (Constans), coin of his reign. American Numismatic Society.

Constans' early reign was marked by continued Byzantine losses in the face of Arab aggression. Egypt fell into Muslim hands in 642, and Byzantium would never again recover the land that had been one of her richest provinces.

As soon as he was old enough, Constans assumed personal command of his army. He proved to be an excellent soldier and, particularly in his struggle against the increasing Slavic pressure in the Balkans, he won some important victories. Later Byzantine chroniclers have little good to say for him, however, since his religious policy was in direct defiance of Orthodox belief. Constans probably cared little about doctrine of any sort; but in an attempt to settle the Monothelete question, he issued an edict, *The Typos*, designed to stop all dispute on this, the bitterest religious issue of the day. *The Typos* simply forbade all discussion of whether Christ possessed only one Divine Will or two Wills, one divine and one human. This moratorium on argument did not work as Constans had hoped. *The Typos* met with vast opposition, particularly from Maximos the Confessor and Pope Martin I. Both were brutally punished for their views. Pope Martin was arrested, spirited away from Rome, and sent into exile in the distant city of Cherson, where he died not long afterwards of the privations he had suffered.

For causes unknown, the emperor Constans also killed his own brother, Theodosios. It is likely that Theodosios was plotting to seize the throne. But whatever the reason, Constans reportedly was so disturbed by horrible nightmares afterwards that he determined to leave Constantinople forever and relocate the imperial capital somewhere in the West.[2] His decision to move may have been prompted, too, by a belief that the defense of the empire against the Arabs could be better conducted from a base in Italy.

After a lengthy tour of Byzantine Italy, Constans decided to settle in the Sicilian city of Syracuse. When he sent word for his wife Fausta and their sons to join him there, the people of Constantinople rioted and would not let them leave.

Constans was determined to remain in Sicily, and it was there that one day while he was bathing, an attendant struck him over the head with a heavy, silver-trimmed soapdish.[3] The blow proved fatal to the thirty-eight-year-old sovereign. With him died all thought of Syracuse as the imperial capital.

---

[1]A. N. Stratos, *Byzantium in the Seventh Century*, Vol. III (Amsterdam, 1975), pp. 2-3, rightly insists that this ruler's legal name was Constantine and urges avoidance of the name Constans. Readers should be warned, however, that in most studies he is still referred to as Constans II. (Further confusion ensues from the fact that Byzantium has no Constans I. That name belongs to a son of Constantine the Great who reigned as emperor in the West, 337-350.)

[2]Cedrenus (Bonn), I, 762.

[3]Theophanes (de Boor), pp. 351-352. See also Stratos, *Byzantium in the Seventh Century*, III, 254.

CONSTANTINE IV
668-685

Constantine IV was sixteen years old when his father Constans was murdered. Though rebel forces in Sicily tried to install another candidate as emperor, Constantine was readily accepted by the people of Constantinople, and his right to the throne was never seriously jeopardized. Although he agreed to accept his two younger brothers, Herakleios and Tiberius, as co-emperors, later in his reign he turned against them, deprived them of their titles, and, according to one report, subjected them both to *rhinokopia*.[1]

The famed mosaic portrait of Constantine IV in Ravenna's Church of St. Appollinaire in Classe depicts the emperor's family in happier days. To the right of Constantine (and on the viewer's left) stand the two imperial brothers and Constantine's son, the crown prince Justinian, later to reign as Justinian II. The golden-haired, hollow-cheeked emperor Constantine is clad in a costume almost exactly like that worn by his hero Justinian I in the mosaic portrait of San Vitale. Although he is here depicted as clean-shaven, on some of his coins he displays a short beard. In no instance does his beard reach the tremendous proportions of that of his father, Constans; for this reason, modern scholars have determined that the epithet Pogonatos, 'the Bearded One', sometimes accorded him on the ancient emperor-lists, actually belonged to Constans instead.[2]

Constantine IV's most important achievement came in his defense of Constantinople during the city's five-year siege by the Muslims from 674 to 678. It was during this struggle that the Byzantines employed for the first time their famous secret weapon, 'Greek fire', a compound recently developed by a Syrian refugee scholar, Kallinikos. Greek fire was a highly combustible liquid; hurled through tubes or in other containers at the enemy fleet, it would burst into flames which water would not quench. Even with this powerful advantage on their side, the Byzantines drove off the enemy only after much hard fighting had taken place and famine had struck the Arab forces. If the battle for Constantinople in the 670s had gone the other way, all of southeastern Europe would have lain open to the Muslim advance and the course of subsequent history would have been profoundly altered.

Constantine also warred, with some success, against the Slavs and Bulgars. Then in 680 he led his forces on a raid deep into Bulgar territory. When the enemy stubbornly refused to appear for battle, the emperor, who was afflicted with gout, left camp to 'take the waters' at a health resort. His departure was misunderstood by his soldiers. Believing that Constantine had fled, his men panicked and hastened to retreat. In the ensuing disorder, the Bulgars fell upon the imperial forces, slaughtering many and pursuing the survivors south across the Danube. The Bulgar problem was much intensified as a result, and Constantine finally had to agree to a regular subsidy payment to this warlike people in order to keep them at peace.[3]

Constantine died of dysentery at the age of thirty-three. His successor was his son, Justinian II.

---

[1]For details see E. W. Brooks, "The Brothers of the Emperor Constantine IV," *English Historical Review* 30 (1915), 42-51.

[2]E. W. Brooks, "Who Was Constantine Pogonatus?", *Byzantinische Zeitschrift* 17 (1908), 460-462.

[3]Theophanes (de Boor), pp. 356-359.

JUSTINIAN II RHINOTMETOS
685-695 and 705-711

The son of Constantine IV and his empress Anastasia, Justinian II succeeded to the throne at the age of sixteen. During his first reign, he demonstrated great ability; unfortunately, he was also very willful and hot-tempered. His arbitrary disposition earned him many enemies, and, when he was twenty-six, he was dethroned as the result of a sudden coup d'etat.

Leontios, the victorious general who became his successor, decreed for Justinian the penalty of *rhinokopia*—the cutting off of his nose. Since no man with a serious physical defect was eligible to reign, Leontios believed Justinian to be permanently disqualified from any claim to the throne. In addition, he was banished to Cherson, a distant port city on the Black Sea.

Deposed and disfigured though he was, however, Justinian II never gave up. After several years in Cherson, he escaped to the land of the Khazars, a barbarian tribe which held much of the Crimea and surrounding lands. The

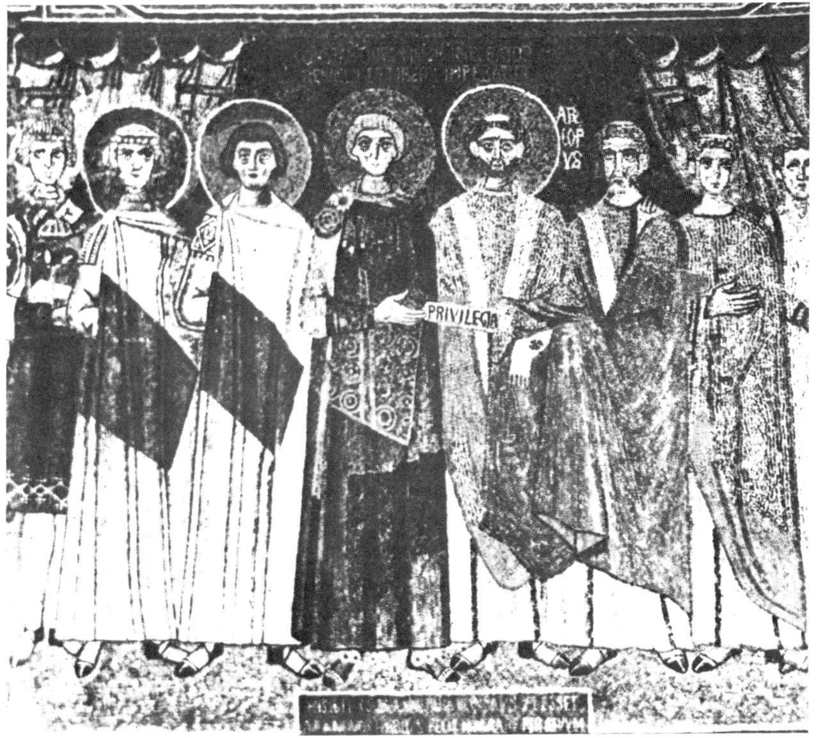

Constantine IV (fourth from left) with his son Justinian II (extreme left), mosaic in the church of Sant'Apollinare in Classe. Ravenna, Italy.

khagan of the Khazars welcomed Justinian, promised him aid in regaining his empire, and gave him his sister as a wife. Justinian named his Khazar bride Theodora in memory of the first Justinian's empress. Like that famous couple in an earlier century, the second Justinian and Theodora proved to be deeply devoted to each other.

The khagan, it turned out, was a false friend, and learning that the emperor in Constantinople was offering a reward for Justinian, he planned to betray him. Theodora, however, learned of the plot and warned her husband so that he was able to escape from Khazaria.[1] After many further adventures, Justinian and a few of his loyal supporters reached Bulgaria. Here he won promises of aid from the khan of the Bulgars, and in 705, Justinian II and his allies marched on Constantinople. It is unlikely that they would ever have taken the city had not the former ruler been aware of a tunnel under the walls. Through it, he and his men effected their entry. The reigning emperor (who was no longer Leontios, but Tiberius Apsimar) fled in dismay.

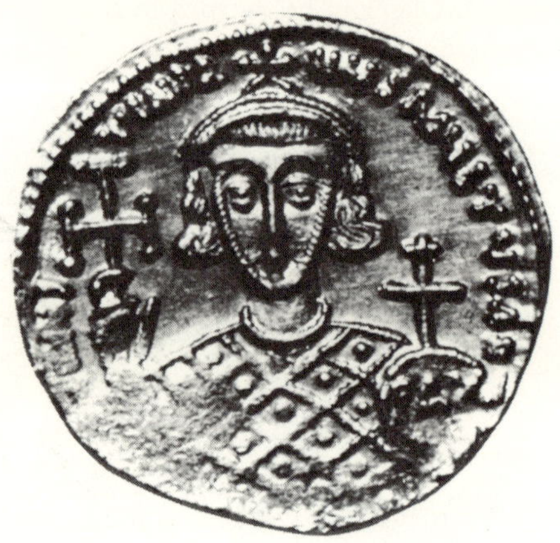

Justinian II, coin of his second reign. Dumbarton Oaks.

Thus Justinian II reigned again, in spite of the ancient rule that should have disqualified him from emperorship. It is said that he hid his disfigurement as best he could by wearing an artificial nose of pure gold.[2]

One of Justinian's first acts after his recovery of the empire was to send to Khazaria for his wife. Theodora of the Khazars was Byzantium's first empress born to a barbarian tribe beyond the empire's frontiers—another shattering of tradition.

The records of Justinian's second reign are difficult to evaluate.[3] Though there is considerable evidence of constructive statesmanship on his part, Byzantine chroniclers generally picture him as obsessed by a drive for vengeance that surpassed all bounds of reason. In any event, in 711, Justinian II lost his life at the hands of a mutinous army.

Other than the childhood portrait of Justinian II with his father in the Ravenna mosaic, the only definitely identified images of this emperor are found on his coins. These are unusually fine, and present a vivid likeness of the emperor's thin face with its prominent pointed chin. Interestingly, the coins of his second reign, including the one pictured, reveal no hint of the mutilation of his nose; to depict the emperor's deformity would not have been consonant with the ideals of Byzantine art.

---

[1]Theophanes (de Boor), p. 378.

[2]Agnellus of Ravenna, "De Sancto Felice." In *Liber Pontificalis Ecclesiae Ravennatis*. Edited by O. Holder-Egger. *Monumenta Germaniae Historica: Scriptores Rerum Langobardicum et Italicarum Saec. VI-IX*. Hanover, 1878, p. 367.

[3]For details see Constance Head, *Justinian II of Byzantium* (Madison, 1972), pp. 112 ff.

LEONTIOS
695-698

The coins of Leontios present one of the most realistic portraits in the entire series of Byzantine coinage.[1] The likeness of the fat, round-faced emperor is strikingly individualized. By birth, Leontios was an Isaurian.[2] He rose to prominence as a general in the reign of Constantine IV and was a close friend of that emperor.

Before his overthrow of Justinian II, Leontios had been imprisoned for three years, probably for some military blunder. Then Justinian suddenly ordered his release, appointed him governor of the newly organized *theme* (military province) of Hellas, and declared that he must depart at once for this new post together with a body of troops assigned to his command.

Instead of carrying out these orders, Leontios seized the moment to stage a coup. With his forces, he stormed the prison where he had been incarcerated and released all its inmates. Meanwhile, his supporters aroused the townspeople, especially the members of the Blue Deme of the city militia. The twenty-six-year-old emperor Justinian was taken prisoner; on the following morning, after the crowds in the Hippodrome had acclaimed Leontios as their new sovereign, he pronounced his verdict upon his fallen rival. Leontios believed himself merciful in decreeing that Justinian suffer *rhinokopia* rather than death. The mutilation of Justinian's nose was carried out forthwith before the throng of spectators in the Hippodrome.

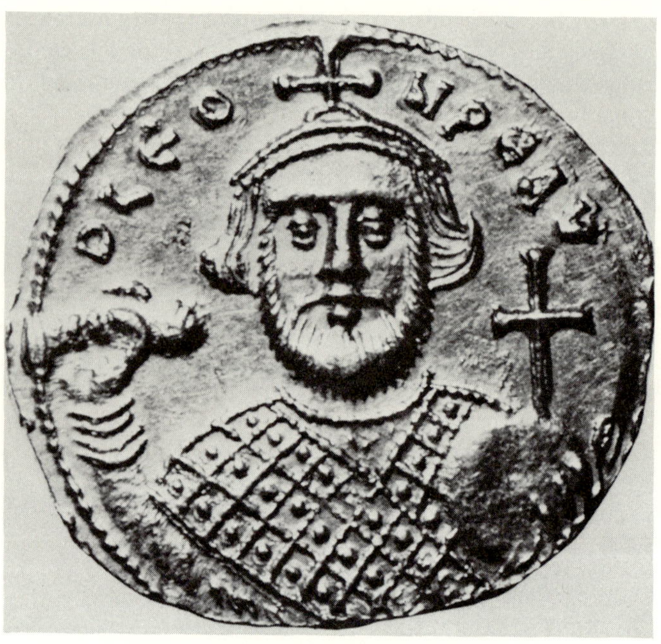

Leontios, coin of his reign. Dumbarton Oaks.

Leontios did not have long to enjoy the throne which he had won. So brief was his reign that later Byzantine historians even forgot his attempt to change his official name to Leo.[3] He is actually the third Leo, but is never numbered as such.

The major crisis of Leontios's short reign was the fall of Carthage to the Arabs. It was this disaster that cost him his crown, for the defeated Byzantine fleet feared to return to Constantinople with a report of their losses; thus on the homeward voyage they selected a naval officer, Apsimar, as a rival contender for the throne.

Leontios was apparently unpopular with many of his subjects in the capital, particularly the Deme of the Greens, and, when they threw their support to Apsimar, the rebel officer's victory was assured.

Apsimar sentenced Leontios to *rhinokopia*, then compelled him to enter a monastery in Constantinople. It was not until seven years later that Leontios was executed, side by side with his adversary Apsimar, when Justinian II returned from exile to reclaim the throne.

---

[1]J. P. C. Kent, "The Mystery of Leontius II," *Numismatic Chronicle*, 6th series, 14 (1954), 217-218, first identified Leontios' coinage as distinct from that of Leo III.

[2]For details see Constance Head, "Who Was the Real 'Leo the Isaurian'?", *Byzantion* 41 (1971), 105-108.

[3]Kent, "Mystery of Leontius II," pp. 217-218.

TIBERIUS APSIMAR
698-705

Very little is known of the emperor Apsimar, the naval officer who seized the throne of Leontios, but the few historical notices of his reign suggest that he was a conscientious and effective ruler. He warred with some success against the perennial enemy, the Arabs, and had he reigned longer, he might well have gone down in history as one of the truly great emperors of Byzantium.

Apsimar selected the additional name Tiberius when he claimed the throne, probably feeling it was more suited to the imperial dignity than the Germanic Apsimar. The custom of selecting a throne name was very popular at this period of Byzantine history, but would disappear completely in later times. So little is known of the emperors of the troubled times from 695 to 717 that in most instances even the names of their empresses have not been preserved. It is recorded, however, that Apsimar had a son, Theodosius, who later became the bishop of Ephesus.[1]

Apsimar was himself the first navy man to succeed to the Byzantine throne; the navy never carried as much prestige among the Byzantines as did the army.

It is perhaps indicative of the defense orientation of Tiberius Apsimar's reign that he is depicted on his coins in military costume, rather than in civil garb like his predecessor Leontios. The imperial portrait is considerably more stylized than Leontios'; while the craftsmanship of the coins throughout this whole period is unusually fine, and while Apsimar may have possessed the thin,

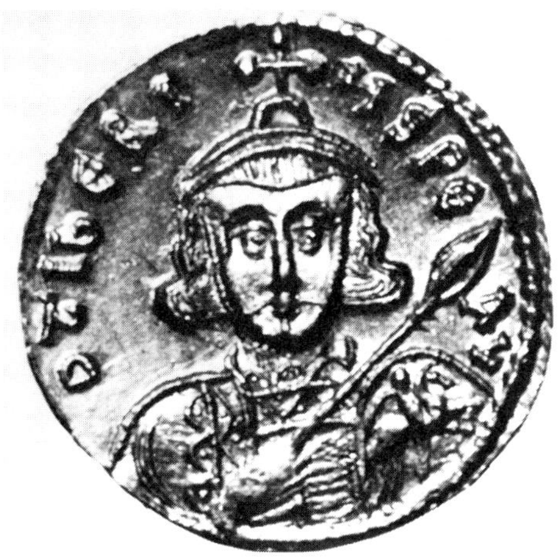

Tiberius Apsimar, coin of his reign. Dumbarton Oaks.

oval face his coins depict, it is disconcerting to discover the very close resemblance he bears to his next few successors, none of whom was related.

Tiberius Apsimar escaped from Constantinople when Justinian II made his surprising return to power. Justinian immediately posted a reward for his capture. Apsimar was found in Apollonias and forcibly returned to Constantinople. There, probably early in 706, Justinian conducted a ceremony in the Hippodrome: while his two fallen rivals, Leontios and Apsimar, knelt before him, a choir chanted the biblically inspired passage, "Thou shalt tread upon the Lion and the Asp." After Justinian had literally placed his feet upon his enemies' backs, the Lion and the Asp, Leontios and Apsimar, were whisked away and beheaded.[2]

---

[1]Theophanes (de Boor), p. 427.

[2]Theophanes (de Boor), p. 375.

PHILIPPIKOS VARDAN
711-713

Vardan was an Armenian by birth and a member of the Monothelete Christian sect considered heretical by the Orthodox. Reportedly, he began to have imperial aspirations when he dreamed that an eagle flew over him and sheltered him. He was rash enough to speak of this dream openly, for which he was imprisoned by Tiberius Apsimar, but he was released when Justinian II returned to power and promoted to a high rank in the imperial army.[1]

In 711, Justinian sent forces to subdue the city of Cherson, where he had spent the years of his exile. Although the chroniclers claim that the emperor acted solely out of a desire for vengeance, it is clear that another reason—and perhaps the prime reason—for this campaign was the alarming expansionist activity of Justinian's brother-in-law, the khagan of the Khazars.[2]

As a result of a complicated series of intrigues, Justinian's forces outside Cherson joined with the Chersonites and the Khazars and nominated Vardan as their contender for the imperial throne. It was at this point that he bestowed upon himself the name of Philippikos, which he must have thought exceptionally elegant, even though it had never been borne by a previous emperor. Philippikos Vardan was reportedly a good-natured, pleasant-tempered man, and no doubt these attributes helped make him the rebel army's choice for emperor. At the time, no one seemed unduly concerned over his Monotheletism.

While Philippikos remained safely with his allies, the Khazars, his Byzantine adherents marched toward Constantinople. Justinian II could probably

Philippikos Vardan, coin of his reign. Dumbarton Oaks.

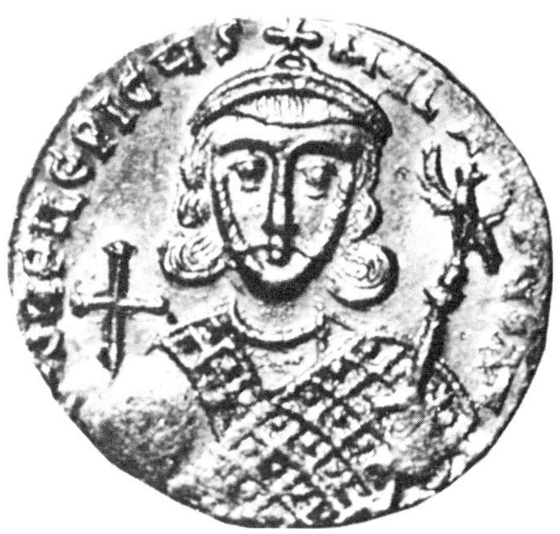

have crushed the revolt had he remained inside his strongly fortified capital, but the hot-headed emperor, unable to bear such inaction, left the city and was captured by Philippikos Vardan's men a few miles outside the walls. He was promptly beheaded.

Installed as emperor, Philippikos Vardan rapidly lost popularity because of his unorthodox religious leanings. After a reign of less than two years, while taking his afernoon siesta, he was seized by a band of conspirators. The old custom of *rhinokopia* was not inflicted upon him, nor would it ever be used again on a fallen monarch, since the second reign of Justinian II had proved that mutilation of the nose was no bar to emperorship. Philippikos was subjected to the even more terrible penalty of blinding and then confined in a monastery. His subsequent fate is unknown.

Philippikos Vardan's coins present a highly stylized portrait of this unfortunate monarch. They are interesting, however, in the unique detail of the eagle-tipped scepter held by the emperor, a symbol that must have been chosen in reference to his prophetic dream of rulership.

---

[1]Theophanes (de Boor), p. 372.

[2]Theophanes (de Boor), p. 379.

ANASTASIOS II ARTEMIOS
713-715

Artemios was a treasury official. Reportedly he was not personally involved in the plot to depose and blind Philippikos Vardan, but, taking advantage of the confusion this intrigue caused, he managed to seize the throne. He followed the now-common practice of adopting a new name at his coronation

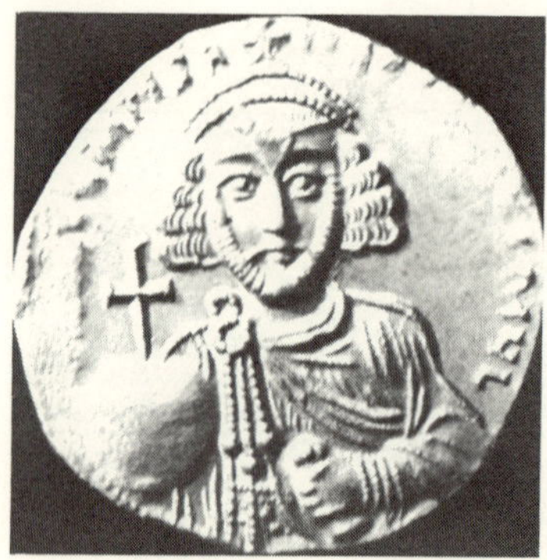

Anastasios II Artemios, coin of his reign. American Numismatic Society.

and chose to call himself Anastasios in memory of the first emperor of that name, who was like himself a civilian and a treasury employee before his accession.

Although he was apparently a dedicated and hard-working emperor, Anastasios II's lack of military experience made him highly unpopular with the Byzantine armies of the various *themes* (military provinces). Few details are known of his reign; even the exact dates are uncertain. In any event, he fell after about two years in power, when the rebel forces of the Opsikion *theme* were able to install their candidate for the throne, Theodosios III.

Anastasios Artemios was allowed to retire unmolested to a monastery and there might have lived out his days in peace had he not become involved in a plot to regain his crown a few years later. Leo III, who was then emperor, defeated this attempt and had Anastasios put to death.[1]

Anastasios is another of the sovereigns whose only contemporary portrait is preserved on his coins. As would be expected, he is dressed in purely civilian garb, tunic and *chlamys*. Though his image is highly stylized, his unusually bushy hair may well represent an authentic characteristic of this emperor.

---

[1]Theophanes (de Boor), p. 400.

THEODOSIOS III
715-717

Most unwilling of all emperors was Theodosios the Reluctant, whose story provides an element of comic relief in the sad chronicle of early eighth-century Byzantium.[1] A local tax-collector in the town of Adramyttion, Theodosios was sitting in his office tending to business when a group of rebel officers from the Opsikion *theme* entered. They asked him his name, and when they dis-

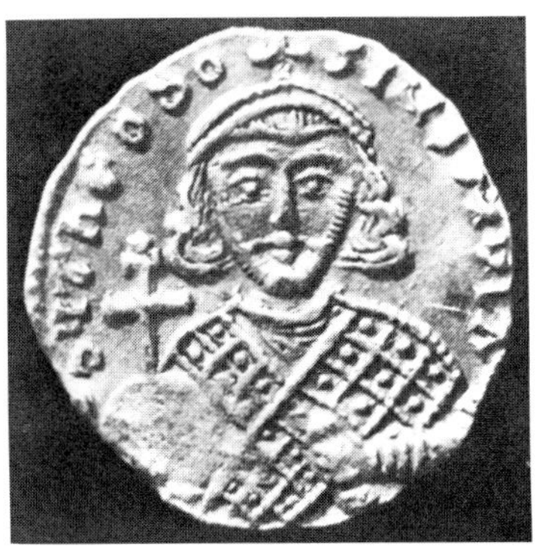

Theodosios III, coin of his reign. American Numismatic Society.

covered it was Theodosios, they assured him that this was a sufficient requisite for emperorship. Actually the position of emperor had become so insecure in recent years that none of the men planning the coup against Anastasios II wanted to claim the title for himself. The obscure tax-collector, they assumed, would be a useful puppet in their hands.

Theodosios of Adramyttion had no imperial aspirations, and protested loudly against accepting the title offered him. The men who had found him, however, forcibly took him from his office and declared that, whether he liked it or not, he would march with them to Constantinople. In the hectic events that followed, Theodosios actually managed to escape his overly-enthusiastic adherents, but they recaptured him, and the intrigue moved forward with their unwilling candidate in nominal leadership.

Constantinople surrendered to Theodosios' forces not long thereafter. The new emperor, still reluctant, was duly crowned, but he was principally concerned with how he might abdicate—as rapidly and painlessly as possible.

Meanwhile, a brilliant young general, Leo, commander of the troops of the Anatolikon *theme*, announced a claim to the throne. At this critical moment, it was widely known that the Arabs were preparing for a siege of Constantinople. A strong and well-qualified emperor was desperately needed if the city were to survive the Arab attack. Against this background, Theodosios gladly gave up his throne to Leo and retired to a monastery in Ephesus. There he lived for the rest of his life. Apparently he found himself ideally suited to the monastic routine and, when he died many years later, his tomb came to be regarded as a holy spot, where many miracles of healing reputedly took place.[2] Thus the Reluctant Emperor is found on many Orthodox calendars as St. Theodosios, a man who was a far better monk than a sovereign.

There is little except his costume to distinguish Theodosios' coin portrait from that of his recent predecessors. As might be expected, coins of his short reign are very rare.

---

[1]Theophanes (de Boor), p. 386.

[2]Philip Grierson, "The Tombs and Obits of the Byzantine Emperors (337-1042)," *Dumbarton Oaks Papers* 16 (1962), 52-53.

LEO III, THE ICONOCLAST
717-741

Leo's real name was Conon; Leo was a childhood nickname bestowed upon him for his lion-like courage, and when he became emperor he made it his official name.[1] Though he is often given the epithet 'Isaurian' on the ancient emperor-lists, Leo was not an Isaurian.[2] By birth he was a North Syrian, and when he was a young boy his family moved to the province of Thrace, not far from Constantinople. Of peasant stock, he volunteered for service in Justinian II's army when that emperor was marching to regain his throne. Leo's quick thinking and intelligence won him rapid promotions, and, by the time of Anastasios II, he was commander of the troops of the Anatolikon *theme*.

Leo became emperor at one of the most crucial points in Byzantine history. Almost immediately after his accession, the Arabs launched their greatest effort thus far against the imperial capital, besieging the city by land and sea. Leo's victory over them after a year's siege is as important to the further development of European civilization as Constantine IV's similar triumph nearly half a century earlier. Never again would the Arabs come so near to conquering Constantinople.

A few years later, Leo III undertook to enforce his new religious policy of iconoclasm—the destruction of religious images and pictures. The underlying causes of the iconoclast movement were many and diverse. It is certainly true that among the more ignorant Byzantines, veneration of images or icons had degenerated to the level of superstition and idol-worship. It is likely, too, that Leo resented the undue influence that the monks, who manufactured icons, held over the common people. Moreover, among the people in the frontier areas between the Byzantine and the Muslim worlds, there was widespread knowledge of the Islamic prohibition of graven images. Perhaps Leo, who was born in such an environment, thought that Muslims might be more readily converted to Christianity if Christians would abandon the matter that caused so much contention. As a soldier, Leo also knew that many of the troops from the eastern *themes* scorned the use of icons, and the policy of iconoclasm proved very popular with them.

The vast majority of Byzantines, however, were iconodules—those who favored the use of icons as aids to worship. As long as he lived, he persisted in trying to enforce iconoclasm, but Leo III's policy was never widely accepted.

Since later Byzantines remembered Leo III as an iconoclast and *ipso facto* a heretic, the chroniclers scarcely gave him credit for his important accomplishments outside the field of theology. Under Leo's sponsorship, a recodification of Byzantine law was promulgated. The *Ekloga*, as this work was called, incorporated many changes and tended to be more merciful than the law code of Justinian I.

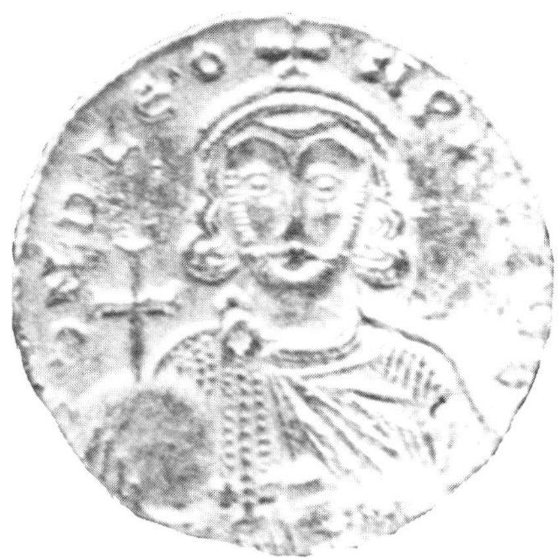

Leo III, coin of his reign.
American Numismatic Society.

Almost nothing is known of the empress Maria, Leo's wife. Their first-born son, Constantine V, was designated co-emperor as an infant, and at Leo's death years later succeeded to the throne.

While the iconoclast emperors did not prohibit the production of their own portraits, the numismatic art of the period became more rigidly stylized, less representational, than ever before. Other contemporary portraits of the unpopular Leo and his son and grandson have simply not survived, and hence there is practically nothing to give a clear indication of the appearance of any of the iconoclast dynasty.

---

[1]Ostrogorsky, *History of the Byzantine State*, p. 155, n.2.

[2]Karl Schenk, "Kaiser Leons III Walten im Innern," *Byzantinische Zeitschrift* 5 (1896), 296 ff.

CONSTANTINE V
741-775

Like his father, Leo III, Constantine V was an iconoclast, and as emperor he pushed for the implementation of iconoclasm more vigorously and violently than Leo had ever done. The Orthodox believers of his time were convinced of his outrageous impiety, and Byzantine historians have preserved many anecdoctes illustrating his radical point of view. Reportedly he so disliked the words saint and holy that these terms had to be dropped from the names of Constantinople's churches; one had to say, for instance, "I am going to Sophia's," rather than to Hagia Sophia. He despised holy relics as well as icons

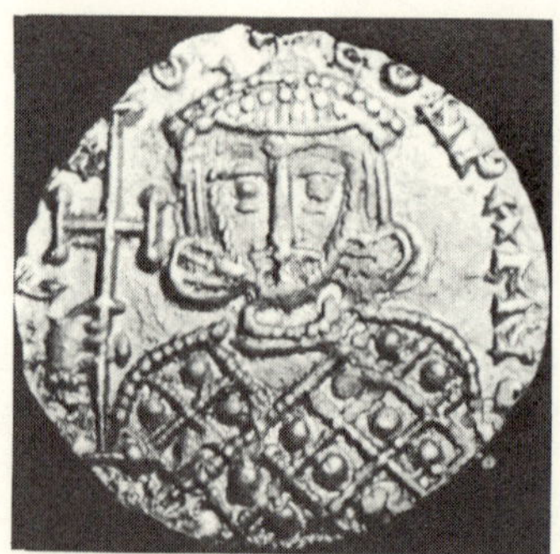

Constantine V, coin of his reign. American Numismatic Society.

and ordered the destruction of many of them. Exhibiting a freethinking viewpoint extremely rare for his time, he denounced the use of the epithet 'Mother of God' for Mary and commented, "Mary gave birth to Jesus just as my mother Mary gave birth to me."[1]

Constantine was particularly harsh in his dealings with monks and nuns. Thousands of them were compelled to leave their cloisters and marry. Hundreds more fled to southern Italy in order to avoid the emperor's decrees.

To Constantine's iconodule opponents, everything the emperor did was scandalous. He played the lute very well, but his enemies even denounced his musical ability as a sinful waste of time. Rumor had it that he practiced black magic, and other serious charges were launched against his moral behavior. It is very difficult to evaluate how true these statements are, since almost nothing has survived that presents his own viewpoint and that of his supporters, the iconoclasts.

Constantine married three times. His first wife, Irene of the Khazars, died giving birth to the throne-heir, Leo, and his second wife, Maria, also died very young. Constantine's third marriage to Eudokia defied the Orthodox tradition prohibiting more than two marriages, but Constantine was never bothered by Orthodox tradition. Eudokia presented her husband with a large family, including a set of twins.

Whatever his religious policies, Constantine was unquestionably a great warrior emperor. Though physically frail and frequently troubled by ill health, he led his troops in person. Much of his reign was spent in campaigns against Bulgaria, Byzantium's aggressive neighbor to the north. Constantine was an outstanding strategist and a good organizer, much admired by his troops.

He died while on campaign against the Bulgars. The fact that some favorable memory of him remained among his subjects is demonstrated by the custom that arose after his death: in times of military crisis crowds would gather around his green marble tomb and invoke his aid against Byzantium's foes.[2]

---

[1]Theophanes (de Boor), p. 415.

[2]Ostrogorsky, *History of the Byzantine State*, p. 175.

Constantine V and his son Leo IV, The Khazar, coin of their joint reign. American Numismatic Society.

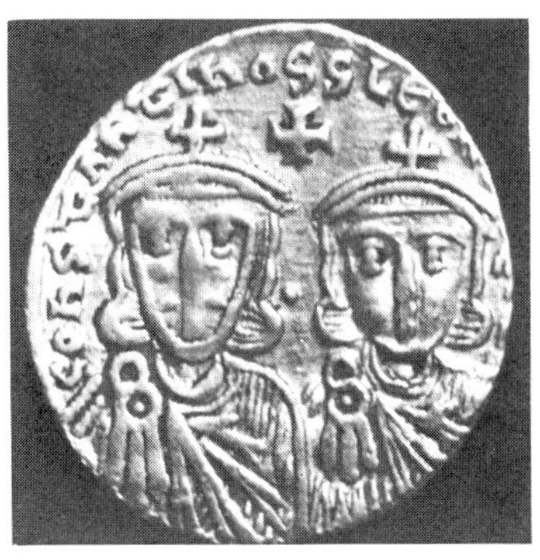

LEO IV, THE KHAZAR
775-789

Leo was really only half-Khazar; his mother Irene was a princess of that exotic tribe of the Russian steppes. After a long period as co-emperor with his father, Constantine V, Leo succeeded to sole emperorship in 775. He was a frail young man and would die after a reign of only five years. It is interesting to note that his favorite hobby was collecting rare and precious stones, a small fact that makes this rather obscure emperor seem a bit more human.[1]

Leo was an iconclast, but not an extremely vigorous one. He did not share his father's hatred of monasticism and allowed hundreds of monks and nuns who had fled during Constantine's reign to return to their cloisters. In adopting more lenient policies, he was perhaps influenced by the weight of public opinion which ran strongly against iconoclasm and in favor of the monastic movement.

Leo's empress was Irene, a Greek girl from the quiet provincial town of Athens. She was not a princess or an aristocrat, and how he happened to choose her is unknown; perhaps it was for her reputedly outstanding beauty. In any case, Irene secretly favored the use of icons. Though she concealed her opinion from her husband, kept her own icons hidden under pillows in her suite, and lied boldly when Leo discovered them there, it is none the less likely that her influence was responsible for Leo's more merciful policies on the matter of icon veneration.[2]

When Leo died in 780, his only child, ten-year-old Constantine VI, succeeded to the throne and Irene of Athens was designated regent. A period of dramatic change and tragic upheaval was about to open for Byzantium.

---

[1]Goodacre, *Handbook of the Coinage of the Byzantine Empire*, p. 146.

[2]Ostrogorsky, *History of the Byzantine State*, pp. 175-176.

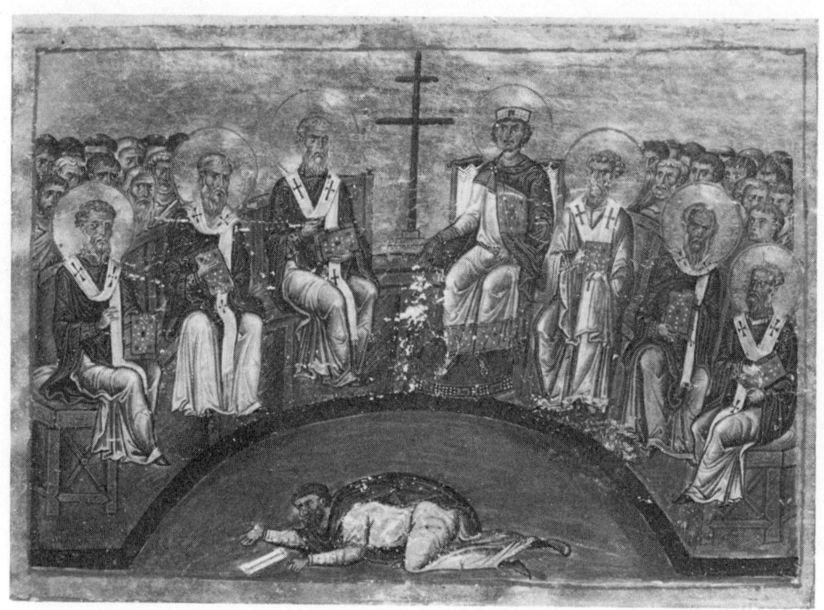

Constantine VI at Council of Nicaea II, manuscript miniature: Cod. Vat. Gr. 1163. Biblioteca Apostolica Vaticana.

CONSTANTINE VI

780-797

Constantine VI reigned while his mother Irene ruled. As the boy grew to manhood, his domineering mother still kept a tight hold on the reins of government. Under her sponsorship the Seventh Ecumenical Council (Nicaea II) condemned iconoclasm and sanctioned the veneration of icons, a decision that has ensured her an esteemed place in the history of Orthodoxy.

It was Irene, too, who selected her son's wife. For years as he was growing up he was betrothed to Rotrude, the daughter of Charlemagne, King of the Franks, but Irene suddenly called off this prospective match and announced a beauty contest at which she planned to choose the fairest girl in the empire to be her son's bride. The winner was Maria of Amnia. A sweet-tempered country girl from an impoverished background, Maria was literally the Byzantine Cinderella, even down to her tiny feet that exactly fit into the tiny red shoes that Irene had selected for Constantine's wife-to-be.[1]

Unfortunately, this Cinderella story does not end "happily ever after," for Constantine VI detested the wife his mother had forced upon him; he schemed to rid himself of her so that he might marry Theodote, one of her ladies-in-waiting. At length, he compelled Maria to enter a convent and married Theodote, an act which the Orthodox denounced as bigamy.

In spite of the muddle he made of his private life, young Constantine was popular with the army, a fact that caused much uneasiness for his power-hungry mother. Even more alarming to Irene was her son's inclination toward the revival of iconoclasm, a policy which, if carried out, would have meant the undoing of her entire life's work on behalf of the icons.[2] The result was much discreditable intrigue by both mother and son and the eventual outbreak of war between them.

Finally Constantine was imprisoned by Irene's henchmen who blinded him, an act which Irene made no effort to stop. The empress then ordered her blind son sentenced to life imprisonment in the room where he was born. It is reported that the faithful Theodote voluntarily shared his imprisonment, but nothing is known of the eventual fate of the fallen emperor.

From a tenth-century prayerbook with illustrations of the seven ecumenical councils comes a portrait of Constantine VI. Although it is not a contemporary likeness, it is believed to be a copy of a much older painting. It is interesting to note that the artist was careful to portray Constantine as beardless, to indicate that he was a mere youth of seventeen when the Council was held in 787.

---

[1]Diehl, *Byzantine Empresses*, pp. 14-16.

[2]R. J. H. Jenkins, *Byzantium: The Imperial Centuries* (New York, 1966), pp. 101-102.

IRENE OF ATHENS
797-802

When Irene consented to the blinding of her son Constantine VI, the Byzantine chroniclers report, the sun did not shine for seventeen days after—an indication of Heaven's displeasure with the cruel act of this unnatural mother.[1] Nevertheless, Irene remained popular with many of her subjects. Through her long years as empress-mother, she had guided the empire back to Orthodoxy, and now the grateful Byzantines, willing to overlook her crime against her son, were ready to accept her as sole ruler. Never before in Byzantine or Roman history had a woman reigned alone, and to silence those who claimed that such a thing could not be, the strong-willed empress signed her pronouncements: "Irene the Faithful Emperor."[2]

Probably in her late forties, 'Emperor' Irene was still beautiful and possessed a dramatic flair for what would now be called public relations. Dressed in solid white, she would ride in a chariot through the city streets, tossing coins to the crowd. Her subjects seemed to adore her, while her contemporary sovereigns, the Caliph Harun al-Rashid (of "Arabian Nights" fame) and Charlemagne, King of the Franks, listened with some alarm to reports of the incredible woman emperor of Byzantium.

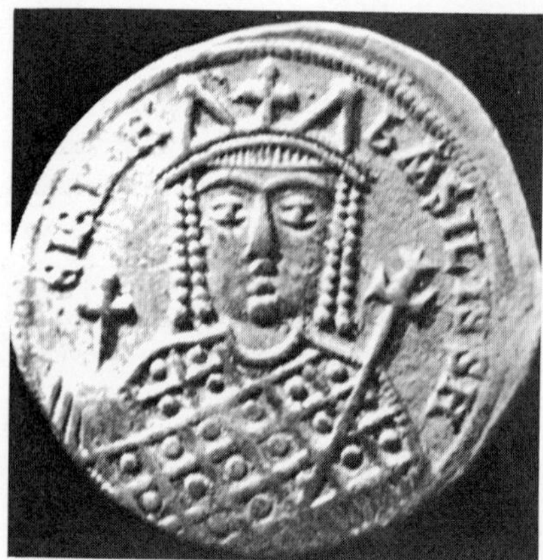

Irene, coin of her reign.
American Numismatic Society.

In the year 800 the pope bestowed on Charlemagne the title of emperor. The imperial throne was vacant, alleged the pope; Irene, as a woman, could not lawfully reign. More realistic, Charlemagne, a widower four times over, contemplated marriage with Irene and a union of their respective empires.[3] Irene was interested; envoys travelled from Aachen to Constantinople and back again, but Irene had no desire to leave her capital and move to barbarian Frankland. It seems she insisted that if the alliance were to take place, Charlemagne must come to live in Constantinople.

What might have been the final result of these negotiations was never carried out, since in 802 Irene was dethroned as a result of a sudden palace coup. Her unsound financial policies—her carefree granting of tax exemptions—had earned her the hatred of her finance ministers, and it was their chief, Nikephoros, who replaced her as emperor.

Nikephoros ultimately banished Irene to a small island where she lived out her life in exile and where, tradition reports, she was compelled to earn her own money as a spinner of thread. Before she died a few years later, legend has it that she repented of all her sins. In any case, she is listed as a saint on Orthodox calendars.

There is little hint of Irene's far-famed but only vaguely described beauty in the portrait of her that appears on both sides of her coins. Numismatic art was still rigidly stylized, and we cannot even be sure if the short bangs across her forehead represent Irene's actual hairstyle. It is interesting that as 'emperor' she had herself depicted in the *loros*—originally a male costume—though her pointed crown with its shoulder-length *pendilia* is thoroughly feminine.

---

[1]Theophanes, as quoted by Diehl, *Byzantine Empresses*, p. 87.

[2]*Cambridge Mediaeval History*, IV, i, p. 90; Jenkins, *Byzantium: The Imperial Centuries*, p.103.

[3]Theophanes (de Boor), p. 475. See also Constantine N. Tsirpanlis, "Byzantine Reactions to the Coronation of Charlemagne," *Byzantina* 6 (1964), 347-360.

NIKEPHOROS I
802-811

Nikephoros was primarily a financier; his years as *Logothete*, or chief finance minister, had gained him an understanding of economics far superior to most emperors. When he set to work to remedy the fiscal chaos caused by Irene, raising taxes and cancelling most of her exemptions, he became vastly unpopular and remained so throughout his reign. One contemporary chronicler, Theophanes, actually made a list of "ten horrible misdeeds" of Nikephoros. Rumors were also spread claiming that the emperor was of Arab descent. While this allegation was probably true, it was an ancestry that no Byzantine would have cared to brag about.

Nikephoros' colonization policies, which caused thousands of Byzantines to be uprooted from their homes and resettled elsewhere, made the emperor still more disliked by his subjects. Present day Byzantine scholars view Nikephoros far more kindly than his contemporaries did.[1] His population transfers, they point out, were crucial in rebuilding a Greek element among the Slavs who inhabited southern Greece in great numbers at that time. His financial policies, though they seemed harsh from the taxpayers' viewpoint, were based on sound common sense. With respect to religion, Nikephoros was an iconodule, but not a rabid one, and he readily tolerated other points of view.

Though his background was thoroughly civilian, Nikephoros (whose name literally means the conqueror) pictured himself as something of a military expert. Unfortunately, he fell far short of living up to his name. Defeated by invading Arab forces of Harun al-Rashid, he was compelled to increase the 'subsidies' that Irene had paid to this powerful neighbor. An even more threatening foe was King Krum of the Bulgars, whose invasion of Byzantine territory inaugurated another round in the long struggle between Bulgaria and the empire.

Nikephoros led his troops in person during more than one campaign, finally undertaking an invasion of Bulgaria. For a brief period, the fortunes of war favored Nikephoros. Pliska, the Bulgarian capital, was taken and burned to the ground. At this point, Nikephoros refused Krum's offer to negotiate. For weeks he sat brooding in his tent, refusing to confide his plans even to his close advisors or his son and heir, Stavrakios. Early one morning, Krum's forces unexpectedly fell upon the Byzantine camp and Nikephoros was slain in his tent, the first emperor to die in battle since Valens, more than four hundred years earlier.

Krum ordered Nikephoros' skull fashioned into a silver-lined goblet, and for years thereafter, when Byzantine ambassadors visited the Bulgar court, they were compelled to drink a toast from this grim trophy.

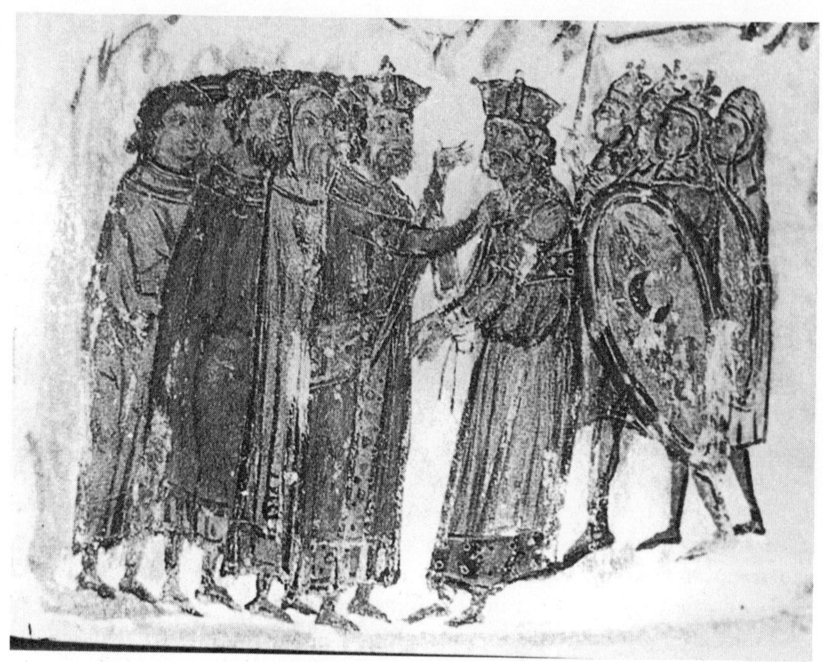

Nikephoros I and Krum the Bulgar, manuscript miniature: Manasses Codex, 1345. Biblioteca Apostolica Vaticana.

A well-known but historically inaccurate manuscript miniature of the fourteenth century depicts Nikephoros as a prisoner standing before Krum, his victorious adversary—an indication that even when the precise details were forgotten, the historical memory of Byzantium's terrible defeat by the Bulgars lived on.

---

[1]*Cambridge Mediaeval History*, IV, i, p. 91.

[2] Ostrogorsky, *History of the Byzantine State*, p. 196.

STAVRAKIOS
811

Stavrakios reigned for less than three months and, throughout this period, he was slowly dying of an injury to his spine that he received in the same battle in which his father Nikephoros was slain. Although Stavrakios was rescued from the battlefield and carried back to Constantinople, it soon became evident that his wound would be fatal, and the question of the imperial succession hung in the balance.

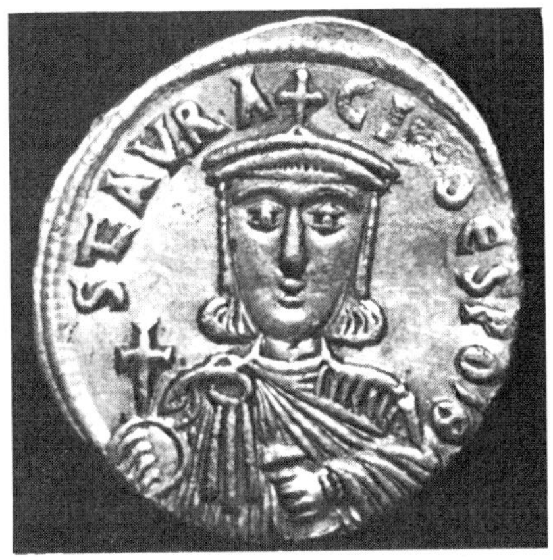

Stavrakios, coin from the reign of his father Nikephoros I. American Numismatic Society.

Stavrakios' wife was Theophano of Athens, a cousin of "Emperor" Irene, whom he had selected as his bride at a beauty show during the time when he was co-emperor with his father. The dying Stavrakios reportedly wanted to name her as his successor; after all, Irene had reigned alone, so why not Theophano?

This plan met with widespread opposition from those who felt that the Bulgar situation called for a warrior emperor who could lead his troops in person. The logical choice was Stavrakios' brother-in-law, Michael Rhangabe, but Stavrakios detested him and was determined to deny him the succession.

In this tense situation, Michael decided not to wait for the death of his brother-in-law. An obliging patriarch crowned Michael as emperor, and Stavrakios was not informed of this event until after the deed was done. Michael, who felt he could depend on the support of the army, then compelled Stavrakios to enter a monastery. He died there a few months later.

Coins minted during the reign of his father Nikephoros provide the only contemporary portraits of the unfortunate Stavrakios, here still a beardless youth.

---

[1]Theophanes (de Boor), p. 492.

MICHAEL I RHANGABÉ
811-813

Michael I is the first Byzantine emperor with a surname in the modern sense of the term, though the meaning of Rhangabé is uncertain.[1] He is also one of the few emperors of this period of whom there is a description of physical appearance. "Michael was in the prime of life, with a round face and skin the color of grain; black hair and a manly beard, handsomely styled," reports the contemporary chronicler known only as Scriptor Incertus.[2] The stereotyped

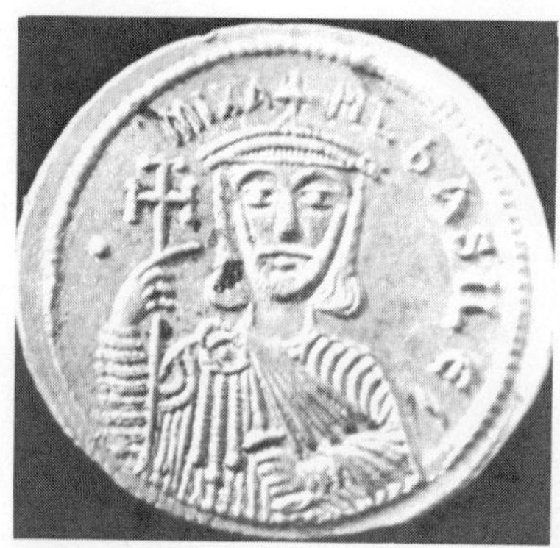

Michael I Rhangabé, coin of his reign. American Numismatic Society.

image on Michael's coins gives no hint of his round face, for the numismatic art of the time was still heavily influenced by the strictures of iconoclasm.

Michael Rhangabé did not prove to be a successful emperor. His one important accomplishment was the conclusion of a treaty with Charlemagne, recognizing the Frankish ruler's right to the title of emperor. Later Byzantine sovereigns, who tended to hold to the concept that the emperor in Constantinople was the only emperor in the world, had cause to regret Michael's generous recognition of the reborn empire of the West.

Michael was devoutly Orthodox, but even among the superstition-prone Byzantines, he was considered unduly superstitious and too easily influenced by the monks who were his chief advisors. While the Bulgarian King Krum and his forces made substantial inroads into Byzantine territory, carrying off great numbers of captives and much plunder, the soldiers of Michael Rhangabé grew daily more disaffected with their emperor. Under the iconoclasts, it was pointed out, Byzantium had won numerous victories; under the iconodules, Nikephoros and now Michael, Krum's Bulgars had the upper hand. Was this not a clear sign that Heaven favored iconoclasm? Propaganda of this sort was widely circulated, so much so that when the Byzantines actually encountered the Bulgars in direct combat, many Byzantines fled from the field rather than fight for Michael.

Michael Rhangabé realized his failure. When one of his generals, Leo the Armenian, claimed the crown, Michael abdicated and became a monk. His wife Prokopia became a nun; and Leo also compelled all their children to enter the monastic life. Ironically one of Michael's sons, Ignatius Rhangabé, later rose to greatness as Patriarch of Constantinople.

Michael himself lived on for many years and from his monastic retreat near Constantinople watched the rise and fall of several future claimants of the imperial throne.

---

[1]Ostrogorsky, *History of the Byzantine State*, 2nd ed., p. 197, n. 2.

[2]*Scriptor Incertus de Leone* (Bonn), p. 341.

LEO V GNUNI, THE ARMENIAN
813-820

Leo Gnuni was commander of the troops of the Anatolikon *theme* and was the prime mover in the intrigue leading to Michael Rhangabé's abdication. It is likely that Leo was not his real name, but one he assumed in memory of his hero, Leo III. Upon his accession, his wife Barca changed her name to Theodosia and their son Sembat became Constantine.

Leo V was apparently the only Byzantine emperor who proudly admitted to being an Armenian, although there were certainly several others of Armenian background. The chronicle of Symeon Magister presents a brief but revealing description of Leo's personal characteristics: "He was a man of very small stature, but heavy set and muscular, handsome, with a full beard and thick hair, and a voice resounding like a lion."[1]

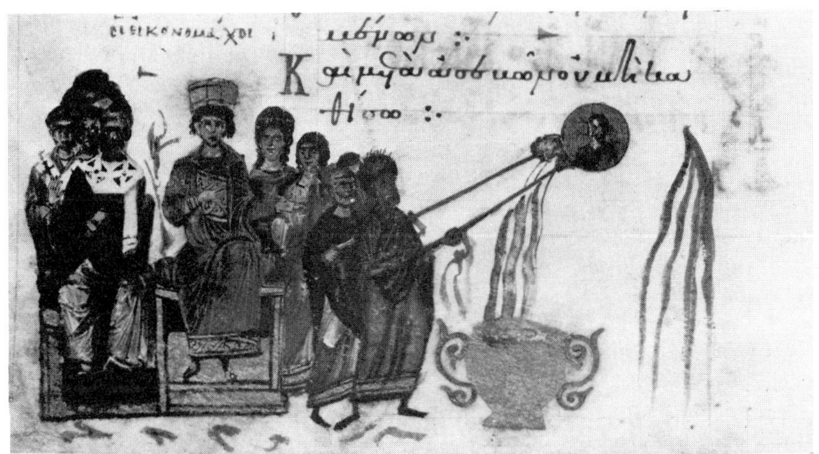

Leo V and the iconoclasts, manuscript miniature: Barberini Psalter. Biblioteca Apostolica Vaticana.

Leo was an iconoclast, and as emperor he heartily championed his theory that iconoclasm led to military victory and iconodulia to defeat. Not long after Leo seized the crown, King Krum besieged Constantinople. While terrorized Byzantines watched from the walls, the Bulgars in their camp offered some of their captives as human sacrifices.

Krum knew, however, that he could not take the strongly-walled city. He offered to initiate peace talks with Leo and came to the negotiations unarmed. The Byzantines tried to kill him, and Krum barely managed to escape with his life. In the weeks that followed, the Bulgars ravaged the territories around Constantinople and carried off an estimated 10,000 prisoners.

The emperor Leo's attempted counter-offensive did not prove successful until some months later, when Krum suddenly died of a cerebral hemorrhage and his successor Omurtag decided to come to terms. A thirty year peace was agreed upon; and to insure the sanctity of their treaty, the pagan Omurtag swore on a Bible while Leo swore, according to Bulgar custom, on a pile of dead dogs topped by a sword. The treaty defined a clear border between Bulgaria and the empire, and the Bulgars were permitted to build along this line a fortification called the Great Fence.[2] Traces of the earthworks of the Great Fence are still visible today.

For the remainder of Leo's reign, the empire enjoyed external peace, while the emperor intensified his iconoclastic activities. A manuscript miniature now in the Vatican Library depicts Leo and a group of dignitaries watching while two of the emperor's men obliterate an icon with whitewash.

Constantly suspicious of plots against his throne, Leo was ordinarily very cautious; but early on Christmas morning of the year 820 he went to sing with the choir in a palace chapel. There he was attacked by conspirators disguised as monks. The unarmed emperor tried to defend himself with a candlestick, but one of the assassins struck him a mighty blow, severing his right arm. Leo fell to the chapel floor, and there the assassins cut off his head.

---

[1]Symeon Magister (Bonn), p. 603. [2]*Cambridge Mediaeval History*, IV, i, p. 98.

MICHAEL II OF AMORION
820-829

The man who benefitted most from the coup against Leo V was Michael of Amorion. On the Christmas morning when Leo was slain, Michael was locked away in a palace dungeon, awaiting execution as soon as the holy season was over, on charges (perhaps true) of conspiring against the emperor. A complicated plot aroused a group of Michael's friends to act on his behalf, and it was they who, disguised as monks, slew Leo V. The next step was to release Michael from his cell. In the confusion, the key to Michael's fetters could not be found and the new emperor was acclaimed still wearing the chains of a prisoner.[1] The Skylitzes miniature reproduced here depicts his coronation, although the chains are conspicuously missing.

In spite of the unsavory intrigue that gained him the throne, Michael II proved a competent emperor. Because he had a serious speech impediment, his subjects made much fun of him and alleged that he was lacking in intelligence.

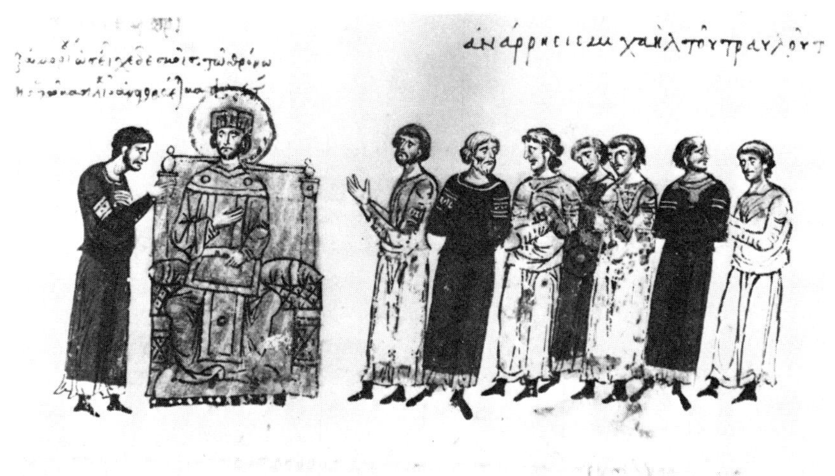

Michael II proclaimed emperor, manuscript miniature: Skylitzes Matritensis. Biblioteca Nacional, Madrid.

This charge was completely untrue. Michael possessed a great deal of common sense, though he had almost no formal education. Born to a peasant family near the town of Amorion in Asia Minor, he had grown up on a farm, and even as emperor he possessed a great love for the rural life. Like many young men of peasant background, Michael had entered the Byzantine army at an early age and had risen to prominence through the military.

Long before he became emperor, he married Thekla, a general's daughter whom he reportedly met under most unusual circumstances: as an obscure young officer, Michael was invited to dine with the general and his family, and, if surprised by this attention, he was even more astonished when, after the meal, the general offered him Thekla as a bride. Michael accepted Thekla's hand and later learned that her father's eagerness to negotiate the match sprang from a vivid dream he had had, revealing that Michael was likely to become emperor.[2]

Upon another occasion, Michael and two fellow officers heard a soothsayer predict that two of them would become emperors and the third make an unsuccessful attempt for the throne.[3] After one of this trio actually became the emperor Leo V, Michael seems to have become involved in plotting to make the next part of the prophecy come true. In any event, Leo believed him dangerous and had him imprisoned, an imprisonment that was ended, as we have seen, when his friends effected not only his release but his coronation.

As regards religion, Michael personally belonged to the iconoclast party but he exhibited a tolerance rare for his time. "Let every man do as seems to him good and right (in matters of religion)," he proclaimed, "and he shall have no vexation to undergo and no penalty to fear."[4] Michael II lived up to his word, and iconodules suffered no persecution in his reign unless they were active rabble rousers.

Michael excited great controversy when, after the death of his wife Thekla, he decided to marry a nun, Euphrosyne. This highly irregular proceeding was permitted only because Euphrosyne was the daughter of the unfortunate Constantine VI and Maria of Amnia and was thus, by right of birth, the best claimant to the imperial throne.

After a reign of nine years, Michael of Amorion died, the first emperor in more than half a century to die a natural death while still in possession of the crown. His successor was his and Thekla's only son, Theophilos.

---

[1]Theophanes Cont., I, pp. 33 ff.
[2]Theophanes Cont., I, pp. 44-45.
[3]Theophanes Cont., I, pp. 7-8.
[4]Quoted in the old *Cambridge Mediaeval History*, IV (New York, 1923), p. 32.

THEOPHILOS
829-842

The magnificent emperor Theophilos was an iconoclast and harsher than his father on matters of religious policy. For this reason Byzantine chroniclers in later years found it impossible to believe he had entered heaven, but legend at least accorded him the most honored place in hell as one of the judges of the dead.[1]

Elegant, cultured, and well-educated, a lover of learning and beautiful surroundings, Theophilos was a striking contrast to his rustic father, Michael II. Much building and redecorating took place at the imperial palace during Theophilos' reign. He borrowed freely from the art and architecture of his military foes, the Arabs. Particularly famous was his golden throne that could be raised to ceiling level and lowered by a hidden mechanism.

Like several of his predecessors, Theophilos selected his bride Theodora at a beauty contest designed to help the emperor find the fairest lady in the land for his empress. He narrowed the field to six semi-finalists; then, on the appointed day, he appeared before the nervous young women holding in his hand a golden apple, the 'prize' derived from a famous Greek myth. To the first of the girls, Kassia, Theophilos addressed a remark to the effect that all of the earth's troubles came from woman, for Eve after all was the first sinner. Yes, Kassia replied, but salvation also came through a woman, through Mary who gave birth to Christ. Kassia's quick thinking did not please Theophilos. He promptly handed the golden apple to the next girl, who became his bride and who would eventually be revered as an Orthodox saint, Theodora the Blessed.[2]

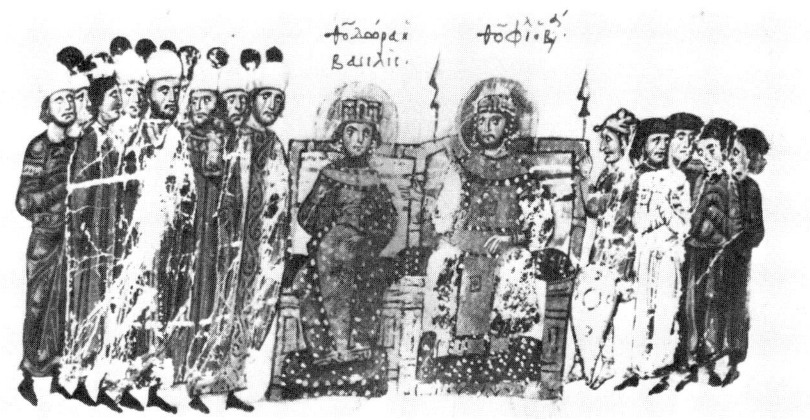

Theodora the Blessed and Theophilos, manuscript miniature: Skylitzes Matritensis. Biblioteca Nacional, Madrid.

She is depicted enthroned beside her husband in the Skylitzes miniature.

Ironically, Theophilos had, without realizing it, chosen a devout iconodule. Though reportedly it was a happy marriage, and Theodora managed for years to conceal her views on the subject of icons from her husband, she brought up their five daughters to venerate icons even as she did.

Apart from iconoclasm, Theophilos had a great reputation for justice, and many anecdotes are told to illustrate his concern for his subjects. He often went in disguise among the ordinary citizenry to learn their candid opinions, and he was especially interested in keeping a close check on food prices in the market place. Once a week, he held audience at a certain church in Constantinople where any of his subjects could come and present their troubles to the emperor in person. Once, it is reported, a poor old woman came to complain that the empress' brother was building a palatial residence next to her cottage and that this new building would shut off all her light and fresh air. Theophilos' reaction reveals much about his dramatic flair for drastic action: when investigation proved the story to be true, the emperor ordered demolition of his brother-in-law's new home and gave the land on which it stood to the old woman. For good measure, the emperor's brother-in-law was publicly whipped.[3]

As Theophilos lay dying, he designated Theodora as regent for their little son, Michael III, and urged her to promise that she would uphold iconoclasm. Theodora swore a mighty oath to carry out her husband's wishes, intending all the while to break this promise as soon as possible. Thus with the death of Theophilos the iconoclastic movement ended forever, and Theodora as empress-regent earned her epithet 'Blessed' for her restoration of iconodulia.

---

[1]Jenkins, *Byzantium: The Imperial Centuries*, p. 148; *Cambridge Mediaeval History*, IV, i, p. 102.

[2]Diehl, *Byzantine Empresses*, pp. 94–95; J. B. Bury, *A History of the Eastern Roman Empire* (London, 1912), p. 82.

[3]Theophanes Cont., III, p. 93.

MICHAEL III, THE DRUNKARD
842-867

Few emperors have excited more controversy than Michael III, both in his own time and with subsequent generations of historians. Much maligned by the Byzantine chroniclers, 'Michael the Drunkard' has his champions among modern Byzantine scholars who believe he was by no means the degenerate wretch his adversaries have pictured.[1] The truth most likely lies between the two extremes, and though he was not a great ruler, his long reign witnessed many important events.

Michael grew up in the shadow of his strong-willed mother, the empress-regent Theodora the Blessed, who seems to have enjoyed power so much that she encouraged her son to pursue a life of pleasure. By the time he reached his mid-teens, he was a heavy drinker who delighted in carousing, coarse jests, and parodies of religious ceremonies. When he was about fifteen, he became enamoured of a lowly-born girl called Ingerina, who was probably of Scandinavian descent and whom he took as his mistress. His mother promptly compelled him to marry someone else, an aristocratic young lady with the interesting name of Dekapolitissa ('Ten Cities'), but he neglected her while openly showering his favors on Ingerina.

Michael had a passion for horses and chariot racing and liked to take part personally in the Hippodrome, an activity that was considered unsuitable to the imperial dignity. As he grew to manhood, Michael felt more and more resentment of his mother's continued rulership, and finally with the help of his uncle Bardas, he compelled Blessed Theodora to enter a convent. For the next ten years, it was the Caesar Bardas who ruled while Michael reigned, and under Bardas' leadership, Byzantium experienced great achievements both culturally and militarily. Bardas was a generous patron of scholarship and of missionary endeavor; he was also determined that Byzantium would take the offensive against the perennial Arab foe. In the ensuing conflict between Byzantines and Arabs, the young emperor Michael, whatever his other weaknesses, proved an excellent military man.[2] It was the beginning of what would be a long period of expansion and military supremacy for the Byzantine empire.

It was Michael's misfortune that he eventually fell under the spell of the low-born, crafty Basil the Macedonian, who contrived the assassination of Caesar Bardas. Soon thereafter Michael, acting upon an unprecedented whim, made Basil co-emperor and gave him Ingerina as his wife, though she continued to be Michael's mistress. In the scene illustrated in the Skylitzes manuscript, the enthroned Michael confers with the bride's father, Inger, while to the left stand Basil and Ingerina awaiting the celebration of their marriage rites.

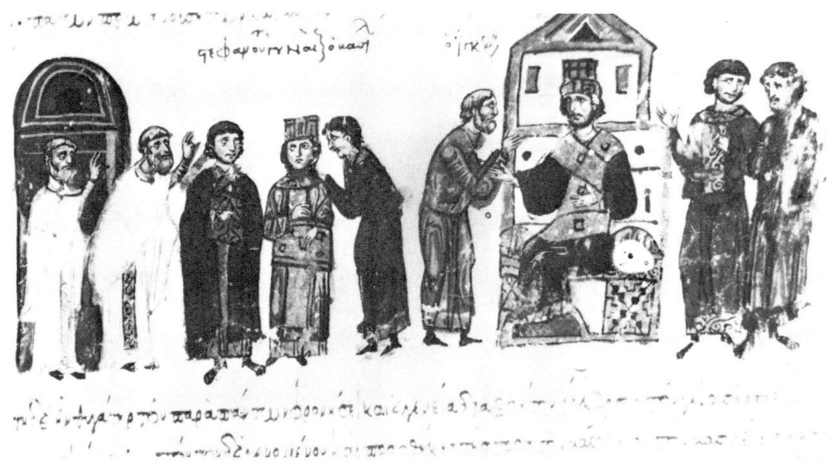

Michael III arranges the marriage of Basil I and Ingerina, manuscript miniature: Skylitzes Matritensis. Biblioteca Nacional, Madrid.

The unusual arrangement between Michael, Basil, and Ingerina lasted for about a year; then Michael suddenly turned against the co-emperor he had created and plotted to have Basil slain. Warned in time, Basil acted first, and invited Michael to a banquet. Then, when Michael was drunk and unable to defend himself, he was murdered by Basil's henchmen. Thus amid tragedy and shame, the dynasty of Amorion ended; the greater dynasty of the Macedonians was about to begin.

---

[1]For details se A. A. Vasiliev, "The Emperor Michael III in Apocryphal Literature," *Byzantina-Metabyzantina* I (1946), 237-248; R. J. H. Jenkins, "Constantine VII's Portrait of Michael III," *Bulletin de l'Academie de Belgique* 34 (1948), 71-77.

[2]*Cambridge Mediaeval History*, IV, i, p. 110.

BASIL I, THE MACEDONIAN 867-886

Basil, whose name means King, was nonetheless a peasant through and through. Although born in the *theme* of Macedonia, he was of Armenian descent on his father's side. A favorite Byzantine folktale relates how, as a young man, Basil came to Constantinople to seek his fortune. Destitute and friendless on his first night in the big city, he fell asleep on the steps of a

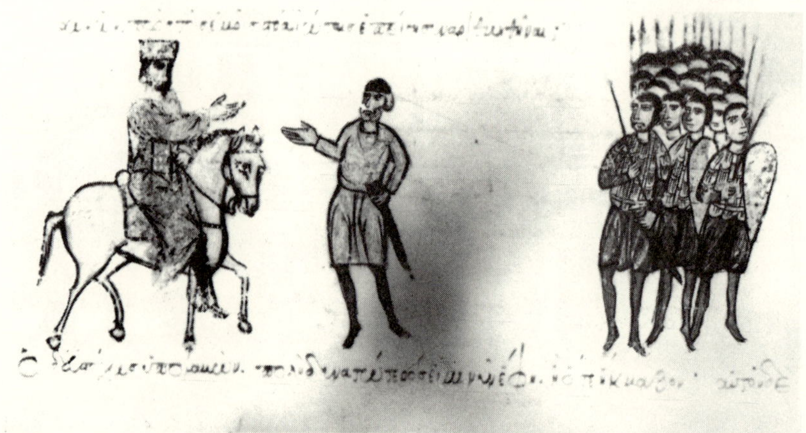

Basil I, manuscript miniature: Skylitzes Matritensis. Biblioteca Nacional, Madrid.

monastery. In the night the abbot was awakened by a strange dream telling him: "Go out! The king is sleeping on the steps!" When the abbot looked out and saw Basil, he could not believe that this ragged beggar youth was a king of anything; but when the dream was repeated three times, he finally summoned Basil in and gave him food and shelter. Thus, the Byzantine storytellers report, the future emperor Basil was started on the road to fame and glory.[1]

Because he was an expert in working with horses, Basil rapidly obtained a job. Powerful and muscular, he also proved to be an outstanding wrestler. When he won a wrestling match against a hitherto undefeated Bulgar champion at the imperial palace, he attracted the interest of Michael III. Soon thereafter, Basil was employed by the emperor as a trainer of wild horses. Within a few years, the ambitious Macedonian, who allowed no scruples to stand in the way of his rise to power, was co-emperor. A year later, Michael III was slain, and Basil reigned alone.

The chronicle of Symeon Magister preserves a brief description of the new emperor: "Basil, Emperor of the Romans, was most outstanding in bodily form, and heavy set; his eyebrows grew together, he had large eyes and a broad chest, and a somewhat downcast expression."[2]

Surprisingly, in spite of his lack of formal education (he was said to be completely illiterate), Basil the Macedonian possessed a real sense of imperial responsibility. He sponsored a thoroughgoing revision of Byzantine law, a project completed by his successor, Leo VI, who named the new code the *Basilika* in memory of its originator. The *Basilika's* emphasis was upon harmonizing civil law with the regulations of the Orthodox church. Translated from Greek into the Slavic languages, the code would later have great influence upon the development of the Bulgarian and Russian legal systems.

Militarily, Basil's reign witnessed a continuation of Byzantine successes against the Arabs, a situation reflected in the Skylitzes miniature of the emperor on horseback addressing his troops.[3] Lands in southern Italy, lost to the empire many years earlier, were reoccupied, and the imperial navy was built up to a position of new strength.

Basil's empress was Ingerina (also called Eudokia), the one-time mistress of Michael III, to whom he remained married for better or worse. Generally their married life could be described as worse, for there seemed to be a perennial spirit of distrust between them. They had a large family, but Basil took comfort in the fact that his heir was Constantine, his son by an earlier marriage. When this young man died, however, Ingerina's son Leo became throne-heir, and Basil, who never knew if Leo was his own son or Michael's, began to suffer severe bouts of depression. He despised the unfortunate prince Leo, who was bookish and frail. Reportedly the temperamental emperor once threw the young man around by his hair.[4] When Leo took a mistress whom Basil disliked, he was imprisoned for many months thereafter.

According to the official report, Basil died as the result of a freak accident. While hunting, he was thrown from his horse; his belt caught on the antlers of a stag which carried him sixteen miles before it was caught and slain. Leo VI—who probably was Basil's son—succeeded to the throne.

---

[1]Symeon Magister (Bonn), p. 820.

[2]Symeon Magister (Bonn), p. 686.

[3]A contemporary manuscript miniature of Basil I exists, but it is so badly flaked that the features of the emperor are obliterated. See Spatharakis, *Portrait*, pp. 96 ff.

[4]Charles Diehl, *Byzantine Portraits*, trans. Harold Bell (New York, 1927), p. 179.

LEO VI, THE WISE
886-912

Leo, who was twenty when he came to the throne, won the epithet 'the Wise' for his scholarly ways and for his reputed (and vastly overrated) ability to predict the future.[1] The mosaic portrait in Hagia Sophia usually identified as Leo VI depicts a middle-aged man, whose long black hair and beard are tinged with grey. His eyes appear to be blue, probably a heritage from the Scandinavian forebears of his mother Ingerina. Leo was well educated; he enjoyed writing poetry and hymns and was very interested in the completion of his father's legal work, the *Basilika*. Though he personally avoided battle, his reign witnessed continued Byzantine successes against the empire's various enemies.

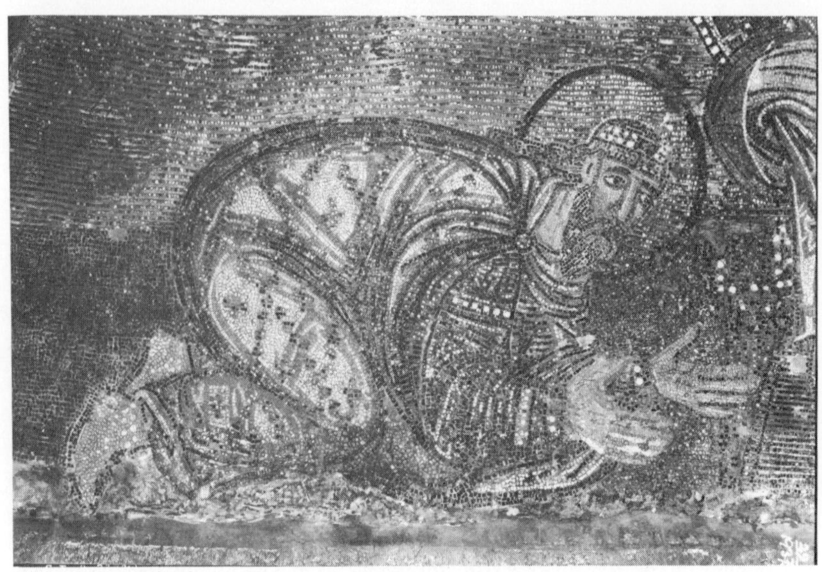

Leo VI, mosaic panel. Hagia Sophia, Istanbul (Photograph: Dumbarton Oaks).

Leo's married life was a series of disasters with far-reaching consequences. At sixteen, his father compelled him to marry Theophano, a very pious young woman who proved so unbearably saintly that Leo soon sought the consolation of a mistress, Zoe Zautzina. When Theophano finally died fifteen years later, Leo married Zoe, but then she also died about twenty months later. Both the Orthodox Church and the *Basilika* code firmly decreed that one must not marry more than twice, but Leo was only in his early thirties and had no heir except the one daughter borne him by Theopano. With a special dispensation from the Patriarch, he selected a third wife, Eudokia Baiane. A year later she died giving birth to an infant son who also died. The Orthodox Church firmly refused the emperor permission to marry again.

Leo took a mistress—another Zoe, who was nicknamed Carbopsina or "Black Eyes." About four years later she gave birth to a little boy, Constantine, who though frail, seemed likely to live. Leo then married Zoe Carbopsina in a secret ceremony, and not until after the deed was done was the Patriarch informed of it.

Orthodox persons—both clergy and laity—considered the emperor's fourth marriage illegal. The Patriarch excommunicated the emperor; Leo disposed of the Patriarch, selected a new one, and fortified himself with a dispensation from the Pope in Rome that recognized his marriage to Zoe as lawful. When Leo died six years later, the controversy about his fourth marriage was still raging.[2]

The coins of Leo VI's reign are particularly beautiful, presenting probably the most individualized portrait of a specific ruler anywhere in the long series of Byzantine currency. The mosaic portrait of an emperor in Hagia Sophia is usually identified as Leo VI on the basis of its approximate date. An additional clue to the identity of the emperor in this famous panel may be its subtle hint of Leo's marital troubles. The emperor kneels before Christ, but on the opposite side of Christ's throne, where one would expect to find the empress, is a large blank spot—a silent witness to the fact that Leo never had for any substantial length of time an empress pleasing both to himself and to public opinion.

---

[1]Cyril Mango, "The Legend of Leo the Wise," *Zbornik Radova Vizantološkog Instituta* 6 (1950), 59-93, gives details.

[2]For details, see Jenkins, *Byzantium: The Imperial Centuries*, pp. 212-226.

ALEXANDER
912-913

As Leo VI lay dying, his younger brother and co-emperor Alexander entered the room. The scholarly Leo had never been on good terms with the shiftless playboy Alexander, yet Leo knew that his own son Constantine was too young to press a claim to the throne and that Alexander would succeed him as senior emperor. "Ah," Leo muttered, "here comes the thirteen-month man!" This term was merely a Byzantine idiom denoting any unpopular person, but when Alexander lived and reigned exactly thirteen months after Leo's death, the remark was remembered and quoted as a great prophecy.

Alexander accomplished little of value during his short reign. Those who disliked him—and they were many—circulated scandalous tales of his behavior. He was extraordinarily superstitious; he believed that a certain statue of a bronze boar in the Hippodrome was his *stoicheion* (an inanimate object whose fortunes are bound up with a person), and he lavished ridiculous attentions upon it, even furnishing it with a new set of teeth, hoping his own teeth would thereby be improved. He reportedly took part in 'Black Mass' services. He was easily influenced by a group of degenerate, lowly-born favorites. He neglected his wife (her name has not even been preserved) and forced his mother-in-law to move out of the palace. He harbored thoughts of mutilating little Constantine, the rightful throne-heir, though actually he did him no harm. So runs the list of Alexander's misdeeds, and the reader is left with the impression that it is fortunate indeed that the Thirteen Month Man lasted no longer.[2]

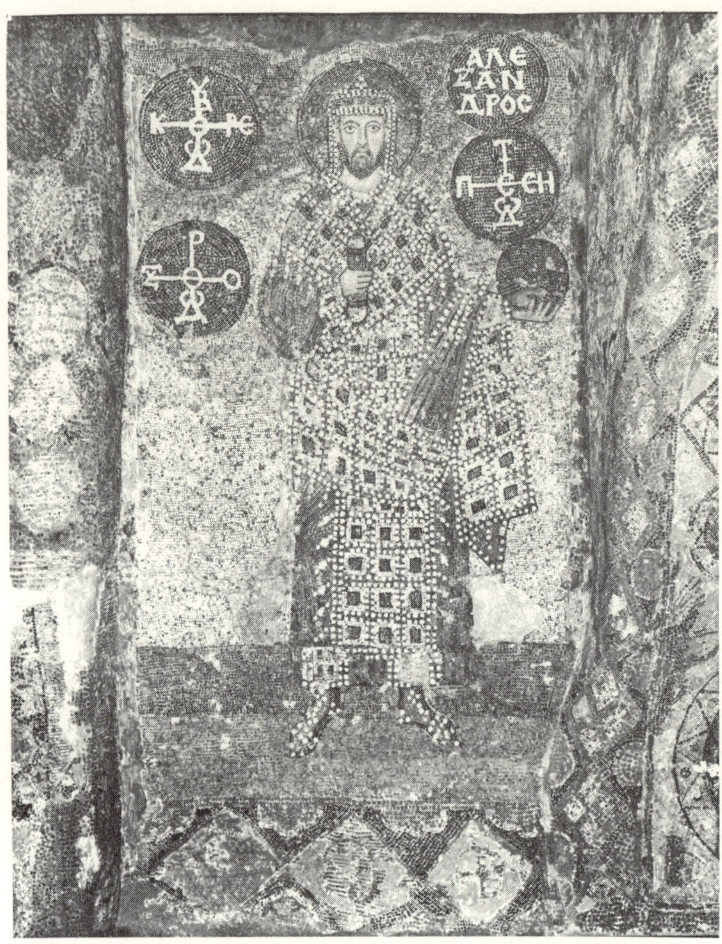

Alexander, mosaic panel. Hagia Sophia, Istanbul (Photograph: Dumbarton Oaks).

Most serious, perhaps, of all Alexander's blunders was the provocation of hostilities with King Simeon of Bulgaria, a heritage that would provide trouble for his successors for years to come.

In recent times (1958) a full-length mosaic of Alexander was uncovered in Hagia Sophia beneath layers of Turkish plaster.[3] The portrait reveals a marked resemblance between Alexander and his brother Leo VI. Alexander's eyes are light brown; his shoulder-length hair is dark. The emperor is clad in the jewelled *loros*; he holds in his hand the *mappa* or *akakia*, a ceremonial cloth; his red enamel crown is adorned with *pendilia* of pearls and red stones; and on his feet are the inevitable red shoes that were considered an especially important part of the imperial costume. The portrait almost certainly was made during Alexander's own reign, for, as its restorers wisely pointed out, there was certainly no future emperor who would have cared so to commemorate the unsatisfactory memory of Alexander the Thirteen Month Man.

---

[1]Theophanes Cont. (Bonn), VI, 377.

[2]For details see Patricia Karlin-Hayter, "The Emperor Alexander's Bad Name," *Speculum* 44 (1969), 585-596.

[3]Paul A. Underwood, "Notes on the Work of the Byzantine Institute in Istanbul: 1957-1959," *Dumbarton Oaks Papers* 14 (1960), 205-219; P. A. Underwood and Ernest J. W. Hawkins, "The Mosaics of Hagia Sophia at Istanbul: The Portrait of the Emperor Alexander," *Dumbarton Oaks Papers* 15 (1961), 189-217.

CONSTANTINE VII PORPHYROGENITOS
913-959

The son of Leo VI and Zoe Carbopsina, Constantine was born in the purple room of the imperial palace. The name Porphyrogenitos, which technically belonged to every imperial child born in this special chamber, was bestowed on him with particular emphasis to enhance his somewhat doubtful claim to legitimacy.

Emperor from early childhood, Constantine did not actually reign in his own right until he was in his forties. At the death of his uncle Alexander, seven-year-old Constantine was recognized as sole emperor, and the government was placed in the hands of a regency council under the direction of his mother Zoe. A few years later, the administration of the empire was seized by the admiral Romanos Lekapenos, who married off his young daughter to the thirteen-year-old Constantine and then had himself proclaimed senior co-emperor. For a quarter of a century Romanos reigned while Constantine devoted himself largely to scholarly pursuits, compiling treatises on Byzantine history, geography, politics, and court ceremonial—works that remain important primary sources for Byzantine historians through the centuries. Constantine was also a talented artist and painted numerous icons. Gossip had it that he sold his paintings to the palace servants, as his father-in-law Romanos kept him short of cash.[1]

Throughout his life Constantine was always frail, almost a semi-invalid, and could never participate personally in the military expansion that continued throughout his reign. Despite his ill health, he was an attractive man. The

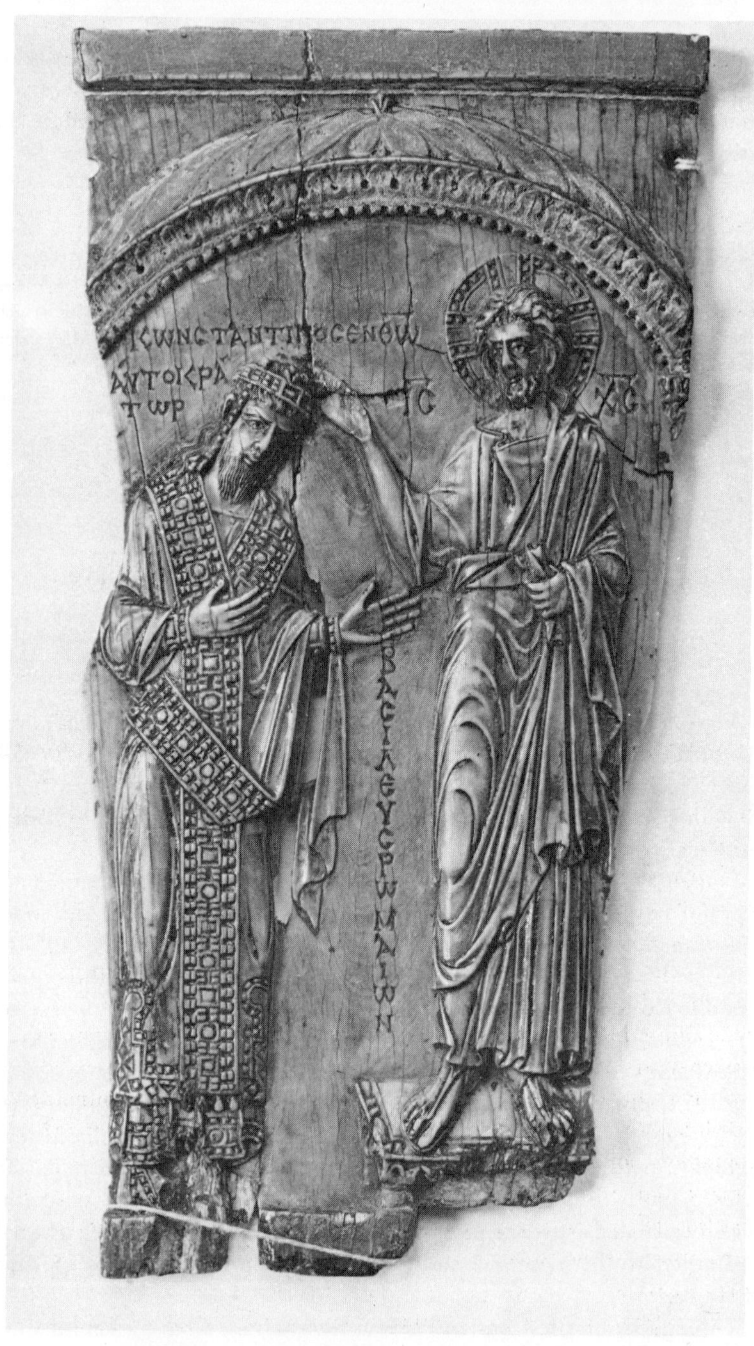

Constantine VII crowned by Christ, ivory relief. Museum of Fine Art, Moscow (Photograph: Hirmer, Munich).

anonymous writer of *Theophanes Continuatus*, Book VI, who was undoubtedly one of the emperor's close associates, reports: "The Emperor Constantine Porphyrogenitos was tall in stature. His skin was milky white; his eyes were blue and genial. He had an aquiline nose, a long face, ruddy cheeks, and a long neck. He stood as straight as a cypress tree, and was broad shouldered."[2] Of several existing contemporary portraits of Constantine, probably the best is the ivory carving now in Moscow which depicts the emperor crowned by Christ.

Though he delighted in the formalities of court ceremonial and etiquette, Constantine was basically a warm-hearted, witty, and approachable man. Liutprand of Cremona, an Italian ambassador who visited the Byzantine court when Constantine had finally reached the position of sole ruler, has preserved in his writings several intimate glimpses of the emperor, revealing his good nature and his genuine delight in generosity.[3]

Constantine and his wife, Helena Lekapena, were the parents of five daughters who shared their father's intellectual interests and served as his secretaries when he compiled some of his books. Above all else, however, Constantine treasured great hopes for his only son, who would be Romanos II. Romanos was a wild boy, with none of his father's scholarly tendencies, yet Constantine loved him greatly and remained oblivious to his faults.

Constantine died in 959, probably of typhoid fever. He was not a great emperor, but he was a gentle soul and a dedicated scholar. Without him, Byzantine history would be much the poorer.

---

[1]Jenkins, *Byzantium: The Imperial Centuries*, p. 257.

[2]Theophanes Cont. (Bonn), VI, 468.

[3]Liutprand, "Antapodosis" (Wright), pp. 207-212.

ROMANOS I LEKAPENOS
919-944

Romanos Lekapenos, who reigned as senior co-emperor with Constantine VII for twenty-five years, was born the son of an Armenian peasant known as Theophlylaktos the Unbearable. His native village was a place called Lekape, and from it Romanos derived his surname.[1]

As a young man, Romanos enlisted in the Byzantine navy as a common sailor. Because of certain daring exploits—including the slaying of a lion single-handedly—he won a series of promotions, and in Alexander's reign

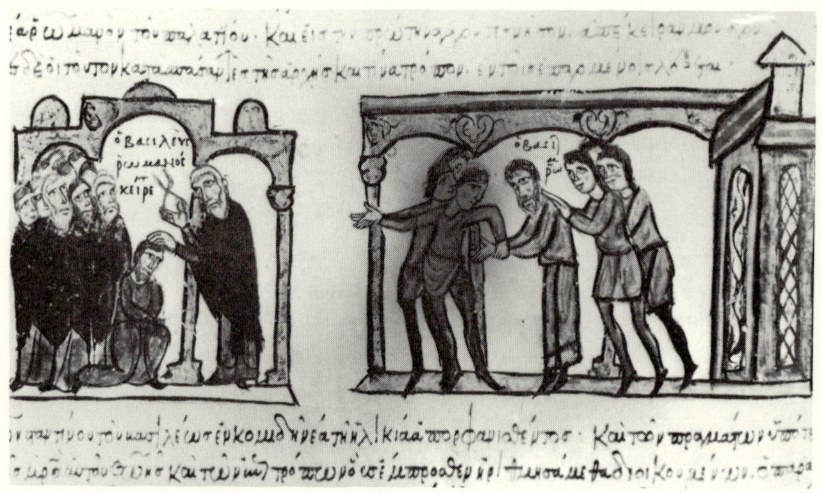

Romanos Lekapenos ousted by his sons (right) and tonsured (left), manuscript miniature: Skylitzes Matritensis. Biblioteca Nacional, Madrid.

finally earned the post of High Admiral of the Byzantine fleet. Much involved in the palace intrigues during the childhood of Constantine VII, Romanos eventually emerged as the young emperor's father-in-law and imperial partner. The Lekapenos family installed itself in the palace. Romanos created co-emperorships for three of his sons, while the fourth son, Theophylaktos, became Patriarch of Constantinople when he was still in his teens. The rightful emperor Constantine VII was reduced to the role of a decorative figurehead with no real voice in affairs of state.

Though Romanos had little formal education (his son-in-law Constantine scornfully considered him illiterate),[2] he possessed much innate ability, cleverness, and wit. He proved to be a serious and dedicated emperor, particularly concerned with promoting social legislation to protect the property rights of the poor but free farmer class and with saving them from bondage to the soil as serfs. The large landowning aristocrats of the empire naturally did not appreciate these efforts, but, in spite of their opposition, Romanos' work took root, providing the original impetus whereby Byzantium delayed the spread of disruptive feudalism for about a century.

Another important accomplishment of Romanos was the establishment of peace with the Bulgars, brought about by the marriage of his granddaughter Maria Lekapena to the Bulgarian King Peter.

Romanos did not share Constantine VII's interest in the arts, and though his reign is part of an era of great productivity by Byzantine artists, no contemporary portrait of Romanos has survived except the stereotyped image on his coins. Nor do the chroniclers give us any details of his personal appearance.

After twenty-five years as emperor, Romanos lost his crown as a result of a surprise coup by two of his sons, who seized him while he was taking an afternoon nap and whisked him off to a monastery on a nearby island. These events are depicted in a double picture in Skylitzes' *Chronicle*; at the right is Romanos being pushed from the palace by his sons; at the left, he kneels for the monastic tonsure. The fallen emperor, who was in his seventies, adapted well to the monastic life. He spent much of his time working in the monastery's vegetable garden, digging in the soil and meditating on the events of his long reign.[3]

Romanos' sons profited not at all by their removal of their father. The inhabitants of the capital, learning of Romanos' fall, rioted on behalf of Constantine VII and refused to recognize anyone else as senior emperor. Within a month, Constantine had the Lekapenos brothers shipped off to join their father in his monastic retreat. There, according to one chronicler's report, old Romanos met them with a sarcastic greeting: "How fortunate that you sent me here first! The monks know nothing of imperial etiquette, but I am an expert on the subject!"[4]

Though his sons were soon removed to more distant monasteries, Romanos Lekapenos remained where he was for the rest of his life. He died in obscurity, yet modern historians of Byzantium tend to agree that this sailor-emperor-monk was truly one of the empire's greatest rulers.

---

[1]Henri Grégoire, "Le lieu de naissance de Romain Lécapène et de Digenis Akritas," *Byzantion* 8 (1933), 572-574.

[2]Constantine VII, *D.A.I.*, 13.145 (Jenkins, p. 73).

[3]Liutprand, "Antapodosis" (Wright), p. 193.

[4]*Ibid.*

ROMANOS II
959-963

Named for his maternal grandfather, Romanos II was the only son of Constantine VII. Strong and athletic, he was very much an out-of-doors person; he had a passion for hunting and horseback riding, but he seemed bored with the elaborate ceremonial of the Byzantine court.

In his early childhood, Romanos was officially married to a little princess from western Europe, Bertha-Eudokia of the Franks. This pair is generally

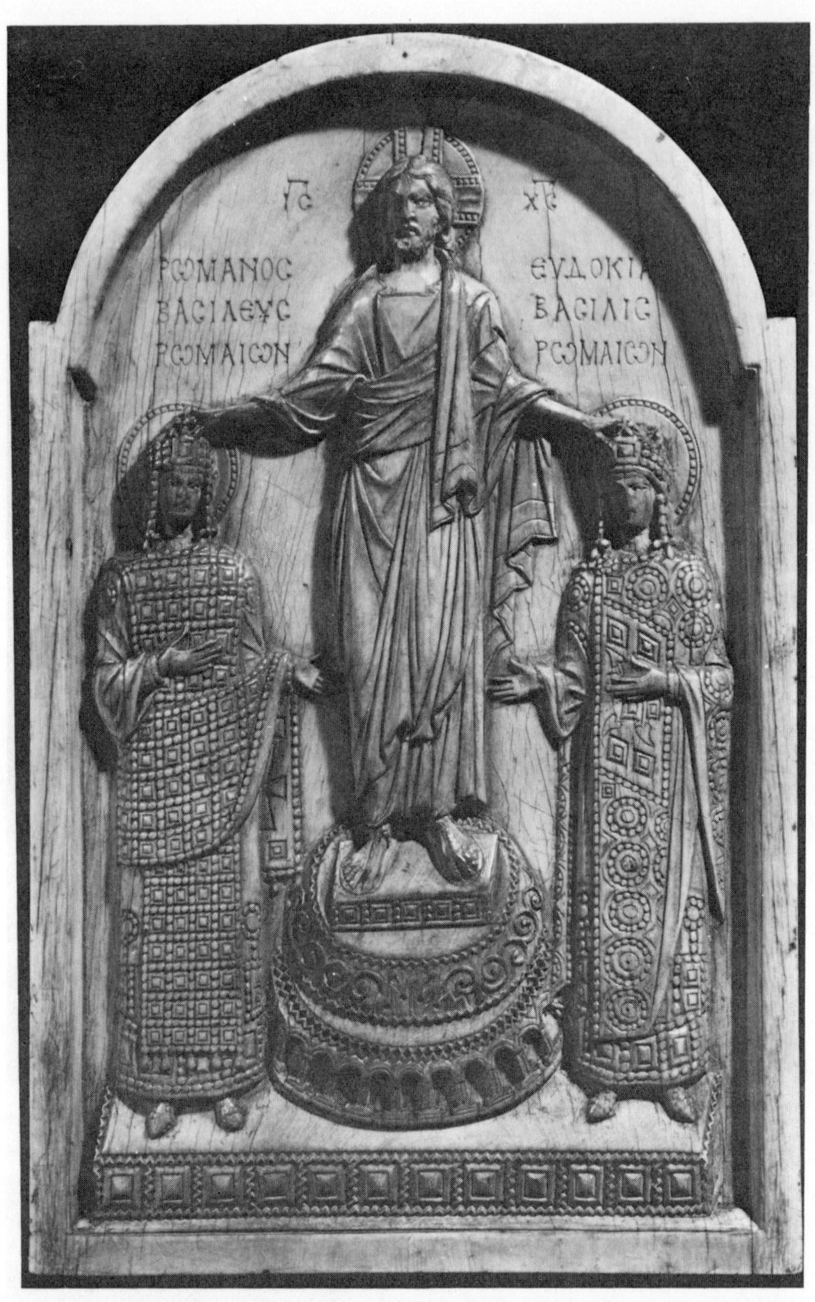

Romanos II and Bertha-Eudokia crowned by Christ, ivory plaque. Bibliothèque Nationale, Paris.

believed to be the young couple pictured as crowned by Christ on a beautiful and well-preserved ivory carving presently found in the Louvre, in Paris. Romanos' beardless state in this portrait is a clear indication of his youth at the time the carving was made, since all mature Byzantine males of that period wore beards as a matter of course.[1]

After little Bertha died, Constantine VII allowed his son to select whomever he pleased as a second wife. Romanos' choice reveals a great deal about the young man's headstrong nature; he selected a tavern-keeper's daughter called Theophano, a very beautiful—and as time would prove, completely unscrupulous—young woman.

Romanos was twenty when his father died. "He was youthful and vigorous of body," reports the chronicle of Symeon Magister, "with skin the color of wheat, beautiful eyes, a hooked nose, pleasant aspect, sweet speech. He stood straight as a cypress tree, with broad shoulders, and was calm and mild in manner."[2] The similarities to his father Constantine are obvious.

Unfortunately, as soon as Romanos II became sole ruler, the new empress Theophano began to exhibit her autocratic nature. To assure more power for herself she banished her mother-in-law and her five sisters-in-law to distant convents.[3] Romanos, who adored his beautiful wife, allowed her to have her way and seemed to delight in indulging her whims.

While Romanos was far too involved with hunting, banqueting, and enjoying himself with Theophano to lead his armies in person, his short reign was marked by a series of brilliant victories over the Arabs, culminating in the conquest of Crete by the great general Nikephoros Phokas.

Given more time, Romanos, who was certainly well-educated and intelligent, might have matured into a capable emperor, but as it turned out he died at the age of twenty-four. There is nothing to support the theory that he was poisoned by Theophano, who seemingly was devoted to him and who had nothing to gain and everything to lose by his death. It seems rather that the young emperor suffered severe internal injuries as the result of a wild horseback ride, and that his untimely death resulted from these.

---

[1]In spite of the emperor's beardless state, which seems to me a decisive argument in favor of his identification as Romanos II, some art historians identify the imperial couple depicted on this ivory as Romanos IV Diogenes and Eudokia Makrembolitissa. Yet, Diogenes was a mature man throughout his brief reign (1069-1071) and to have depicted him as beardless would have been a grave insult to his manly dignity.

[2]Symeon Magister (Bonn), pp. 756-757.

[3]Charles Diehl, *Byzantine Empresses*, p. 118; Ostrogorsky, *History of the Byzantine State*, p. 284.

NIKEPHOROS II PHOKAS
963-969

Romanos II left two small sons, Basil and Constantine who, although they were proclaimed co-emperors, were far too young to rule. The empress-mother Theopano was designated regent. Fearful of losing power she sought the help of the famous general, Nikephoros Phokas.

Nikephoros, who was in his early fifties, had a long and distinguished military career behind him. His given name means 'bearer of victory', and he was, his admirers claimed, "well named indeed," for under his leadership Byzantium had won greater triumphs over the Arabs than at any time since the rise of Islam three centuries earlier. His soldiers, who idolized him, bestowed upon him the complimentary epithet 'the Morning Star'.[1]

Besides his abilities as a strategist and leader of men, Nikephoros displayed a strong ascetic bent to his character. After the death of his wife when they were both young, he had vowed himself to a life of celibacy. He often asserted that when he retired from military life, he planned to become a monk and had a cell reserved for himself on Mt. Athos. In the meantime he fasted regularly, abstained from wine and meat, slept on the ground, and often wore a hair shirt.

It was this man who Theophano selected as an ally to help her safeguard the throne of her sons. With her support and the enthusiastic acclaim of the Constantinople citizenry, Nikephoros was crowned as senior co-emperor.

A few weeks later, the ascetic old warrior, his vow of celibacy forgotten, married the beautiful widow Theophano. At the outset, he may have agreed to the match to strengthen his claim to the throne, but it was soon evident that he was deeply infatuated with the charming empress. Though there were many who criticized their alliance and the Patriarch threatened excommunication unless he would give her up, Nikephoros refused to abandon his bride. He even took her with him when he resumed personal leadership of his forces.

Militarily, Nikephoros' successes continued. The Byzantines reoccupied much of Syria, a land that had been in Muslim hands for three centuries. In Constantinople, however, the emperor grew increasingly unpopular because of the higher taxes he demanded to finance his war efforts.

Also ominous was the growing estrangement between Theophano and her husband. She no longer accompanied him on campaign; he reverted to his ascetic way of life while she dallied at the palace with handsome young John Tzimiskes, Nikephoros' cousin.

In December, 969, when Nikephoros came home from the campaign for the winter, Theophano pretended a reconciliation with her husband. The emperor, who apparently still loved her, little realized that she aimed to destroy him and place John Tzimiskes on the throne. With Theophano's connivance,

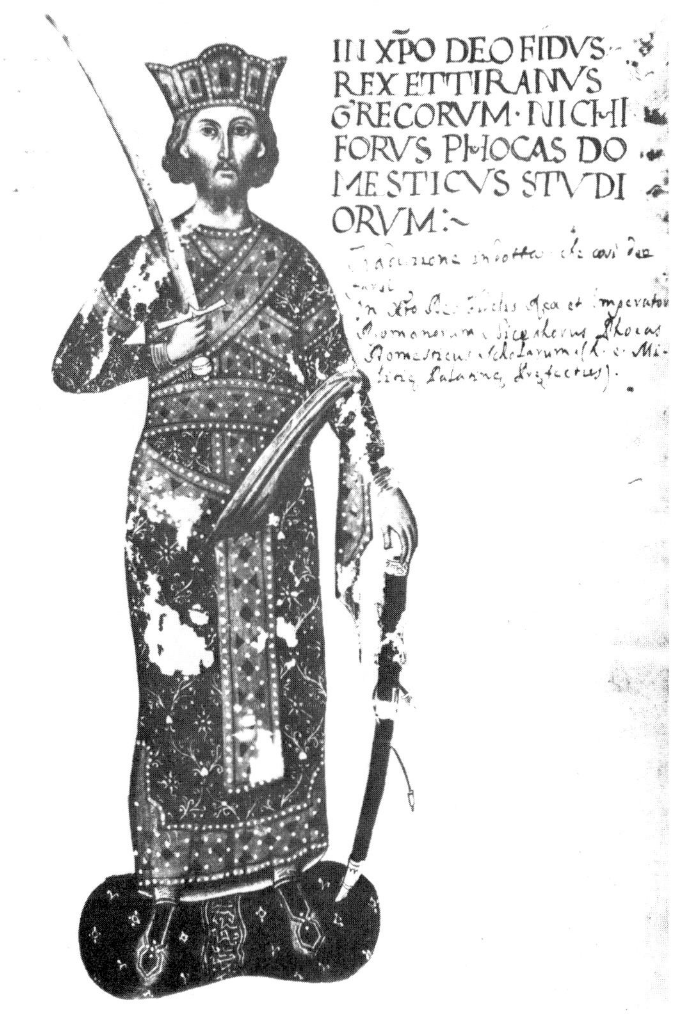

Nikephoros Phokas, manuscript miniature: Cod. Lat. 342. Marcian Library, Venice.

John and some of his henchmen entered the palace through a window, and with her help, too, they were guided to the unlocked door of Nikephoros' bedroom. The emperor's bed was empty; the old emperor by preference was sleeping on the floor. There they found him and killed him; his head was placed for exhibit on a pike and his body tossed out into the snow. The next morning John Tzimiskes would be acclaimed as emperor.

Contemporary sources give vivid descriptions of Nikephoros' personal appearance. "The color of his face tended more to black than white," writes Leo Diaconus, who knew him well. "He had long dark hair, black eyes that seemed deep in thought, and thick eyebrows. His nose was midway between narrow and broad, and a little crooked; he had a fine beard, turning grey around the jaws. His body was round and firm, with a broad chest and shoulders; in vigor and strength he was next to the celebrated Hercules."[2] Less flattering are the descriptions reported by the Italo-German ambassador, Liutprand of Cremona, who emphasizes that Nikephoros was unusually short in stature.[3] Even as emperor he often wore old, ill-fitting clothes, and was so lacking in imperial grace that Liutprand describes him as a "clodhopper."

It is obvious that the miniature of Nikephoros from a post-Byzantine manuscript of the sixteenth or seventeenth century accords ill with these particulars. It is, however, a particularly striking example of how Greek artists of the post-Byzantine period felt an emperor should look.[4] The fact that Nikephoros is clad in the *loros* fashion of his own time (rather than that of the late empire) may be a hint that this portrait had an earlier prototype.

---

[1]Liutprand, "The Embassy to Constantinople" (Wright), p. 241.

[2]Leo Diaconus, III.8 (Bonn), p. 48.

[3]Liutprand, "The Embassy to Constantinople" (Wright), pp. 236-237.

[4]This portrait was used as the design for a postage stamp issued in Greece in 1961 to commemorate the millenium of Nikephoros' conquest of Crete.

JOHN I TZIMISKES
969-976

John Tzimiskes, the treacherous kinsman of Nikephoros Phokas, claimed both the throne and the hand of Theophano. But when the patriarch Polyefktes agreed to crown him only on the condition that he give up his mistress and partner-in-crime, he readily agreed and banished Theophano to a convent. A miniature in the Skylitzes chronicle depicts their parting; while John sits enthroned in imperial splendor, the reluctant Theophano is escorted out of the palace to be rowed away to her monastic retreat. John then married a daughter of Constantine VII, Theodora, a safe, respectable match.

Historians of John's time report that he was a very handsome man. Leo Diaconus recalls, "Such he was: white of complexion, just the right color: his hair was golden and receding in front, he had sharp-sighted blue eyes, a slender nose of the right size. His moustache was red and thick rather than sparse, his beard of a good, appropriate length, not too short. As for his stature, his chest and back were broad. He appeared short, but there was gigantic strength in this man, agility in his hands and a certain power against which it was vain to

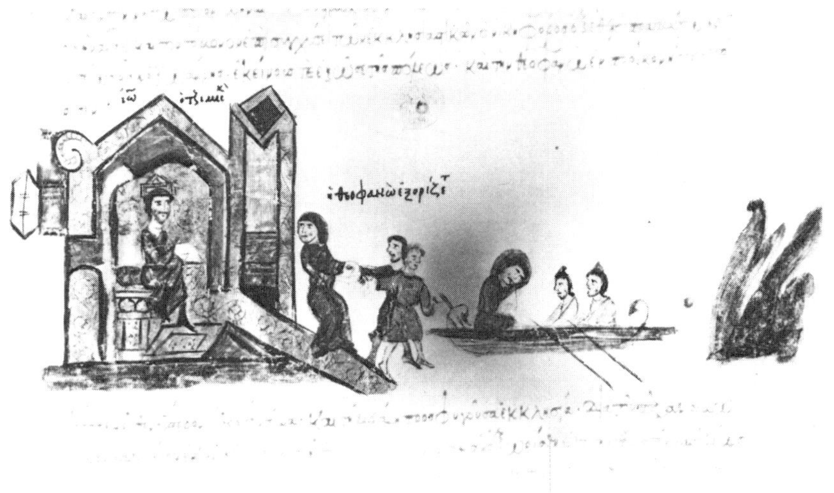

John Tzimiskes banishes Theophano, manuscript miniature: Skylitzes Matritensis. Biblioteca Nacional, Madrid.

resist."[1] John was famed as an expert horseman and, before becoming emperor, had delighted in trick riding and displays of dare-devil ability.

Like Nikephoros, John was a great soldier who insisted on leading his troops in person. The push into Syria continued throughout his reign. Many towns and villages surrendered without a battle as the Byzantines approached. The emperor's frequently announced goal was the reconquest of the Holy Land lost by Herakleios three centuries earlier. Had he lived longer, this objective well might have been fulfilled.

Not all of John's military efforts, however, were directed against Islam. He also warred with the Bulgars and annexed a part of Bulgaria to the Byzantine realm.

In his dealings with western Europe, John took the important and hitherto unheard-of step of sending a Byzantine princess, Theophano, to wed Holy Roman Emperor Otto II. Scholars have been at a loss to ascertain the exact identity of this princess, who is described as John's 'niece', but it is possible that she was the daughter of the notorious Theophano and Romanos II.[2] Her journey to the German realm was an important step in bringing a deeper knowledge of Byzantine culture and civilization to the medieval West.

John Tzimiske's death in 976 was the result of typhoid fever. His successor was Basil II, who had been co-emperor since 963.

---

[1]Leo Diaconus, VI.3 (Bonn), p. 96.

[2]Jenkins, *Byzantium: The Imperial Centuries*, pp. 294-295.

BASIL II, THE BULGAR-SLAYER
976-1025

The longest reign in Byzantine history and one of the most successful is that of Basil the Bulgar-Slayer, son of Romanos II and Theophano. Basil was, however, anything but a typical emperor. He hated court ceremonial and almost never wore jewelled ornaments or robes of imperial purple. He had little regard for learning or the arts. His chief interest—practically his only interest—was war, and in that realm he succeeded very well.

Basil never married.[1] He never bothered to explain why, but it seems likely that his childhood memory of how his mother Theophano had contrived to kill his stepfather Nikephoros made him distrustful of all women.

Basil was in his late teens when he succeeded John I as senior co-emperor. The early years of his reign were marked by civil wars launched by various claimants to the throne. In the course of these struggles, Basil sought the help of the pagan prince Vladimir of Kiev in Russia. Vladimir agreed to become an Orthodox Christian and was rewarded with an imperial bride, Basil's sister Anna. This alliance proved of utmost significance for the spread of Orthodoxy and Byzantine civilization into Russia.

Most of all, Basil is famed for his wars against King Samuel of the Bulgars. While Samuel sought to detach the conquered Bulgar territories from the Byzantine realm, Basil's goal was the incorporation of all of Bulgaria into the empire. The struggle was long and hard. According to tradition, the end came when Basil rounded up fifteen thousand Bulgar prisoners of war, placed them in groups of one hundred, and then ordered ninety-nine men in each group blinded. The hundredth man was blinded in only one eye, that he might lead his comrades home.[2] Though this tale is probably a vast exaggeration, it accords well with Basil's basic ruthlessness. And it is historical fact that when King Samuel saw some of these unfortunates returning home, he dropped dead from shock.

Bulgaria became an imperial province. Basil governed the defeated land with surprising mildness. The Bulgars were allowed considerable local self-government. In absorbing this powerful neighbor, the Byzantine empire reached its greatest size since the days of Herakleios.

Basil was not, however, able to maintain a firm hold over all the Syrian lands taken by his recent predecessors. The opportunity for the reconquest of Jerusalem was lost as Basil contended with foes nearer home.

From a prayer book which belonged to Basil himself comes a famous miniature of the emperor clad in full military dress, with spear in hand, while small figures of defeated Bulgars grovel in subjection before him. The famous Byzantine historian Michael Psellos was a small child when Basil was an old

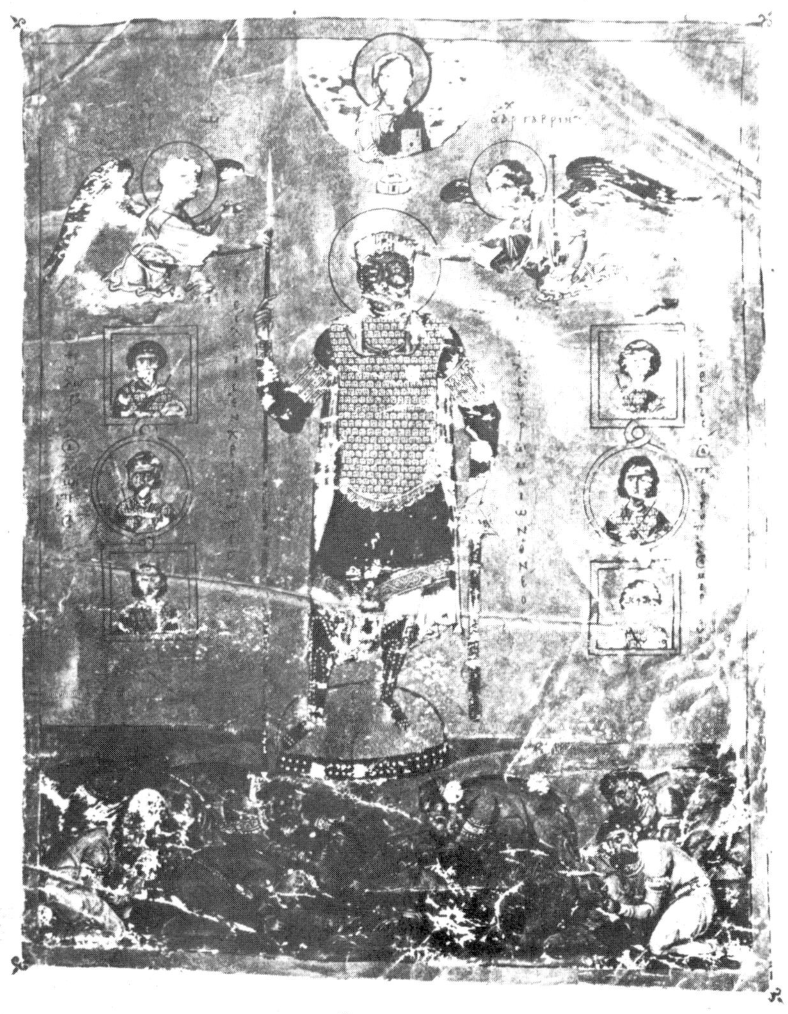

Basil II, manuscript miniature: Cod. Gr. 17. Marcian Library, Venice.

man, but he gives a vivid description of the emperor that accords well with this portrait:

> As for his personal appearance, it betrayed the natural nobility of the man, for his eyes were light blue and fiery, the eyebrows not overhanging nor sullen, nor yet extended in one straight line like a woman's, but well-arched and indicative of his pride. The eyes were neither deep-set . . . nor yet too prominent . . . but they shone with a brilliance that was manly. His whole face was

> rounded off, as if from the center into a perfect circle, and joined to his shoulders by a neck that was firm and not too long. . . .
>
> As for height, he was of less than normal stature, but it was proportionate to the separate parts of his body, and he held himself upright. If you met him on foot, you would find him much like other men, but on horseback he afforded a sight that was altogether incomparable. . . .
>
> In his old age the beard under his chin went bald, but the hair from his cheeks poured down, the growth on either side being thick and very profuse, so that wound round on both sides it was made into a perfect circle and he seemed to possess a full beard.[3]

Psellos adds, too, that Basil had a loud laugh, and when he spoke he sounded more like a country fellow than an emperor, for he cared nothing for the fashionable rhetoric of the time. He was unquestionably Byzantium's greatest soldier-emperor, yet his failure to marry and provide a son to succeed him was an immediate cause of the Byzantine 'Time of Troubles', soon to undermine the empire's strength beyond repair.

---

[1]For details see Martin Arbagi, "The Celibacy of Basil II," *Byzantine Studies* 2 (1975), 41-45.

[2]Cedrenus II (Bonn), 457-459.

[3]Psellos, *Chronographia*, I.36 (Sewter, pp. 48-49).

CONSTANTINE VIII
1025-1028

Basil II's brother Constantine had been an honorary co-emperor since his infancy but had never taken an active part in affairs of state. Though as a young man he had shown considerable military ability, he spent most of his life in luxury and leisure. Gambling at dice was one of his favorite pastimes. He also enjoyed cooking and prided himself on the rare sauces he concocted.[1] As might be expected of such a gourmet, Constantine was fat, a fact that is evident even on his highly stylized coins. And though Michael Psellos certainly exaggerated when he reported that Constantine was "nine feet tall," he was considerably taller than the average Byzantine. "He was a man of enormous size," Psellos comments. "His constitution, moreover, was more than usually robust, and his digestive powers were extraordinary, with a stomach naturally adapted to assimilate all kinds of food with ease."[2]

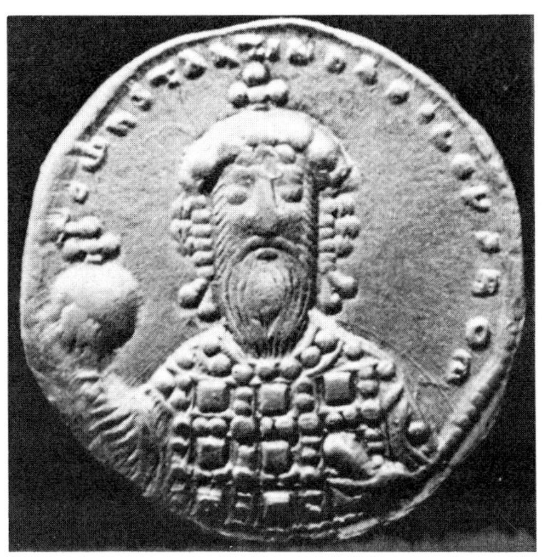

Constantine VIII, coin of his reign. American Numismatic Society.

With the death of Basil II on Christmas Day, 1025, the sixty-four-year-old Constantine became sole emperor. Inheriting power so late in life, he was not well prepared for the serious responsibilities of emperorship. His decisions were often ill-planned and impulsive, and he spent altogether too much time enjoying his old hobby of dice. The power-hungry nobles found it easy to convince him to grant them extensive favors when he was in a good humor. In his reign of less than three years, he carelessly began to destroy the strong, central governmental machinery that Basil II had built up and to squander the great reserves of cash in the imperial treasury.

Probably his most serious mistake was his scatter-brained method of providing for the succession. Constantine and his wife Helena Alypia had no sons, but they were the parents of three daughters. One had died; the other two, Zoe and Theodora, were spinsters in their late forties by the time of their father's reign. Constantine realized that his elder daughter Zoe was unquestionably his heir, but for many months he postponed a definite announcement on the subject. Finally as he lay on his deathbed, he arbitrarily selected a husband and consort for Zoe: Romanos Argyros, who was given the choice of matrimony or blinding.

Romanos and Zoe were married; three days later, Constantine VIII died. A new chapter in the Time of Troubles was about to begin.

---

[1]Psellos, *Chron.*, II.7 (Sewter, p. 57).

[2]*Ibid.*

ZOE PORPHYROGENITA
1028-1050

Zoe was one of those women who retained her striking beauty even in her mature years. As Michael Psellos, who knew her well, reports:

> Her eyes were large, set wide apart, with imposing eyebrows. Her nose was inclined to be aquiline without being altogether so. She had golden hair, and her whole body was radiant with the whiteness of her skin. There were few signs of age in her; in fact, if you marked well the perfect harmony of her limbs, not knowing who she was, you would have said that here was a young woman, for no part of her skin was wrinkled, but all smooth and taut, and no furrows anywhere.[1]

To the Byzantines, she was 'Little Mother', the idolized heiress of the Macedonian dynasty. Whatever her shortcomings—and these were many—she always managed to hold the loyalty of most of her subjects.

Unfortunately, Zoe was woefully unprepared for rulership. When she was in her early twenties, she had journeyed to Italy to wed the German emperor Otto III, only to discover that the prospective bridegroom had died shortly before her arrival.[2] She returned to Constantinople; and because her uncle Basil II never located another man whom he considered royal enough to be her husband, she was forced to remain single until she was almost fifty. It was then that her father Constantine VIII hastily married her off to Romanos Argyros. This was the first of three marriages for Zoe, none of which proved happy.

Psellos, who served as an official at Zoe's court, has much to report of the empress' personality. She regarded matters of state with a giddy, carefree attitude that sometimes proved utterly disastrous. Like her father, she was inclined to make spur-of-the-moment decisions, little thinking of long-range consequences. She was extremely generous; she loved to spend the money her uncle Basil had piled up through his long reign, but gave no thought to where new revenues were coming from.

Strangely enough, Zoe cared little for the gorgeous bejewelled robes in her imperial wardrobe and preferred to wear light, airy dresses of solid white. She was not at all interested in the usual pastimes of aristocratic women, such as needlework; but Psellos reports that she was very good at sitting still and looking serene. She often spent many hours a day at her favorite hobby of concocting perfumes and, because she hated fresh air, her apartments were always full of the heavy odor of these essences.[3]

In her quest for someone to love, Zoe was doomed to disappointment. Not one of the three husbands with whom she shared her throne fulfilled her hopes. Finally, becoming disillusioned and perhaps a little wiser as she grew older, she

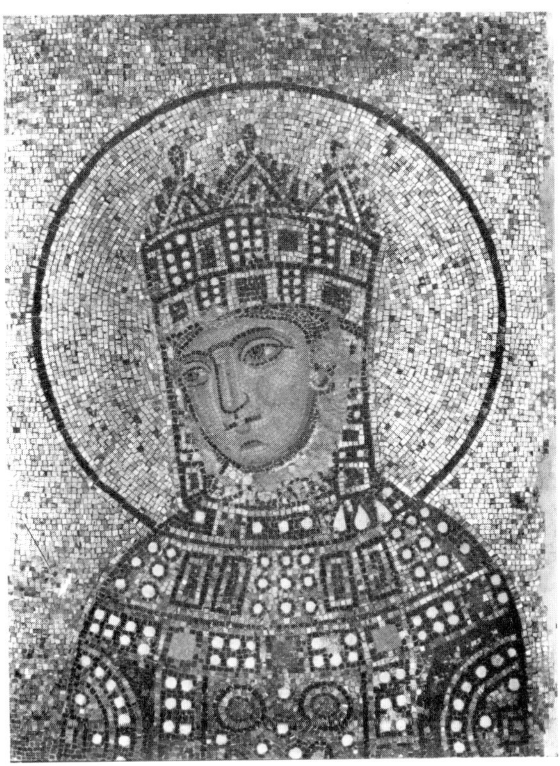

Zoe Porphyrogenita, mosaic. Hagia Sophia, Istanbul (Photograph: Dumbarton Oaks).

granted her third husband, Monomachos, permission to install his mistress in the imperial palace, where Zoe welcomed her as one of the family.

In her old age, Zoe grew increasingly pious—or superstitious—and spent much of her time holding and talking to a certain icon which she believed endowed with miraculous powers.[4] Her tumultuous and often unhappy life ended when she was in her early seventies.

On a wall in Hagia Sophia is a mosaic portrait of the empress Zoe; her blond hair and smooth, unwrinkled skin accord well with Psellos' description of her. The emperor who stands opposite her in the portrait is Monomachos, but there is evidence to suggest that the mosaic originally depicted Romanos Argyros, the first of her husbands, whose memory she had reason to wish to erase.[5]

---

[1]Psellos, *Chron.*, VI.6 (Sewter, p. 158).

[2]Jenkins, *Byzantium: The Imperial Centuries*, pp. 324-325.

[3]Psellos, *Chron.*, VI.64 (Sewter, pp. 186-187).

[4]Psellos, *Chron.*, VI.66 (Sewter, p. 188).

[5]Thomas Whittemore "A Portrait of the Empress Zoe and of Constantine IX," *Byzantion* 18 (1948), 223-227.

ROMANOS III ARGYROS
1028-1034

Romanos Argyros was about sixty when he was compelled to marry Zoe. "He was," says Psellos, "a man of heroic stature, who looked every inch a King."[1] For forty years he had been happily married to the bride of his youth, but the fact that she was still living was no deterrent to Constantine VIII when he decided that Romanos was the ideal man for Zoe. Romanos' wife was hastily sent to a convent; had she refused to go, Romanos would have been blinded. The aging but still handsome nobleman was then promptly married to Zoe. It was not the most promising start for a happy marriage or a successful reign.

Before the sudden stroke of fate that granted him a new wife and the imperial throne, Romanos had served for years as the eparch (mayor) of Constantinople and had a reputation as a capable administrator. He was a descendant of Romanos Lekapenos and a distant cousin of Zoe. His family name, Argyros, means silver.

Zoe at first seemed very much in love with Romanos. In spite of her advanced age, she was hopeful that they might have a child, and she supplied Romanos with numerous love charms and potions in hopes of furthering this goal. While Zoe dreamed of producing a family, Romanos envisioned himself, just as unrealistically, as a great soldier-emperor. Though he had practically no military background, he assumed personal command of his forces for an expedition against the Arabs. The campaign turned out to be a complete fiasco. When the enemy came into sight, the undisciplined Byzantines broke rank and scattered in all directions, Romanos as frightened as any of them. Hours later he was found riding aimlessly by some of his men who recognized him by his red boots. He was rescued and his military career was over.[2] It is a sad commentary on the rapid decline of the empire to see how much the Byzantine army had deteriorated in the few years since Basil II's death.

Meanwhile back in Constantinople, Zoe turned her affections to a handsome palace servant called Michael, who was young enough to have been her son. Since Romanos tended to ignore her and since he seemed oblivious to her affection for Michael, Zoe and her young lover carried on a blatant affair.

After a while, Romanos began to exhibit a number of alarming symptoms; he was unable to sleep well, he had no appetite, his face appeared swollen, and almost all his hair fell out. In great pain, he lost his pleasant, even-tempered disposition and was most disagreeable to his associates. Psellos and other contemporaries suspect—probably correctly—that he was being slowly poisoned.[3]

Finally, early in the morning of the day before Good Friday, 1034, Romanos suffered a fatal accident while bathing in one of the palace swimming pools. No one knows the exact circumstances: gossip held that a bath attendant

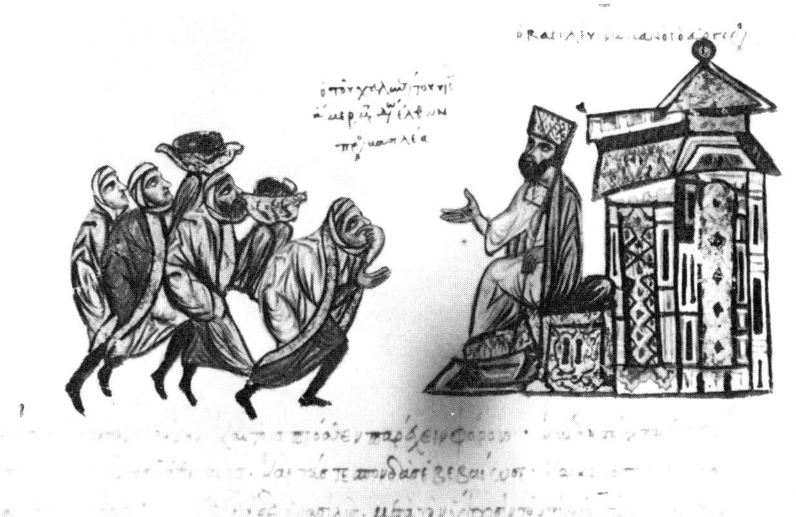

Romanos Argyros receiving envoys from Aleppo, manuscript miniature: Skylitzes Matritensis. Biblioteca Nacional, Madrid.

pushed the old emperor under water and forcibly held him there. He called for help and another attendant aided him to the side of the pool where moments later, gasping for breath, he died.

It was widely suspected but never proved that Michael and Zoe were behind the plot to kill Romanos. In any case, no one was more relieved to learn of his death than they were.

Zoe certainly was to blame for the disappearance of any contemporary portraits of Romanos; the Skylitzes miniature from several centuries later depicts him on one of the happier occasions in his reign, receiving gifts from Arab envoys from Aleppo.

---

[1]Psellos, *Chron.*, III.2 (Sewter, p. 63).
[2]Psellos, *Chron.*, III.10 (Sewter, pp. 68-69).
[3]Psellos, *Chron.*, III.26 (Sewter, p. 81); Cedrenus (Bonn), II, 505.

MICHAEL IV PAPHLAGON
1034-1041

Claiming that the empire could not be left without an emperor, Zoe had herself married to her young lover Michael on the very day of Romanos' death, a scene depicted with typical Orthodox pageantry in Skylitzes' Chronicle.

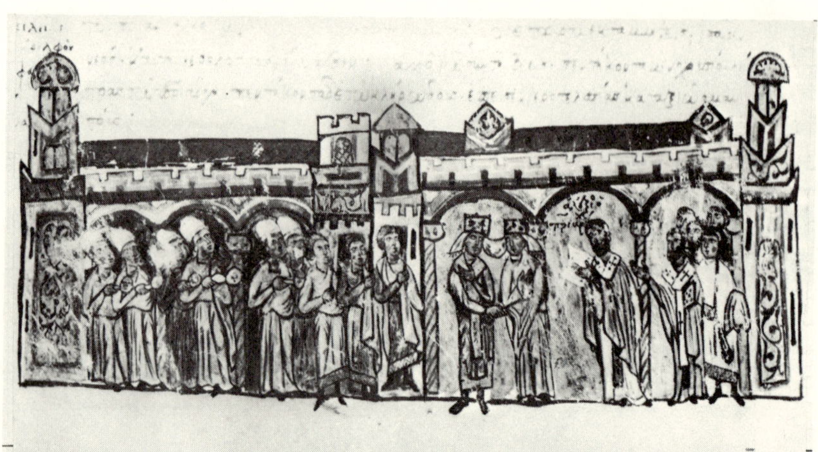

The wedding of Michael Paphlagon and Zoe, manuscript miniature: Skylitzes Matritensis. Biblioteca Nacional, Madrid.

Until their marriage, Michael had been most attentive to the aging empress; as her husband he would soon change completely. Not only did he ignore her as much as possible but he would keep her closely guarded and would curtail her spending money. The unhappy Zoe nevertheless seemed as devoted to him as she had ever been and was constantly hopeful of winning back his love.

Of lowly, obscure birth, Michael had no proper family name; Paphlagon simply indicates that he came from the province of Paphlagonia. "He was a finely proportioned young man," recalls his contemporary Psellos, "with the fair bloom of youth in his face, as fresh as a flower, clear-eyed and in very truth red-cheeked."[1] Nowhere is Michael's exact age indicated, but he was apparently at least thirty years younger than Zoe. Before he won the heart of the old empress, he had been a very minor functionary at the palace, and now, as emperor, he was secretly scorned by many of the aristocrats.

To the surprise of almost everyone, Michael proved to be a surprisingly able ruler. Psellos, who knew him well, wrote long afterwards that history would place him "in the forefront of Roman emperors."[2] Though he lacked advanced education, he was an excellent speaker and appeared so dignified in public appearances that one would have thought him born to the imperial family. While he entrusted much of the business of civil administration to his crafty brother John, Michael led his troops in person and, in spite of the fact that he suffered from epilepsy, he was an outstanding leader.

With the passing of time, Michael's epileptic seizures became increasingly more frequent, and whenever he gave audience he sat on a throne surrounded by red curtains. If he experienced an attack, attendants promptly closed the curtains.[3] When he went anywhere on horseback, he was closely surrounded by bodyguards, but even this precaution did not save him from falling from his horse on several occasions while suffering an epileptic attack.

Michael worried a great deal that his illness was a divine punishment for having married the empress Zoe in order to win the throne. He spent much of his time on visits to the shrine of St. Demetrios in Thessaloniki, where he conversed with the monks and began to think increasingly of becoming a monk himself. Obsessed with the hope of finding divine forgiveness, he invited many poor and sick beggars to his palace, waiting upon them and dressing their sores himself. Meanwhile, his epilepsy grew no better, and he was also afflicted by terrible swelling in his hands—probably dropsy. Realizing that death was near, he was carried to a monastery that he had founded in Constantinople and there asked that he be tonsured immediately. Psellos reports that Zoe went on foot to the monastery and begged for the chance to see him once more, but it was refused. A few hours later, Michael IV died, leaving as his successor his nephew Michael Kalaphates.

---

[1]Psellos, *Chron.*, III.18 (Sewter, p. 76).
[2]Psellos, *Chron.*, IV.7 (Sewter, p. 90).
[3]Psellos, *Chron.*, IV.18 (Sewter, p. 97).

MICHAEL V KALAPHATES
1041-1042

Michael V's mother was a sister of Michael IV: his father had once been a ship's caulker (kalaphates in Greek) and from this occupation he obtained his surname. When Zoe and Michael IV were persuaded to adopt young Michael Kalaphates as their son, they bestowed upon him the title of Caesar and he was openly acknowledged as heir to the throne. The very ambitious but not so clever young man longed for the day when he would possess absolute power.

It was not long after the death of Michael IV that Michael V decided to rid himself of the old empress Zoe, his adoptive mother. By his order, she was shipped off to a convent on a nearby island, a scene depicted in the Skylitzes miniature. In the cloister Zoe's long hair was cut off at the roots—the first step toward making her a nun.

Michael Kalaphates had failed to reckon with Constantinople's inexplicable but very real sense of loyalty to 'Little Mother' Zoe. When the townspeople learned of her fate, a widespread riot broke out in her behalf. "All were ready to lay down their lives for Zoe," Psellos reports.[1] Armed mobs stormed through the streets and to the palace, determined to force Michael Kalaphates to return Zoe to her rightful place as empress.

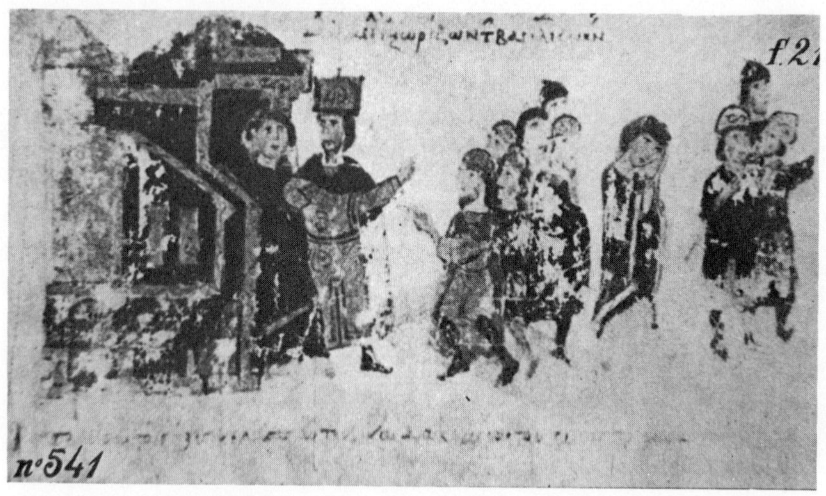

Michael Kalaphates banishes Zoe, manuscript miniature: Skylitzes Matritensis. Biblioteca Nacional, Madrid.

Zoe was duly recalled, Surprisingly, she was apparently ready to forgive Michael and forget his ungenerous treatment of her. The enraged citizenry felt otherwise: if Zoe would not condemn Michael, they would find an empress who would—Zoe's sister Theodora.

Theodora was a nun, living quietly in a convent in Constantinople. The rioters located her, dressed her in a beautiful robe, placed her on horseback and escorted her through the streets, proclaiming her empress. Michael fled for sanctuary to a local monastery, but some of the mob found him and dragged him out. He was then blinded by the palace guards, among them a Viking hero, Harold Hardrada, who later became King of Norway. Norse tradition claims that it was Harold who personally inflicted the drastic punishment upon the fallen emperor. In any case, Michael died not long afterward of the injuries he received. So short was his tenure of power that there are no known coins of Michael V's reign.[2]

With Michael's fall, the empire had no emperor but two empresses, Zoe and Theodora. The two sisters, who had never been close, now sat on identical thrones, wearing identical dresses and crowns. Neither of the empresses was really knowledgeable in affairs of state; the odd partnership scarcely had a chance of success. Zoe solved the problem by taking a third husband, Constantine Monomachos. Thus after a joint reign of about two months, the two empresses yielded precedence to a male ruler, but Monomachos was careful to make it clear that he considered both of the ageing ladies his partners in the honors due the sovereigns of Byzantium.

---

[1]Psellos, *Chron.*, V.26 (Sewter, p. 138).

[2]P. D. Whitting, *Byzantine Coins* (London, 1973), p. 197.

CONSTANTINE IX MONOMACHOS
1042-1055

Constantine Monomachos, the man whom Zoe selected as her third husband, is pictured with her in the famous mosaic panel in Hagia Sophia. His likeness there well accords with Psellos' description of him: his hair was like "the rays of the sun," (which probably indicates a reddish-auburn); his eyes grey. "It was a marvel of beauty that Nature brought into being in the person of this man, so justly proportioned, so harmoniously fashioned, that there was no one in our time to compare with him," Psellos recalled effusively some years after the emperor's death.[1]

Zoe was in her mid-sixties when she summoned Monomachos to Constantinople to marry her; he was probably in his early forties. Since both of them had been married twice before, the Church had to grant them a special dispensation to marry.

Monomachos soon charmed practically everyone who knew him. He was unusually good-natured; he loved to laugh and was easily amused. His generosity was notorious; like Zoe, he spent money without restraint and delighted in making lavish gifts to his associates. Yet beneath his surface charm, many Byzantinists find Monomachos to have been an inept, rather foolish emperor. His moral conduct was the subject of much gossip. His outspoken attachment to Sklerina, an aristocratic young lady of the court, was notorious, and yet even Zoe was so enthralled by Monomachos that she welcomed Sklerina as one of the family and raised no objection to her being accorded the title Augusta (Empress).[2]

Early in his reign, Monomachos was stricken by a terrible illness that caused intense pain and swelling throughout his body. His courage and resignation in bearing his suffering won him much admiration. As far as possible, he continued to carry out his imperial duties, even when he was bedridden. Eventually his health improved considerably.

It was during Monomachos' reign in 1054 that the permanent schism between Roman Catholicism and Eastern Orthodoxy came about. The emperor and his subjects had no realization of the seriousness of the split. Similar incidents had occurred many times before in Christian history, and heretofore had always ended in reconciliation.

Nor was Monomachos as worried as he should have been about the incursions of Patzinaks and Seljuk Turks in the far provinces of the empire. Byzantine military strength had suffered a sharp decline since the days of Basil the Bulgar-slayer, but, oblivious to the problem, Monomachos ordered additional troop reductions in order to have more money to spend on more pleasant things.

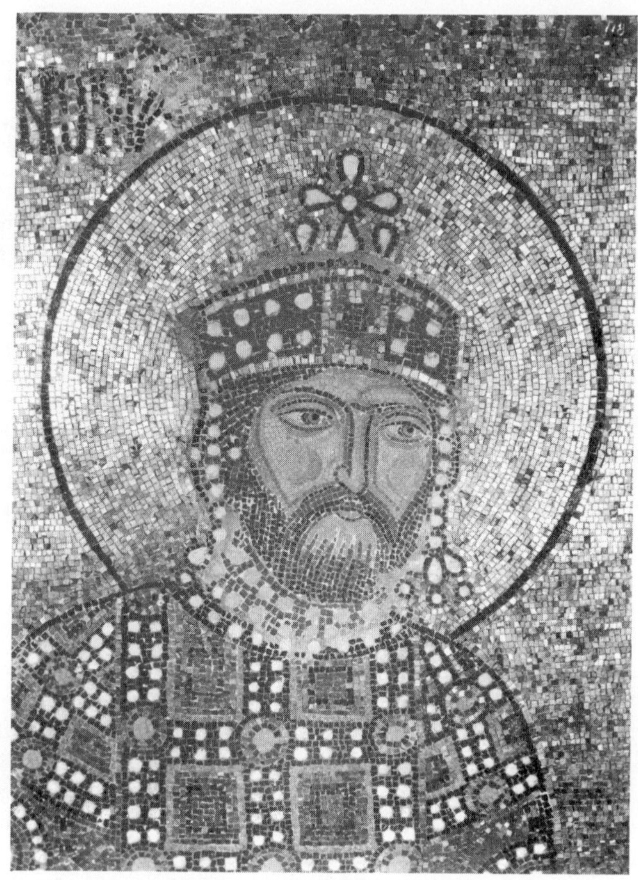

Constantine Monomachos, mosaic. Hagia Sophia, Istanbul (Photograph: Dumbarton Oaks).

When his aged empress Zoe died in 1050, Monomachos mourned her loudly and even tried to convince the Patriarch to recognize her as a saint, a request which was sensibly refused.[3] The emperor did not remarry, but only because the Church forbade a fourth marriage. Zoe's sister Theodora, a straight-laced old maid whom Monomachos had never really liked, continued to perform the ceremonial role of empress.

On a warmish day in January 1055, Monomachos went swimming in an outdoor pool and caught a chill which developed into pneumonia. His death soon thereafter left Theodora in sole possession of the imperial throne.

---

[1]Psellos, *Chron.*, VI.125 (Sewter, pp. 220-221). For additional information on portraits of Monomachos, Zoe and Theodora, see Spatharakis, *The Portrait in Byzantine Illuminated Manuscripts* (Leiden, 1976), pp. 99-102.

[2]Psellos, *Chron.*, VI.61 (Sewter, p. 185).

[3]Psellos, *Chron.*, VI.183 (Sewter, p. 250).

THEODORA PORPHYROGENITA
1055-1056

Theodora was in her mid-seventies when she became sole ruler of the empire early in 1055. Parsimonious by nature, she avoided paying any of the bonuses customary at the start of a new reign, pointing out that she had actually been empress since her short co-reign with her sister Zoe thirteen years before.

Although she had taken the vows of a nun years earlier, Theodora's advisors expected and urged her to marry now that she was sole monarch. The empress rejected these suggestions, believing herself thoroughly capable of reigning alone. Vigorous in spite of her advanced age, she delighted in making long speeches. Her courtiers flattered her with the idea that she was growing younger all the time and predicted that she would have a long and successful reign. On the whole, the aged empress-nun selected competent advisors, and no one except the patriarch Kerularios actively protested the idea of a woman's sole rule. After all, Theodora was the last living member of the much-loved Macedonian dynasty, and for this reason, if for no other, she commanded the loyalty of her subjects.

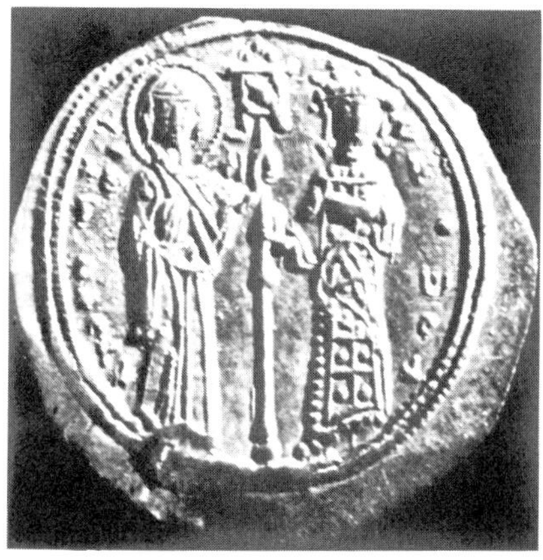

Theodora Porphyrogenita, coin of her reign. American Numismatic Society.

According to Psellos, who was one of her close confidants, Theodora had never been a beauty like her sister Zoe; she was tall and thin with an unusually small head. Even in her old age, "her body was in no way bent despite her exceptional height, and her mental powers were quite equal to more than usually long spells of work or conversation."[1] Psellos found her very talkative and noted, too, how her brother-in-law, Monomachos, always stood in awe and dread of her long harangues.

There is a stylized enamel portrait of Theodora on the so-called "Crown of Monomachos," and though it is not a reliable indication of her personal appearance, it does give the interesting hint that she did not always wear a nun's habit, enjoying instead the jewelled robes and red shoes of an empress. This enamel, along with similar portraits of Zoe and Monomachos, adorned a crown presented by the Byzantine monarchs to the Hungarian court and came to light again in modern times when a farmer in Hungary plowed up this long lost and forgotten treasure.[2] Theodora's coins also depict her in full imperial regalia, far more an empress than a nun.

Because she was the last of the Macedonian line, speculation was rife throughout Theodora's reign as to the identity of her successor. As long as she was in good health, the empress refused to consider naming an heir. Then after a reign of little more than a year she became very ill with an intestinal disease. Knowing that she was soon to die, she 'adopted' Michael Bringas, a retired bureaucrat, as old or even older than she was. With her death soon thereafter and the extinction of the Macedonian dynasty, the Byzantine Empire entered the most disturbed period of the Time of Troubles.

---

[1]Psellos, *Chron.*, VI.new 5 (Sewter, p. 262); see also VI.6. (Sewter, p. 158).

[2]Magda Barany-Oberschall, "The Crown of Constantine Monomachos" (Budapest, *Archaeologica Hungarica; Acta Archaeologica Musei Nationalis Hungarici*, vol. XXII), pp. 50-52. Unfortunately, no photograph has proven available.

MICHAEL VI BRINGAS
1056-1057

Before he became emperor, Michael Bringas had served for years as a 'stratiotikos', a high ranking civil official in the war department, and he had a profound contempt for al! things military. Psellos made a vast overstatement when he commented that Michael "was pretty well the best candidate [for emperor]."[1] As a matter of fact, Theodora could hardly have made a worse choice. Michael was so senile and so lacking in good judgment and tact that he soon alienated practically all his court, except those to whom he awarded undeserved promotions. His innate hatred of the army caused him to reduce military spending even more sharply than Monomachos had done, and at a time when the empire could ill afford to weaken its defenses.

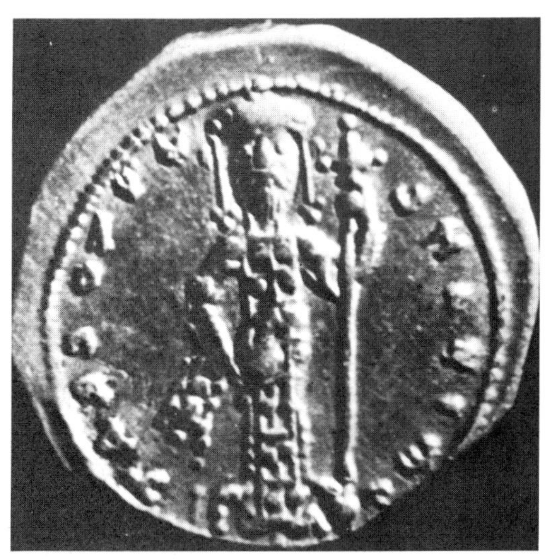

Michael VI Bringas, coin of his reign. American Numismatic Society.

Bringas' follies reached their climax in the spring of 1057. It had long been the custom of the emperor to award an annual Easter bonus to the great officials of the realm, both civil and military. But when the empire's leading generals arrived at the palace to claim their expected rewards, Bringas had nothing for them but a "torrent of abuse," particularly for Isaac Komnenos whom he unfairly accused of numerous mistakes. The generals were not allowed to reply to Bringas' charges, but the unfortunate incident was not forgotten. Isaac withdrew to his country estate and began planning a coup d'etat. Many of the great aristocratic families joined him together with their men at arms, forming a sizable private army.

When Michael Bringas learned that these troops were marching on Constantinople, he had no clear idea of what to do to save his throne. Desperately, he sent a message suggesting that he might adopt Isaac as his heir. When this plan proved futile, the old emperor decided to abdicate. Isaac generously allowed him to retire to private life unmolested. He died not long thereafter.

Psellos gives no details of Michael Bringas' appearance except to remark, "He was already in the autumn of his years . . . and his hair was completely grey."[2] No contemporary portraits survive other than the highly stylized image on his coins.

---

[1]Psellos, *Chron.*, VI.new 21 (Sewter, p. 271). [2]*Ibid.*

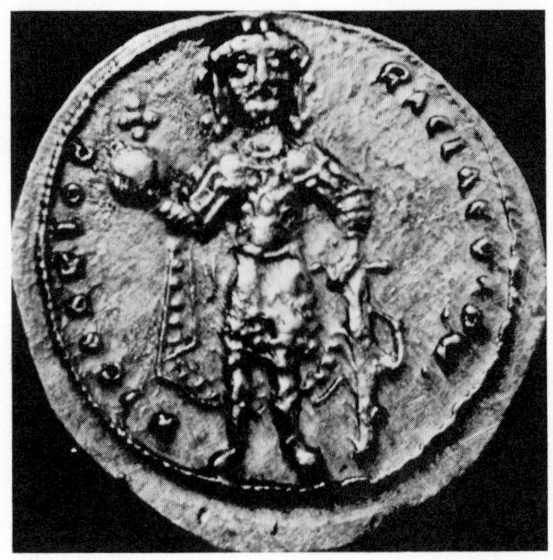

Isaac Komnenos, coin of his reign. American Numismatic Society.

ISAAC I KOMNENOS
1057-1059

Isaac's coins show him with a drawn sword in his hand, a reminder that he seized the empire from Michael Bringas by military force. During his short reign, Isaac endeavored to rebuild the Byzantine army and to undo some of the damage done by his recent predecessors. He cut the salaries of the great crowd of civilian bureaucrats at the court and withdrew many of their tax exemptions. These worthwhile changes naturally were unappreciated by the bureaucratic faction, and Isaac rapidly became a most unpopular emperor. The fact that he was often tactless and brusque did not improve his public image.

Isaac's empress was Aikaterini (or Catherine) of Bulgaria, a princess whom he married years before he became emperor. The fact that he secured a prince's daughter as awife while he was still a private citizen reveals something of the prestige and vast wealth of the Komnenos family.

One of Isaac's greatest enemies was the fiery tempered Patriarch of Constantinople, Michael Kerularios. Isaac dealt with him by removing him from office. Kerularios died soon thereafter, and the people, who esteemed the Patriarch far more than the emperor, considered him a martyr. It was a serious blow to Isaac's already sinking popularity. The figures on a fragment of an enameled cross now located at Dumbarton Oaks are believed to be the likenesses of Isaac Komnenos and his bitter adversary the Patriarch, though presented under the guise of Constantine the Great and St. Sylvester.[1]

Isaac led the Byzantine army in person. In 1059, a successful campaign was waged against the Patzinaks along the northern frontier, but as the Byzantines were returning to winter quarters they ran into severe snow and ice storms. The emperor insisted that they keep marching and, as a result of this terrible journey, he contracted pneumonia. He returned to Constantinople certain that he was dying.

In the weeks that followed, as Isaac lay dangerously ill, there was much intrigue for the succession to the throne. Isaac had no son, but he did have a brother whom some expected him to name as heir. Unable to resist the pressure from the bureaucrats, Isaac nominated instead one of their number, Constantine Doukas. He then abdicated and took monastic vows. Although his health then improved considerably, Isaac could not regain his throne. The monastic vow was deemed irrevocable and he was forced to remain a monk for the rest of his life.

---

[1]Ostrogorsky, *History of the Byzantine State*, 2nd American Ed., plate 46.

CONSTANTINE X DOUKAS
1059-1067

According to Michael Psellos who was his close friend, Constantine Doukas was a paragon of virtue: modest, generous, merciful, even-tempered, a loyal husband and a loving father. The pages of Psellos' *Chronographia* are full of personal glimpses of Doukas, though there is no detailed description of his appearance. Before he succeeded to the throne, Psellos reports, Doukas "used to dress in a rather careless fashion, going about like a country yokel,"[1] since he cared very little about appearing wealthy or powerful. As emperor he was noted for his mercy; he never sentenced anyone to death and allowed no mutilation of offenders more serious than shaving off their beards. Psellos also emphasizes Constantine Doukas' devotion to his four sons and three daughters: "With his children he was delightful, joining gladly in their games, laughing at their baby-talk, often romping with them."[2]

But however charming Doukas may have been as a person, modern Byzantine historians are forced to admit he was not an effective emperor. Although he had been an officer in the Byzantine army, his interests were thoroughly those of the civilian bureaucratic class. The bureaucrats soon won

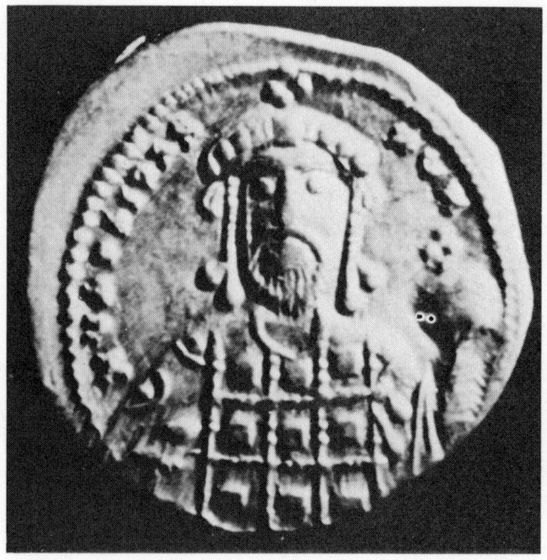

Constantine X Doukas, coin of his reign. American Numismatic Society.

back the privileges and tax exemptions denied them by Isaac. Administrative corruption was widespread; government offices were blatantly for sale to the highest bidder, while taxes were collected by the ancient method of extortion known as tax-farming, which allowed the collectors to keep for themselves all they could collect over the amount they owed the state.

Incredibly foolish as it was, Doukas also instigated further troop reductions. The troops that were maintained were mainly mercenaries. Underpaid and underfed, they had no reason to remain loyal to Byzantium.

It was Doukas' good fortune to die before the inevitable outbreak of trouble from hostile tribes that could not be held off much longer. He planned to leave his throne to his eldest son Michael, but since Michael was very immature and inept, Doukas decided instead, on his death-bed, to leave the authority of the *autokrator* (chief ruler) to his wife, Eudokia Makrembolitissa, with Michael as co-emperor and heir apparent. According to her husband's dying wish, Evdokia swore a solemn oath that she would never remarry.[3]

Doukas' death left a problem-packed situation in which difficulties were sure to develop. Not for many years would there be another emperor to die peacefully in his bed, still in possession of the throne.[4]

---

[1]Psellos, *Chron.*, VII.87 (Sewter, p. 327).

[2]Psellos, *Chron.*, VII.second part 20 (Sewter, p. 340).

[3]For details see N. Oikonomides, "Le serment de l'impératrice Eudocie," *Revue des Études Byzantines* 21 (1963), 101-128.

[4]A silver reliquary, now reportedly located in Moscow, provides a contemporary portrait of Constantine Doukas and his empress Eudokia, but no photograph is available. Another contemporary manuscript miniature of Doukas and Evdokia also exists but is so badly flaked that their features are completely obliterated. Spatharakis, *Portrait*, pp. 104-106.

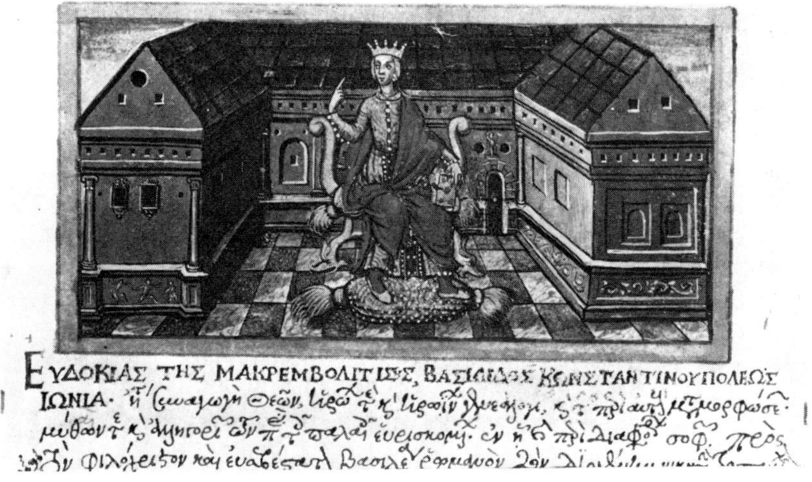

Eudokia Makrembolitissa, manuscript miniature: Cod. Gr. 3057. Bibliothèque Nationale, Paris.

EUDOKIA MAKREMBOLITISSA
1067

"When the empress Eudokia, in accordance with the wishes of her husband, succeeded him as supreme ruler, she did not hand over the government to others," Psellos reports. "She assumed control of the whole administration in person . . . Her pronouncements had the note of authority which one associates with an emperor. Nor was this surprising, for she was in fact an exceedingly clever woman. On either side of her were her two sons, both of whom stood almost rooted to the spot, quite overcome with awe and reverence for their mother."[1] Psellos adds, too, that Eudokia was "beautiful," but gives no details of her appearance. The manuscript portrait of her on this page dates from the fourteenth century and is scarcely a reliable likeness, though her uncommonly plain dress accords well with Psellos' comment that she avoided extravagance in clothes.

Among the problems facing Eudokia was the question of what to do with Romanos Diogenes, a Byzantine rebel general who claimed the throne and who went about in imperial garb, red shoes and all, before he was betrayed by one of his own men and sent to Constantinople under guard. Eudokia had the rebel officer imprisoned, and (more severe than her late husband) she planned to sentence him to death. There was, however, much public clamor for his pardon. Eudokia decided, therefore, to review the case. She had Romanos brought before her, and, it is reported, from the moment she saw the handsome, dynamic rebel, she knew she could not have him killed. He received instead a full pardon, and in the weeks that followed Eudokia was busy trying to decide how she might be absolved from her vow of perpetual widowhood.[2]

The written copy of Eudokia's vow had been filed with the Patriarch of Constantinople. At last, the empress hit upon the idea of sending one of her attendants to the Patriarch, instructing him to hint strongly that she wanted to be married again—to the Patriarch's brother. This 'Byzantine intrigue' was a complete success. The Patriarch handed over the document, and Eudokia, who had no interest whatsoever in his brother, began planning her wedding to Romanos Diogenes.

They were married on New Year's Day, 1068, and Romanos was proclaimed *autokrator*, much to the dismay of Eudokia's teen-aged son, Michael Doukas.

As the wife of Romanos Diogenes, Eudokia would have two more sons. (She had seven children by Constantine Doukas.) Her last years, after Diogenes' fall, were spent in a convent. It does not seem, however, that she became a nun, for a few years later, hoping to be empress again, she proposed matrimony to the widower emperor Nikephoros Botaneiates, an offer which Botaneiates did not accept.[3]

---

[1]Psellos, *Chron.*, VII.third part, I (Sewter, p. 345).

[2]Oikonomides, "Le serment," p. 126.

[3]Anna Komnene, *Alexiad*, III.2 (Dawes, p. 75).

ROMANOS IV DIOGENES
1068-1071

Modern Byzantine historians are often inclined to depict Romanos IV as the noblest Byzantine of them all, one of the few men of the Time of Troubles who made a genuine attempt to improve Byzantium's worsening situation. Physically, he was well cast for the hero's role: "He was a distinguished man, tall of stature, with a fine chest, broad shoulders, and beautiful eyes," records the Cedrenus chronicle.[1]

The romantic story of how Romanos won the heart of Eudokia Makrembolitissa marks the beginning of a short and tragic reign. From the start Romanos was hated by the Doukas family, who saw him as an over-bold

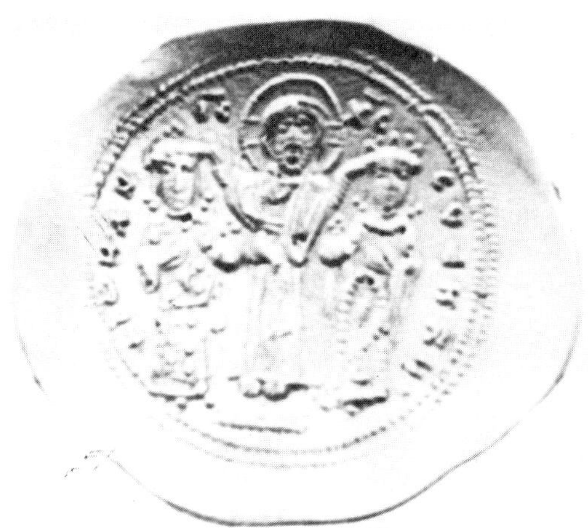

Romanos Diogenes and Eudokia Makrembolitissa crowned by Christ: coin of their reign. American Numismatic Society.

adventurer who had stolen the crown from young Michael Doukas, the rightful heir. Psellos, who was Michael's tutor, was one of the leading spokesmen of the anti-Romanos faction, and his description of the emperor's character is far from complimentary. Psellos and the Doukai expended considerable effort trying to convince Eudokia that Romanos did not really love her; if he did, why was he gone from home so often?

The actual reason for Romanos' lengthy absences from the palace was his determination to rebuild a strong Byzantine army and to push back the Seljuk Turks, who recently had accelerated their periodic raids into eastern Asia Minor. Only by undoing the damages caused by the recent anti-military emperors, Romanos felt, could the Seljuk menace be effectively curtailed. With years of military experience behind him, he was determined to lead his forces personally.

For two years, Romanos conducted fairly successful military operations against the Seljuks. Among his top officers were several of the Doukai, and Romanos little realized that they hated him more than they hated the Turks.

The climax came in August, 1071, near the Armenian town of Manzikert, where the Byzantines encountered a large force of Turks under the personal command of the Seljuk sultan Alp Arslan. During the conflict, the traitorous general Andronikos Doukas started a false rumor among the rear guard that the battle was already lost, urging that they flee from the field. Widespread panic ensued, as Doukas' troops and then other Byzantines scurried off in complete disarray. The brave emperor, realizing that he had been betrayed by his own men, kept fighting along with a few loyal troops who refused to desert him. Then Romanos was severely wounded in the hand and taken prisoner by the Turks.[2]

The sultan Alp Arslan was surprisingly generous to his fallen foe. Though he had Romanos' ears pierced and slave earrings inserted in them, he was otherwise not vindictive, and he even sent his own physicians to attend the emperor's wounded hand. In the days that followed, the emperor and the sultan worked out peace terms: Romanos was to pay a large ransom, yield several frontier forts to the Turks, and send mercenaries to fight in the sultan's army.

On the whole, these were not bad terms; given a few years, Romanos could perhaps have undone the damage.[3] As he was returning home, however, he learned that rebellion had broken out in Constantinople; Romanos was declared deposed, while the Doukai placed their protege Michael on the throne.

Faced with these circumstances, Romanos sent an offer to surrender himself and to become a monk provided that he was not physically harmed. The Doukai agreed, but as soon as they had Romanos in their custody they attempted to poison him. When this effort failed, they ordered him blinded, and the sentence was carried out with excruciating torture designed to be fatal. It is reported that he bore this torture with almost superhuman courage. His enemies then sent him, blind and terribly injured, to a monastery. There he died a few months later.

---

[1]Cedrenus (Bonn), II, 664.

[2]Psellos, *Chron.*, VII.13 ff. (Sewter, pp. 356 ff.); Cedrenus (Bonn), pp. 698-699.

[3]Jenkins, *Byzantium: The Imperial Centuries*, pp. 369-370.

MICHAEL VII DOUKAS
1071-1078

It is widely agreed that young Michael Doukas was not personally to blame for the terrible fate of his stepfather, Romanos Diogenes. Michael seems to have been an extremely shy, withdrawn young man, perhaps rather slow, though Psellos, who was his tutor, praises his intellectual accomplishments. "In appearance," Psellos added of his young pupil, "he somewhat resembles an old man, with something about him of the thinker or pedagogue. His eyes are intent, his brow neither haughty nor beetling, like that of a man who suspects his fellows. His expression is frank, marked with a suitable gravity. . . . He is very prone to blush. . . ."[1]

Michael proved to be a most incompetent emperor, and in his reign the full effects of the Battle of Manzikert became amply clear. With Diogenes no longer emperor, the Seljuks felt free to break their treaty and came pouring into Anatolia. They destroyed practically everything in their path, since they

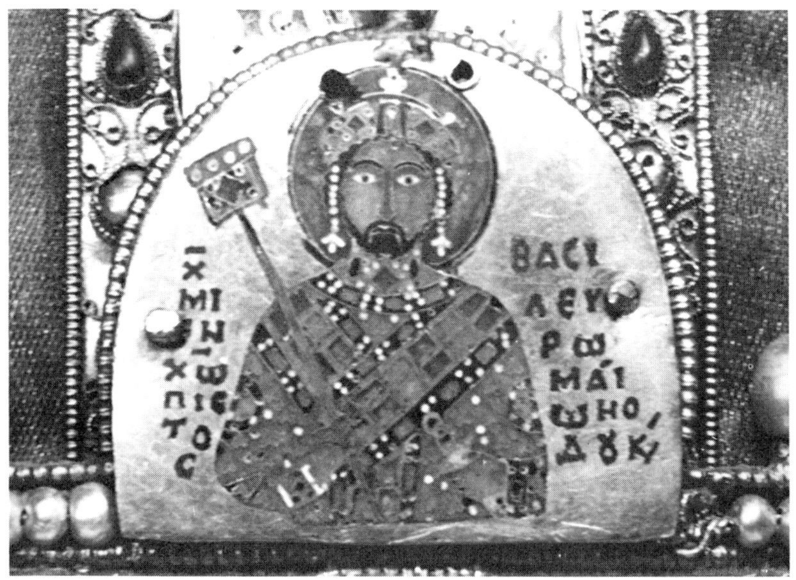

Michael Doukas, enamel plaque on the Holy Crown of Hungary (Bildarchiv Foto, Marburg).

wanted grazing land for their flocks and cared nothing for cities. A historian of the time described the situation in Asia Minor: "Almost the whole world has been destroyed and become empty of population, for all Christians have been slain and all houses and settlements crushed and reduced to nothing."[2] Byzantium would never fully recover from these disasters.

Beside the losses in Asia Minor, Michael's reign also witnessed the fall of Bari, the last Byzantine stronghold in Italy, to Norman adventurers under Robert Guiscard. Along the northern frontiers of the empire, the great menace to Byzantium came from the Pechenegs, a fierce nomadic people akin to the Turks.

As these disasters engulfed the empire, the emperor Michael showed no signs of growing in leadership ability. He preferred writing poetry to state business, and he left much of the direction of affairs of state to the anti-military Doukai and to Psellos. Incidentally, the emperor's poetry had no literary merit whatsoever.

Michael earned much hostility from the people of Constantinople for his devaluation of the coinage and his attempts to inflate the price of grain. His incompetence and unpopularity resulted in the rise of several rival claimants to the throne. When one of these, Nikephoros Botaneiates, took Constantinople, Michael agreed to abdicate. He took monastic vows, which meant that he had to give up his wife, Maria of Alania. He little dreamed she would soon be the wife of his victorious rival.

As for Michael, it seems that the monastic life suited him well. He lived many years longer and, before he died, was rewarded with the post of Bishop of Ephesus.[3]

An enameled plaque depicting the emperor Michael appears at the center back of the famous Holy Crown of Hungary. The Holy Crown, it is generally agreed, is made from at least two earlier crowns, the lower section including the imperial Byzantine portrait, being part of a diadem originally presented by Michael to his ally, King Geza of Hungary.[4]

---

[1]Psellos, *Chron.*, VII.5 (Sewter, p. 370).

[2]An anonymous chronicle quoted by A. A. Vasiliev, *History of the Byzantine Empire*, 2nd ed. (Madison, 1952), p. 355.

[3]Demetrios I. Polemis, *The Doukai* (London, 1968), p. 44.

[4]Patrick J. Kelleher, *The Holy Crown of Hungary* (Rome: American Academy in Rome: Papers and Monographs, vol. XII, 1951).

NIKEPHOROS III BOTANEIATES
1078-1081

Although the elderly general Nikephoros Botaneiates who replaced Michael Doukas reigned only three years, there are several excellent portraits of him preserved in a book of St. John Chrystostom's sermons that once belonged to the emperor and that is now housed in the Bibliotheque Nationale in Paris. This series of portraits is extremely valuable in revealing the different costumes in the imperial wardrobe, but the emperor's likeness probably flatters him a great deal.[1] He was an old man when he took the throne, but in the portraits he seems no more than middle-aged, with jet black hair and beard and soulful dark eyes. Nor do we see any hint of the fact recorded by the chronicler Manasses: "his whole body was covered with scars."[2]

Botaneiates claimed kinship with the Phokas family and was himself named for the emperor Nikephoros Phokas.[3] In his youth he was married to a woman called Verdenia, but as emperor he sought a second wife who would help improve his shaky claim to the throne. Rejecting a proposal from the ex-empress Eudokia Makrembolitissa, who was near his own age, he chose instead Maria of Alania, the former wife of Michael Doukas. 'Beautiful Maria' had red hair and bright blue eyes; she was not a Byzantine, but came from the Alan tribe located in what is now southern Russia. Botaneiates thought her an excellent choice as a wife, for it meant he would have no in-laws close by to make trouble.[4]

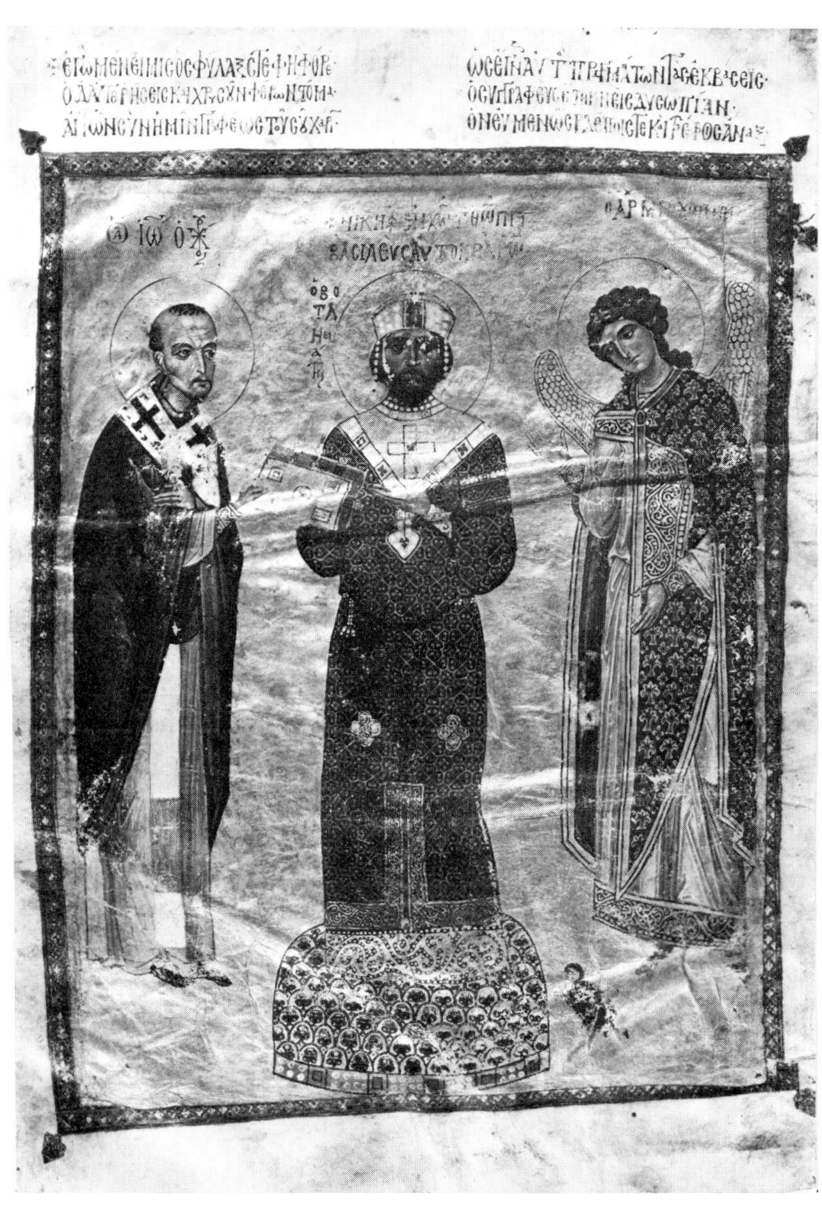

Nikephoros Botaneiates with St. John Chrysostom and St. Michael, manuscript miniature: Ms. Coislin 79. Bibliothèque Nationale, Paris.

Maria did have, however, a little son, Constantine, by her first husband, and her major preoccupation was to have Botaneiates to recognize him as his heir. The emperor proved most uncooperative. He was far more susceptible to the influence of certain of his corrupt favorites than to that of his beautiful young wife. He refused to designate an heir, and even deprived little Constantine of his right to wear red shoes. It was no surprise when Maria began to engage in intrigues with Botaneiates' enemies, especially the Komnenos family. Her prize protege was the young general, Alexios Komnenos, and it was he who deposed Botaneiates by military coup early in 1081.

Botaneiates, like so many fallen emperors before him, became a monk. Later, when asked if he missed his former life, he replied that he missed nothing but the privilege of eating meat.[5]

With the fall of Botaneiates, the Time of Troubles that had produced fourteen reigning monarchs in little over half a century comes to an end. Things would be very different with the Komnenoi on the imperial throne.

---

[1]Spatharakis, *Portrait*, pp. 107 ff., believes that the famous series of portraits of Botaneiates are actually portraits of Michael Doukas, only slightly, and rather unsuccessfully, retouched.

[2]Manasses (Bonn), p. 283.

[3]Ostrogorsky, *History of the Byzantine State*, p. 348.

[4]A. Komnene, *Alexiad*, III.2 (Dawes, p. 74).

[5]A. Komnene, *Alexiad*, III.1 (Dawes, p. 71).

ALEXIOS I KOMNENOS
1081-1118

Dynamic, determined, and clever, Alexios of the aristocratic house of Komnenos put an end to the Time of Troubles when he seized the throne of Botanieates. He would become the founder of an imperial family that would reign for a century, and, under the Komnenoi, stability and a considerable measure of prosperity returned to the Byzantine world.

Alexios was in his early thirties when he became emperor. According to his daughter, Anna Komnena, who years later wrote his biography, he was an impressive figure.

> Alexios indeed was not especially tall but rather broad, and yet his breadth was well proportioned to his height. When standing he did not strike the onlookers with such admiration, but if when sitting on the imperial throne, he shot forth the fierce splendor of his eyes,

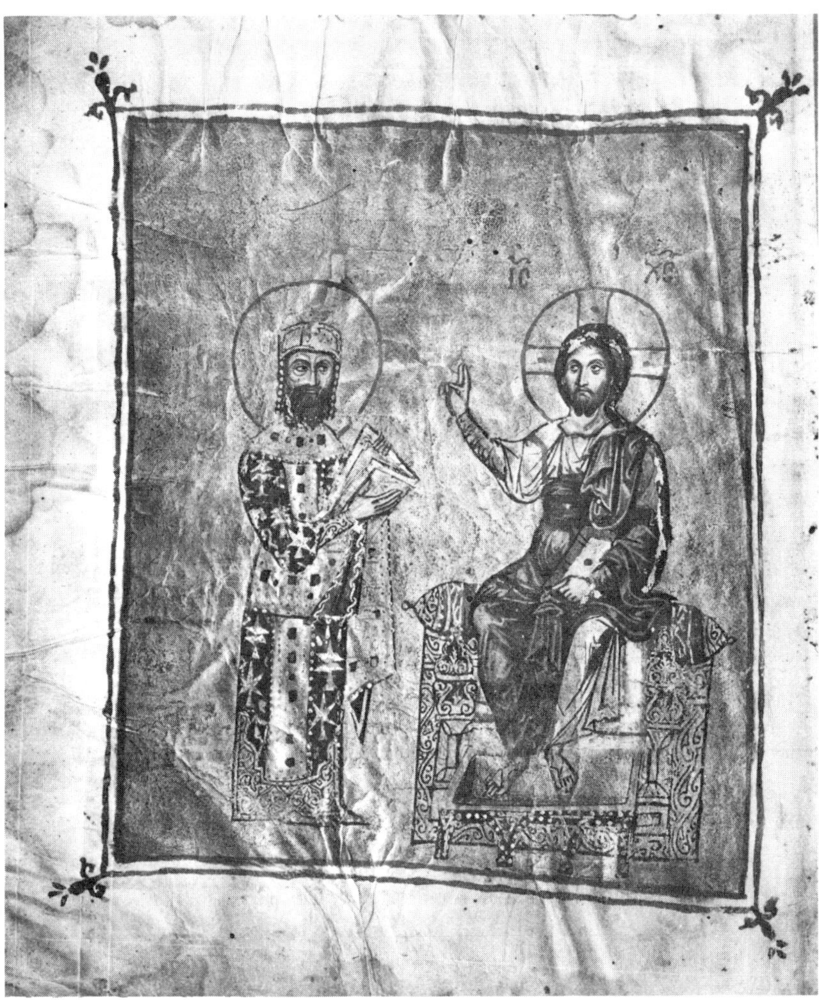

Alexios I Komnenos before the throne of Christ, manuscript miniature: Ms. Gr. 666. Biblioteca Apostolica Vaticana.

he seemed to be a blaze of lightning, such irresistible radiance shone from his face, nay from his whole person. He had black arched eyebrows, from beneath which his eyes darted a glance at once terrible and tender, so that from the gleam of his cheeks and the ruddy color that suffused them, both awe and confidence were awakened. His broad shoulders, muscular arms, mighty chest, in fact his generally heroic appearance, evoked in the multitude the greatest admiration and pleasure.[1]

Alexios' second wife, the mother of his seven children, was Irene Doukaina, whom he married shortly before he became emperor. At first, the match was a very unhappy one. Alexios was infatuated with Botanieates' empress Maria and contemplated divorcing Irene to marry her. He abandoned this idea only because he needed the support of the Doukas family. Ironically, as time passed, Alexios and Irene became deeply devoted to each other. The empress often accompanied her husband on his military campaigns and was ever alert to plots against him, so that on several occasions she saved him from great danger.

Alexios led his forces in person, even as he grew older and was severely troubled by gout. His reign was a period of almost constant war against Normans, Pechenegs, Seljuks, and other enemies. His daughter Anna delighted in recounting tales of her father's great personal courage in battle, but, as a typical Byzantine, she was just as proud of instances where he outwitted his enemies by his craftiness or retreated judiciously to fight again another day.

Among the major events of Alexios' reign was the First Crusade, an enterprise for which he was in part responsible. When Alexios appealed for a few well-trained mercenaries from western Europe to aid him in his struggle against the Turks, he surely did not anticipate the overwhelming response: undisciplined hordes of Crusaders who came trooping through the empire, pillaging as they went.[2] Alexios made every effort to utilize all this fighting energy for the empire's good. Individual Crusader lords were pressured into swearing loyalty oaths to the emperor, and an alliance of sorts was worked out. In the months that followed, Crusaders and Byzantines launched an offensive against the Turks. Though they met with considerable success, there was vast lack of understanding between the allies, and, when the Crusaders moved southward against the Holy Land, the Byzantines did not accompany them.

Not the least of Alexios' claims to fame lies in the fact that his learned daughter Anna is the western world's first great woman historian. Anna was Alexios' first-born child. Disappointed in her hope of obtaining the throne (which went to her brother John), she spent many years after her father's death collecting data for her book, *The Alexiad*, a detailed biographical history of his reign. Although Anna adored her father and does not attempt to conceal it, she also strove to be an accurate and careful reporter. Her book is one of the masterpieces of medieval literature.

From Anna's work come many details concerning her father's last illness and death. When Alexios was in his early sixties he began to suffer from a severe respiratory complaint. Often, Anna reports, his wife Irene would sit up all night with Alexios propped in her arms, in an attempt to ease his breathing difficulties. After weeks of intense agony, he died, surrounded by his wife and daughters.[3]

Alexios was unquestionably one of the great Byzantine emperors: a talented soldier, statesman, and diplomat. He was also greatly loved, best by those who knew him best.

A contemporary manuscript portrait, now in the Vatican Library, pictures Alexios, book in hand, standing before the throne of Christ.

---

[1]A. Komnene, *Alexiad*, III.3 (Dawes, p. 76).

[2]For details see A. Komnene, *Alexiad*, X.5-11 (Dawes, pp. 248-268).

[3]A. Komnene, *Alexiad*, XV.11 (Dawes, pp. 419 ff.).

JOHN II KOMNENOS
1118-1143

According to his sister Anna, who disliked him heartily, John Komnenos was an unusually ugly baby. "The child had a swarthy complexion," she recalls, "broad forehead, lean cheeks, a nose neither snub nor aquiline but something between the two, . . . and very black eyes."[1] Ironically he grew up to be known as Kaloioannes—Handsome John. Perhaps this nickname originated in jest, for other writers beside Anna note that John was anything but good-looking. Or perhaps the emphasis was intended to be on his character, for kalos can indicate 'good' as well as 'handsome', and John Komnenos, a merciful and humane emperor, much beloved by his subjects, certainly merits the title of John the Good. In his long reign of twenty-five years, he never sentenced anyone to capital punishment, and his high-principled, ethical dealing with friend and foe alike won him much admiration.

The emperor's home life seemed ideally happy. His wife Priska-Irene, daughter of King Ladislaus of Hungary, presented him with a family of four sons and four daughters, including a set of twins. When Irene died, still young, John vowed to remain true to her memory, a promise which by all accounts he kept.

Among the most famous mosaics of Hagia Sophia is a panel depicting John and his Irene on either side of the Virgin and Christ Child. John is magnificently clad in a jewel-studded *loros* and holds a bag of money symbolizing his beneficence to the church. Sandy-haired Irene is garbed in similar splendor. Her face is cool and serene beneath a high *modiolos* crown, and, instead of the usual *pendilia*, two very long tresses cascade over her shoulders. Near his parents in the mosaic portrait is a figure of their eldest son, Prince Alexios, who did not live to inherit the throne.

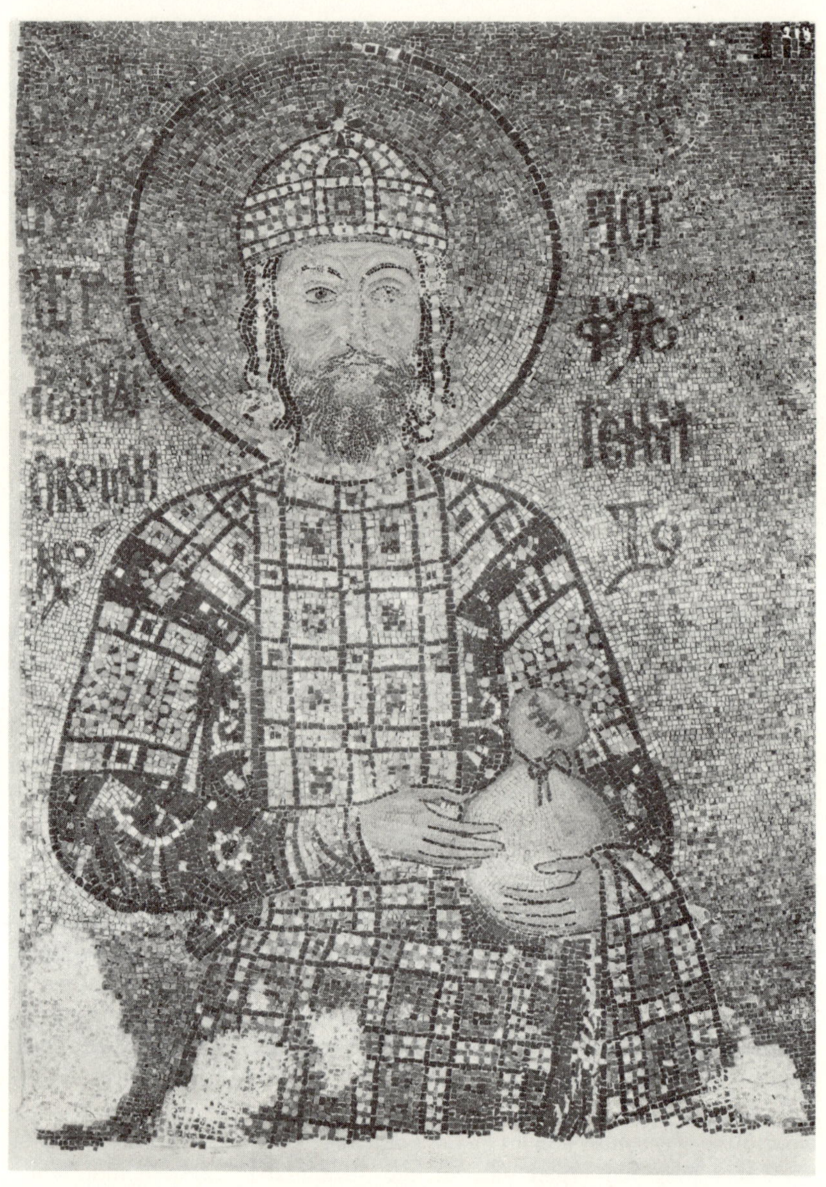

John Komnenos, mosaic. Hagia Sophia, Istanbul (Photograph: Dumbarton Oaks).

Almost the whole of John's reign was spent in warfare against the empire's enemies on all sides. His spectacular victory over the Pechenegs and subsequent scattering of the defeated tribesmen to various parts of the empire put an end to the tribe's marauding activities once and for all. For many years thereafter, the Byzantines annually celebrated 'Pecheneg Day' to commemorate this great triumph. In the east, John won important victories over the Turks and the Crusader state of Antioch. The Prince of Antioch at one point recognized John's overlordship but later rebelled.

It was this happening which caused John to plan a new campaign against Antioch, and in all likelihood he had additional plans for bringing the other Crusader states, including Jerusalem, under Byzantine lordship. What he might have accomplished, however, history can only guess, for John, while hunting, accidentally scratched his hand on a poisoned arrow. Almost immediately he became seriously ill. His physicians advised him that they could probably save his life if they amputated his hand, but John refused, feeling that with such a disability he would no longer be eligible to reign.[2] Before he died, he nominated his youngest son Manuel as his heir.

---

[1]A. Komnene, *Alexiad*, VI.8 (Dawes, p. 152).

[2]Robert Browning, "The Death of John II Comnenus," *Byzantion* 31 (1961), 229-235, gives details and raises the question of a deliberate assassination plot.

MANUEL I KOMNENOS
1143-1180

Manuel Komnenos "was tall of stature," reports his younger contemporary Niketas Choniates, "but ever so slightly stooped. In color, he was not so white and pale as one who is brought up in the shade, nor so dusky as those who are scorched by the sun, but somewhere between black and white and tending more to swarthiness; nevertheless he was very handsome."[1] Twenty years old when he succeeded to the throne, Manuel was well-educated, with a particular interest in medicine and science. He was also much attracted by the customs of western European chivalry, which the Byzantines were gradually absorbing from the Crusaders. He introduced tournaments in the Hippodrome and delighted in taking part in person. Because he liked the more informal relationship between ruler and subjects that the Crusaders evidenced, he abolished some of the lavish court ceremonies. When on campaign with his

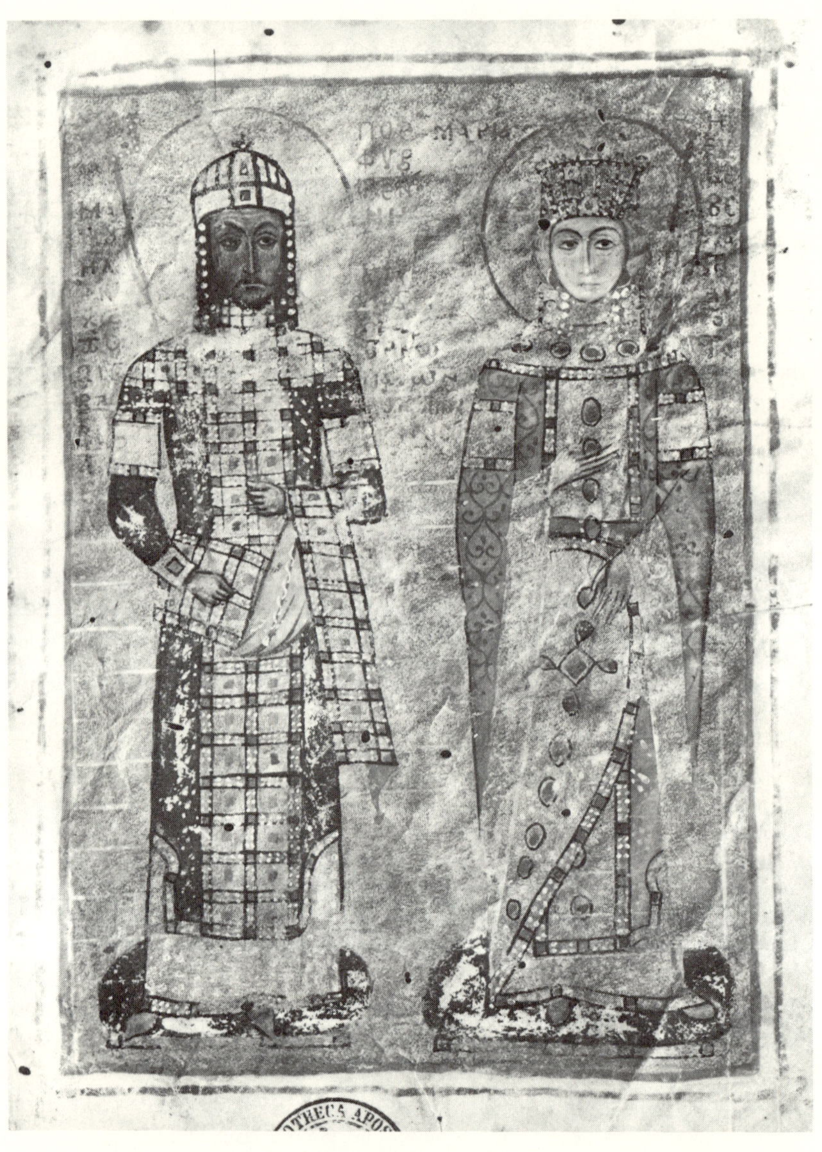

Manuel Komnenos and Marie of Antioch, manuscript miniature: Ms. Gr. 1176. Biblioteca Apostolica Vaticana.

troops, he made it a point to work along with his men, and he was often seen taking part in laborious duties, such as digging of fortifications, that his predecessors would have shunned as beneath their dignity.[2]

Manuel's liking for Frankish ways meant that many westerners flocked to his court and found lucrative positions there. Both of Manuel's wives were western princesses. He cared little for the first of them, the German Bertha-Irene of Sulzbach, who bore him only two daughters. His numerous infidelities were notorious. After Bertha's death, he married French-speaking Marie of Antioch, who became the mother of his only legitimate son, Alexios II. He is pictured with her in the contemporary manuscript miniature on the opposite page. In spite of his admiration for the West, 'Black Manuel' in this portrait is a typical Byzantine sovereign in his stiff, bejewelled *loros*, while his long black hair is in striking contrast with the close cropped style favored by contemporary Franks.

One of the major crises of Manuel's reign was the Second Crusade, which began in 1144. Much as he liked westerners, he was no more eager than his grandfather Alexios I had been to have thousands of them streaming through Byzantine territory. When news of the forthcoming Crusade reached him, Manuel promptly effected a truce with his Turkish neighbors, and both sides settled down to await the common foe. Manuel was most unhappy when he discovered that, although his brother-in-law, the German ruler, Conrad III, was one of the Crusade's leaders, Conrad's forces were marching through Byzantine territory, plundering and killing Byzantines without a qualm. Conrad himself refused to meet with Manuel face to face. The French Crusaders under Louis VII, who followed soon after Conrad's Germans, were even more of a menace. Manuel could only try to hasten their departure through his territory as rapidly as possible.

When the Second Crusade was cut to pieces by the Turks and the survivors started struggling home, Conrad actually stopped in Constantinople to visit his imperial brother-in-law. While there the German ruler became very ill and Manuel had an opportunity to put his medical knowledge to use as he personally took charge of his guest's convalescence. Conrad recovered fully, and the two rulers became firm friends.[3]

Like Justinian I, Manuel cherished the hope of restoring Byzantine authority in Western Europe. For a short time, these plans seemed on the way to fulfillment when imperial forces won several battles against the Normans of southern Italy; however, no lasting expansion of Byzantine territories there resulted. Manuel was more successful in the East; practically all the Crusader states recognized his overlordship. Then in 1176, the Byzantines suffered a devastating defeat by the Turks at the battle of Myriokephalon: a setback which undid practically all of the century-long efforts of the Komnenoi to curtail the spread of these enemies at Byzantium's expense.

In the years immediately following Myriokephalon, Manuel's health began to deteriorate. Exceedingly superstitious, he tried to find out how long he had left to live. A soothsayer warned him to prepare for a "great earthquake," and he was having vast subterranean shelters constructed under the palace when suddenly his health became much worse.[4] Repenting of his habit of seeking to learn the future, he became a monk and died almost immediately thereafter. His heir was his son, Alexios II.

---

[1]Niketas Choniates (Bonn), p. 69.
[2]*Cambridge Mediaeval History*, IV, i, p. 226.
[3]Diehl, *Byzantine Empresses*, p. 241.
[4]N. Choniates (Bonn), pp. 284-288.

ALEXIOS II KOMNENOS
1180-1183

The second Alexios Komnenos was a frail boy of eleven, more interested in sports and games than in learning the business of government.[1] His mother, Marie of Antioch, assumed the regency; her obvious pro-western policies and the fact that she was easily influenced by corrupt favorites meant that discontent with her regime was rife in the capital city. The predicted earthquake so feared by the late emperor Manuel was coming—not a literal one but a far-reaching shake-up of the government that would claim numerous victims.

Young Alexios II and his intended bride, Princess Agnes-Anne of France, who was growing up with him, were oblivious to the gathering storm, while the empress mother Marie did nothing to allay popular discontent. Then in 1182, a cousin of the imperial family, Andronikos Komnenos, appeared in Constantinople as the self-proclaimed champion of the boy emperor and foe of the 'Latins' and their allies. Andronikos was welcomed with wild enthusiasm. Many inhabitants of the capital city, long disgusted by the preferential treatment accorded to western Europeans, took the arrival of Andronikos as a signal for widespread revolt. Mobs roamed the streets, killing any and every westerner they could find. The victims of this 'Latin Massacre' of 1182 numbered in the thousands, and the uprising would prove a major step in the growth of East-West hatred.[2]

Meanwhile, Andronikos obtained complete sway over the young emperor. The boy was even compelled to sign the death warrant of his own mother, Marie of Antioch. Next, Andronikos had himself crowned co-emperor. Publicly he put on a great show of good will toward Alexios: in one public procession, he even carried the young emperor on his shoulders.[3] Actually, however, Andronikos was not content with an imperial partner, and only a few

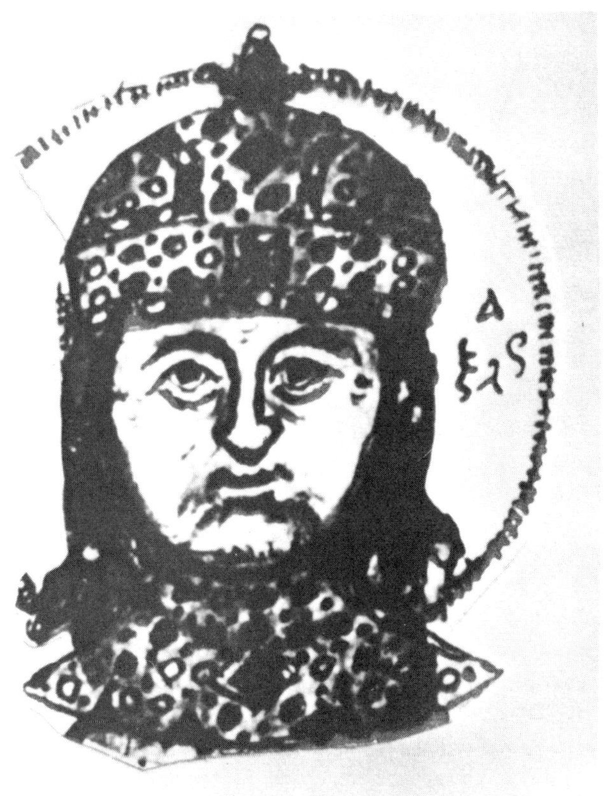

Alexios II Komnenos, pen and wash drawing. Cod. Gr. 122. Biblioteca Estense, Modena.

months passed before he secretly ordered his henchmen to strangle Alexios. The boy emperor was duly killed, and his head was presented to Andronikos. A short and tragic reign had ended; the complete destruction of the house of Komnenos was not far in the future.

For a portrait of the tragic and short-lived boy emperor Alexios one must turn to the fifteenth-century copy of the Zonaras Chronicle, now in Modena. Byzantine artists were rarely successful in their portrayal of children, and this sketch is no exception. Though most of the later imperial portraits in this Modena manuscript are reasonable likenesses, Alexios II's portrait suggests his youth only through the fact that he is beardless.[4].

---

[1]N. Choniates (Bonn), pp. 329-330.

[2]Charles M. Brand, *Byzantium Confronts the West* (Cambridge, Mass., 1968), pp. 41 ff.

[3]Brand, *Byzantium Confronts the West*, pp. 44 and 327, n. 34.

[4]Spatharakis, *Portrait*, pp. 172-183, presents a detailed description of the imperial portraits in the Zonaras ms., contending that most of them are attempts at genuine likenesses of the figures depicted.

ANDRONIKOS I KOMNENOS

1182-1185

In spite of his merciless removal of Alexios II, Andronikos was undoubtedly one of the most popular emperors at the start of his reign. He was a striking figure with a long white beard which he wore in the fashionable forked style, a characteristic faithfully portrayed in the Modena manuscript. "The condition of his body was excellent, of venerable aspect, erect, of heroic stature, and even in his old age, he had a youthful face," reports Niketas Choniates. "His body was outstandingly healthy because he was neither voluptuous nor gluttonous, nor a drunkard, but like the Homeric heroes he lived simply and moderately."[1]

In his sixties when he seized the throne, Andronikos had no sooner disposed of the boy Alexios than he married the young widow, Agnes-Anne of France, who was about twelve or thirteen, an act which scarcely fit with Choniates' praise of his moderation.

Andronikos made no secret of the adventurous details of his life before he became emperor.[2] As a young man he had served nine years in prison for attempted assassination of his cousin, the emperor Manuel. Once during that period, he dug his way out of his cell through a sewer pipe, only to be recaptured. The second time he escaped, it was for good. He fled from Byzantine territory, travelled far and wide in the Middle East, winning fame as a soldier of fortune. He possessed charm that most women found utterly devastating; his romantic conquests were innumerable, but none so spectacular as his affair with his cousin Theodora, the widowed queen of Jerusalem, whom he carried off with him to share his life of adventure. Later when she and their two sons were captured by Byzantine authorities, Andronikos returned to Manuel's court to beg their release and pardon for himself. The generous emperor granted Andronikos' wishes but sent him to serve as governor of a distant frontier outpost, an honorable exile, designed to keep him away from Constantinople.

It was from this outpost that Andronikos came in 1182 to seize the throne of the empire. He brought with him a motley army, including many tenant farmers as well as some Turkish mercenaries. The discontent of the Byzantines with the empress Marie's regime insured their success.

As sole emperor Andronikos undertook an extensive reform program that has remained controversial even to the present day. "Either cease from ill doing," he frequently reminded his officials, "or you will cease from living." He was ruthless in carrying out his threats, and as the number of his victims grew, so did the number of his live opponents in the capital city. Yet, he seems to have striven conscientiously for a fairer system of tax collection, and for the

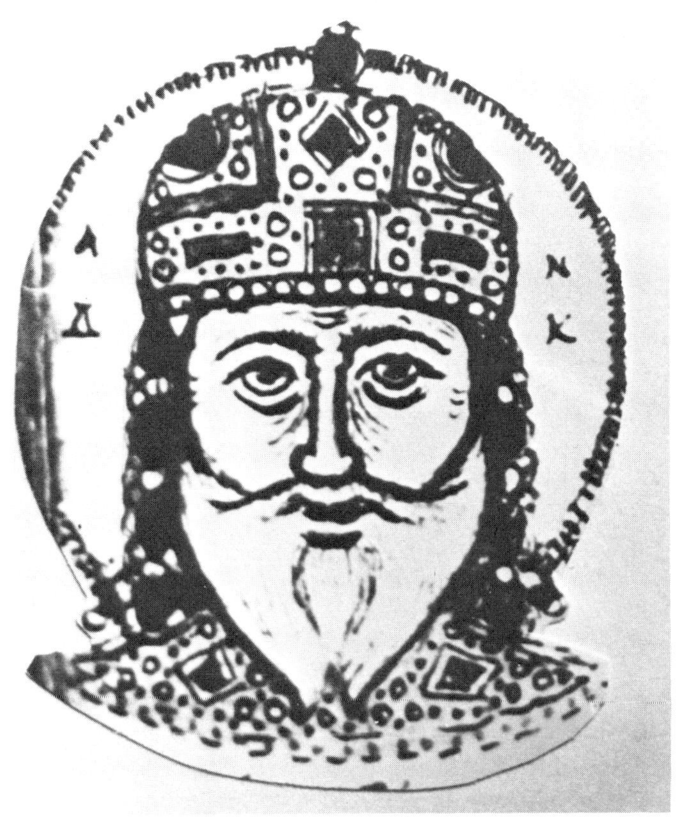

Andronikos I Komnenos, pen and wash drawing. Cod. Gr. 122. Biblioteca Estense, Modena.

worthwhile reforms he undertook, or at least promised, he was popular in the provinces.

Andronikos' troubles were compounded by an invasion of Italian Normans who sacked Thessaloniki, claiming they sought vengeance for the recent Latin Massacre. The emperor could not command the loyalty of his own army officers, and the state which he had intended to reform was seemingly falling to pieces.

Worried that he had no legitimate son to succeed him, Andronikos sought to learn the name of his successor by magic and was warned by a soothsayer that the person who would succeed him had a name beginning with the letters 'Is' . . . The emperor's suspicions immediately fastened on a young nobleman, Isaac Angelos.[3] He commanded his arrest, little dreaming that Isaac would seize the moment to launch a revolt against him.

Andronikos attempted to flee when rioting broke out but was captured. Days later, the new emperor Isaac released Andronikos to the city mob, who subjected him to unspeakable tortures before they finally killed him in the Hippodrome. Whatever had been his shortcomings, Andronikos Komnenos died with truly imperial dignity and courage. While there were many who rejoiced at his fall, there were others who mourned him deeply, most of all his child-bride, the empress Agnes-Anne.

---

[1]N. Choniates (Bonn), pp. 458–459.

[2]For details see Charles Diehl, "Les romanesques aventures d'Andronic Comnène," *Figures byzantines*, 2nd ser. Paris, 1908.

[3]N. Choniates (Bonn), pp. 440–444.

ISAAC II ANGELOS
1185-1195

Isaac Angelos experienced the most dramatic moments of his life when, confronted by the official sent by Andronikos to arrest him, he replied by drawing his sword, striking a fatal blow, and then dashing off, shouting "Follow me!" Thousands of Constantinople's inhabitants, weary of Andronikos' severities, followed the dynamic young nobleman, and within hours Andronikos' government had collapsed.[1]

The new emperor Isaac was thirty years old, a distant relative of the Komnenos family. "His face was florid, his hair red; he was of medium height and robust of body," reports Choniates.[2] The artist of the Modena manuscript, who is believed to have worked from earlier imperial portraits now lost, emphasizes Isaac's prominent hooked nose. Though his disposition was far from angelic, Isaac delighted in puns on his family name indicating that Byzantium was ruled by an angel.[3]

As emperor, Isaac was determined to enjoy life to the fullest. The food and entertainment at the palace were more lavish than anyone could remember, while the emperor's magnificent wardrobe outshone that of any of his recent predecessors. It was not unusual for him to wear a robe only once before discarding it. Rumor had it that he bathed "every other day," which seemed entirely too often to most of his contemporaries.

Isaac's outspoken love of luxury led to substantial tax increases and to a return to much of the administrative corruption that Andronikos had tried to

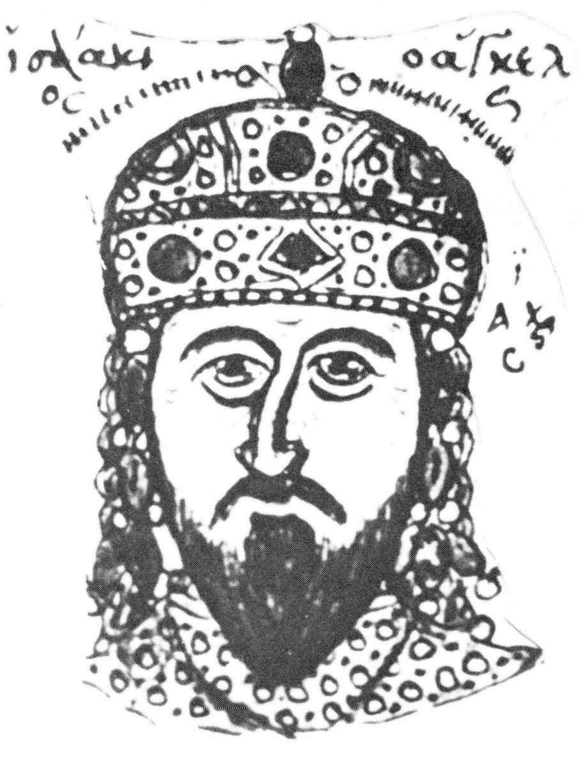

Isaac II Angelos, pen and wash drawing. Cod. Gr. 122. Biblioteca Estense, Modena.

abolish. There was particular complaint when the widowed emperor levied a special tax to pay for his wedding to Princess Margaret-Mary of Hungary.

On the other hand, Isaac was not inefficient as a military man. He coped effectively with the Norman crisis he had inherited from Andronikos and these invaders were driven off. Later in his reign, a revolt of devastating proportions broke out in Bulgaria, long a Byzantine province, now seeking independence under the leadership of a Bulgarian nobleman, Asen. Though Isaac was compelled to recognize Asen as Tsar of the Bulgars, he by no means intended to abandon efforts to bring the rebellious province back into the empire, and the struggle continued off and on for several years.

Then in 1195, just as Isaac was planning to set out on another campaign against the Bulgars, he was seized by his older brother, Alexios, who had long resented Isaac's position. Mercilessly, Alexios Angelos had Isaac blinded to disqualify him for rulership and then sentenced him to imprisonment, together with Isaac's young son and heir, a boy who was named Alexios for his uncle.

During the years that the blinded Isaac remained a prisoner, he could scarcely have dreamed that eventually, for a brief time, he would reign again as honorary co-emperor. This strange turn of fate, however, did come about, a story best told in connection with the reign of Isaac's son Alexios IV.

---

[1]N. Choniates (Bonn), pp. 444–446.
[2]N. Choniates (Bonn), p. 596.
[3]Brand, *Byzantium Confronts the West*, p. 180.
[4]N. Choniates (Bonn), p. 578.

ALEXIOS III ANGELOS
1195-1203

The reign of Alexios III, the emperor who gained the throne by blinding his own brother, did not improve as years went by. Alexios lacked any qualities of leadership ability; he failed completely in his attempts to restore imperial rule in Bulgaria, while his taxes were even more oppressive than his brother Isaac's had been. His court was a nest of corruption; his domineering wife, Euphrosyne Kamatera, openly carried on an affair with another man. Though Alexios once banished her for her infidelities, she was soon recalled to the palace.[1] Apparently he was much swayed by her advice. Alexios and Euphrosyne had no sons and spent considerable effort in arranging advantageous marriages for their daughters, though they little realized that two of their eventual sons-in-law would reign as emperors.

Alexios III faced his first crisis with the West when, early in his reign, the German emperor Heinrich von Hohenstauffen (Henry VI) demanded tribute from the Byzantine emperor. Alexios was so desperate that he ordered the plundering of the tombs of many of the former Byzantine sovereigns in the Church of the Holy Apostles. This loot did not satisfy Heinrich, who continued to threaten invasion of the Byzantine state and who undoubtedly would have made good his threats had he not died suddenly in Italy.

Meanwhile, the deposed Isaac's young son Alexios was growing up, under arrest along with his blinded father. Young Alexios continually dreamed of vengeance on the wicked uncle for whom he was named. On the other hand, the emperor Alexios seemingly considered his nephew a harmless boy. When young Alexios reached his mid-teens, the emperor granted him a certain amount of freedom. He was allowed to ride out on campaign with the imperial forces. It was only a matter of time until the young prince, disguised as a 'Latin' with a short haircut, escaped on a Pisan ship.[2]

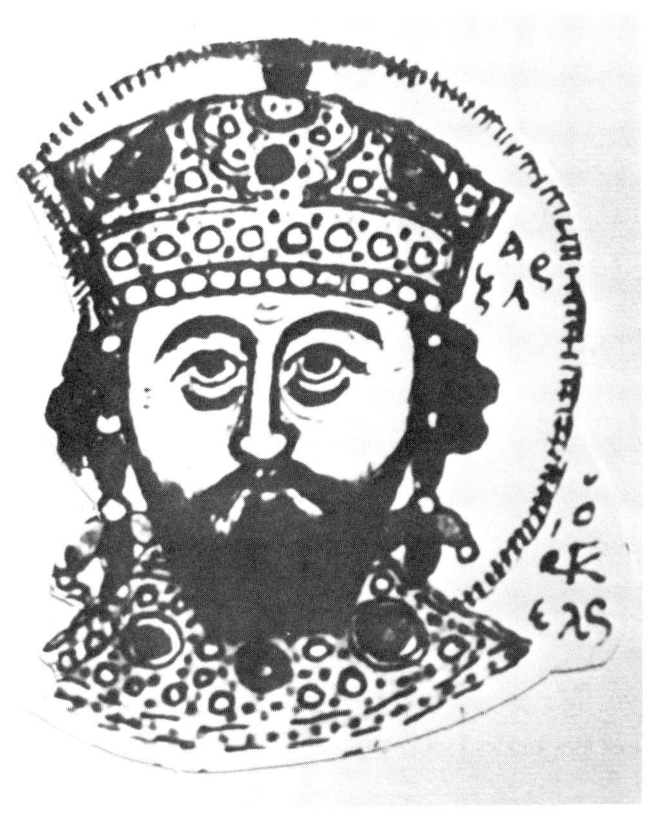

Alexios III Angelos, pen and wash drawing. Cod. Gr. 122. Biblioteca Estense, Modena.

The adventures of the fugitive Byzantine prince in western Europe are best noted in connection with the next reign. In any case, when young Alexios appeared outside Constantinople with an army of Crusaders and a Venetian fleet, the cowardly Alexios III could think of nothing but his own personal safety. Gathering up the crown jewels and as much cash as he could lay his hands upon, he fled from his capital, along with one of his daughters. (The empress Euphrosyne was left behind.)

In subsequent years, after Constantinople had suffered the ravages of the so-called Fourth Crusade, the fugitive Alexios III continually schemed to regain his throne, but without success. His end was probably better than he deserved: taken as a prisoner of war by his son-in-law Theodore Laskaris, he was incarcerated in a monastery where he lived as a monk for the rest of his life.[3]

The portrait of Alexios III in the Modena manuscript is distinctively individual. His short beard is shovel shaped; his hair dark and very curly. Most notably, Alexios' crown is shaped differently from that of any of the other emperors of his time, a strong clue that this sketch was based on an earlier portrait now lost.

---

[1]N. Choniates (Bonn), pp. 644-646.

[2]N. Choniates (Bonn), pp. 710-712.

[3]Alice Gardner, *The Lascarids of Nicaea* (reprint, Chicago, 1967), p. 83.

ALEXIOS IV ANGELOS

1203-1204

As a teenaged boy, young Alexios, son of Isaac Angelos, escaped from his life of captivity in Byzantium and journeyed to the West to seek aid from his sister, Irene Angelina and her husband, the German emperor, Philip of Swabia. In the course of his travels, Alexios fell in with a host of Crusaders and Venetians who realized that the fugitive Byzantine prince was an excellent tool for furthering their own ambitions. Alexios, apparently well intentioned but sadly naive in the game of politics, promised the Crusaders lavish payment if they would help him conquer Constantinople and depose his wicked uncle, Alexios III. The aged Doge of Venice, Enrico Dandolo, enthusiastically sponsored this plan. It was thus that the so-called Fourth Crusade was diverted to Constantinople.

When the Venetian fleet with its host of Crusaders and young Alexios aboard attacked the Byzantine capital early in 1203, the wretched Alexios III's primary concern was to betake himself to safety. He fled the city, and the Byzantine defenders, left without an emperor, made the surprising move of releasing the blind Isaac II and attempting to restore him to the throne.[1]

The Crusaders and Venetians were not prepared for this act, but they countered by sending young Alexios into the city to see Isaac. A joyful reunion of father and son took place; Isaac agreed that his son should be crowned as Alexios IV. They would do their best to pay off their debts to the Crusaders and to Venice, Isaac added, though in view of the fact that Alexios III had absconded with most of the treasury, it would be most difficult.

In the months that followed, Alexios IV worked desperately to collect funds to pay off the allies he no longer needed or wanted. The Crusaders and Venetians made it clear that they were staying in the area until they received their full rewards. Young Alexios frequently visited their camp, attempting to keep their good will by paying as much of the debt as he could. It was rumored

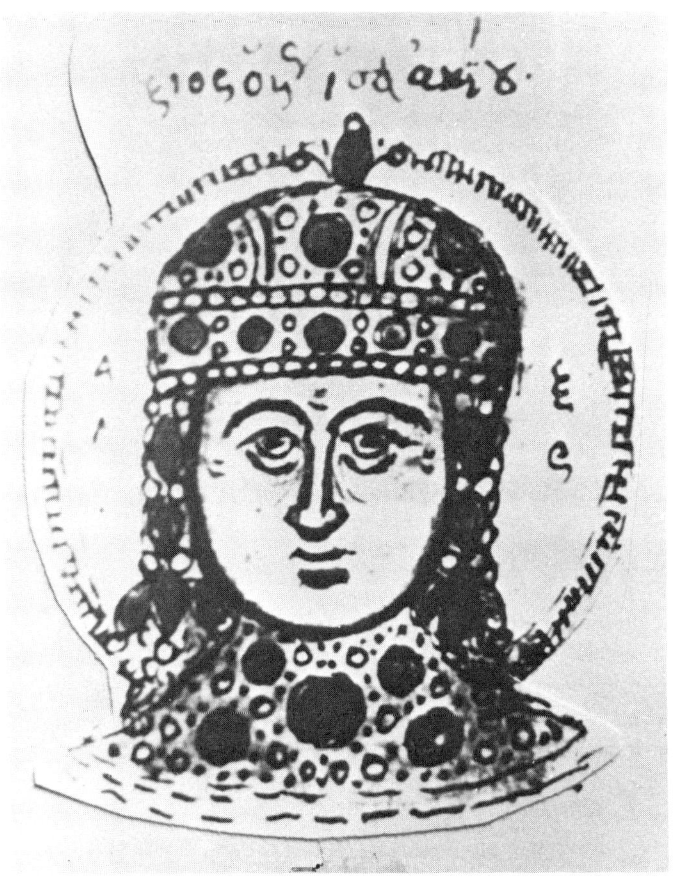

Alexios IV Angelos, pen and wash drawing. Cod. Gr. 122. Biblioteca Estense, Modena.

that when visiting the 'Latins', young Alexios would take off his crown and pass it around among them, allowing any who pleased to try it on. All this, it was felt, was a sure sign of the young man's lack of maturity and respect for his imperial office.

Most of the inhabitants of Constantinople, oppressed by their heavy tax burdens and angered over the host of foreigners surrounding the city, felt that any emperor at all would be preferable to young Alexios. The setting was ripe for a coup, and in January, 1204, the imperial wardrobe master, Alexios Doukas Mourtzouphlos, seized Alexios IV, strangled him to death, and claimed the throne. Old Isaac Angelos perished immediately thereafter, reportedly of shock when he learned of his son's fate, though many believed that he too was murdered.[3] In any event, the new emperor Alexios V had now inherited a crisis of major proportions: how to cope with the Crusaders and Venetians.

The Modena manuscript gives us our only portrait of Alexios IV: his exact age during his brief reign is unknown but his beardlessness suggests he was probably no more than fifteen or sixteen at the time.

---

[1]N. Choniates (Bonn), p. 727.

[2]Brand, *Byzantium Confronts the West*, p. 245.

[3]Brand, *Byzantium Confronts the West*, p. 251 upholds the theory that Isaac died of natural causes.

ALEXIOS V DOUKAS MOURTZOUPHLOS

1204

The confusing abundance of men named Alexios who held the Byzantine throne in succession is mitigated a bit by the fact that Alexios V was commonly called Mourtzouphlos. This nickname was bestowed, Choniates explains, "because his eyebrows grew together and were bushy, overhanging his eyes."[1] Though the throne was his by the fact of his having slain Alexios IV, Mourtzouphlos attempted to strengthen his claim by his marriage to Eudokia Angelina, daughter of Alexios III.

Though Mourtzouphlos' reign is one of the shortest in Byzantine history, it is also one of the most important. With his capital encircled by hostile forces, the emperor faced a crisis of vast proportions. Had he been able to cope with the situation successfully, he would no doubt have gone down in history as a great Byzantine patriot and hero. Sadly for Byzantium, the fortunes of war went the other way. When a plot by the Crusaders to assassinate the new emperor failed, they decided on an all-out assault on the city. Early in April the Crusader and Venetian forces attacked the sea walls of the capital on the side facing the harbor of the Golden Horn. The Byzantine defenders fought bravely and repulsed the first assault, but three days later the enemy forces returned. This time they were successful in scaling the walls and entering the city. Thousands of Byzantines were killed or enslaved; thousands more fled, among these the emperor Mourtzouphlos.[2]

While Crusaders and Venetians parcelled out the vast spoils of war between them and then proceeded to crown a Latin emperor, Baldwin of Flanders, the fugitive Mourtzouphlos wandered through the countryside seeking refuge. Within a short time, his father-in-law, Alexios III, contacted

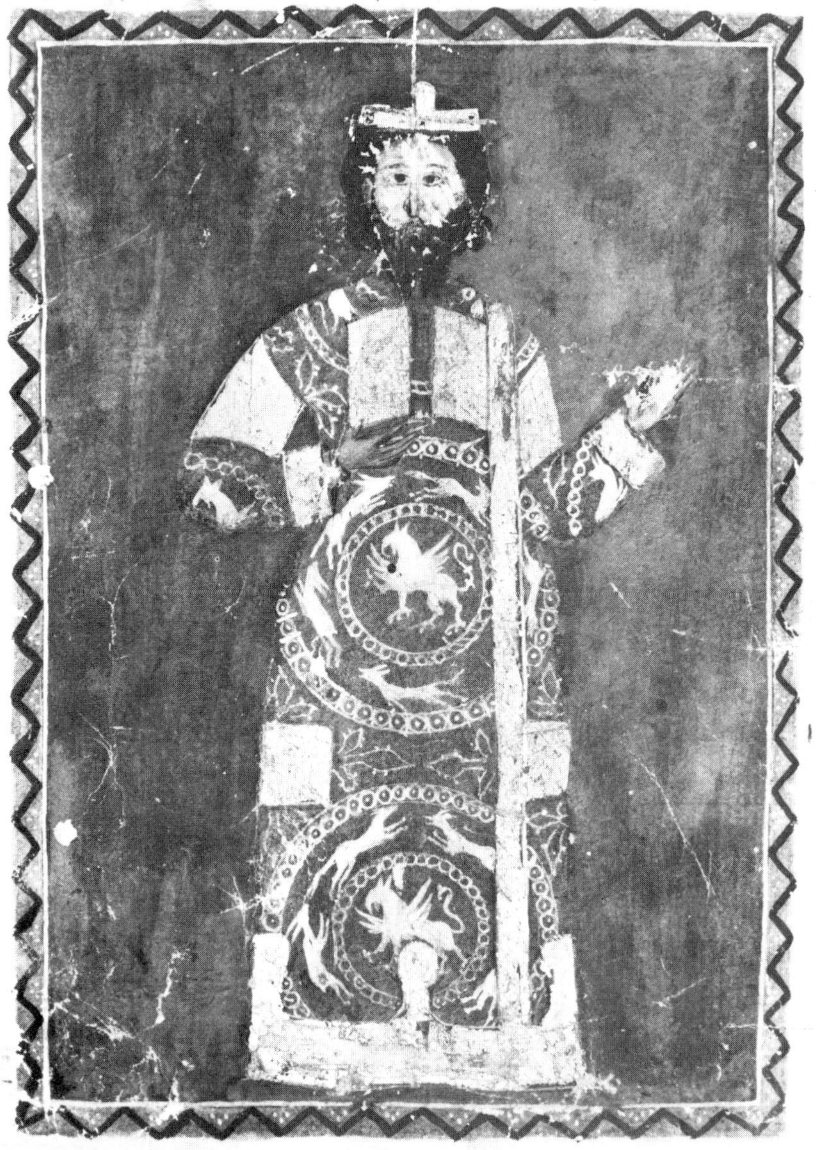

Alexios Doukas Mourtzouphlos, manuscript miniature: Cod. Hist. Gr. 53. Österreichische National-bibliothek, Vienna.

him, suggesting that since they were both ex-emperors, they might make common cause. Mourtzouphlos trusted him, but when he reached Alexios III's hideout, he was seized and blinded by his father-in-law's orders.

Not long afterward, the unfortunate Mourtzouphlos was captured by the Crusaders who conducted him back to Constantinople. There he was executed—pushed to his death from atop the column of Theodosius.[3]

A portrait of Mourtzouphlos, from a manuscript copy of the historian Niketas Choniates, disappointingly gives no hint of his famous bushy eyebrows. Once believed to be a contemporary work, it is now generally believed that the Mourtzouphlos portrait dates from about a century after his reign.[4].

---

[1]N. Choniates (Bonn), p. 742.

[2]N. Choniates (Bonn), pp. 754-755.

[3]*Cambridge Mediaeval History*, IV, i, p. 291.

[4]See Spatharakis, *Portrait*, pp. 152 ff.

THEODORE I LASKARIS
1204-1222

While Baldwin of Flanders sat in the imperial palace of Constantinople enjoying his title of Emperor, a young Byzantine nobleman, Theodore Laskaris, set about to organize a government-in-exile across the Straits in Nicaea, some forty miles from Baldwin's capital. Loyal Byzantines have considered these Nicaean emperors—Theodore and his successors—as representing the true line of the imperial succession, for all that Baldwin and other Latins after him held the old imperial capital.

Theodore Laskaris scarcely looked the part of a great leader. "In body he was very small, moderately dark, with a long beard which was divided at the ends," reports the slightly later historian George Akropolites.[1] "His eyes differed one from the other," Akropolites adds, probably indicating that one of them did not focus properly. Looks notwithstanding, Theodore was a brave soldier; he had played an important part in trying to defend Constantinople from the Crusaders. As the husband of Anna Angelina, Alexios III's daughter, his claim to the throne was better than that of anyone else available after the fall of Constantinople, though exactly what sort of empire he had inherited was by no means clear. The cautious Theodore actually contented himself for several years with the lesser title of Despot, until his position in and around

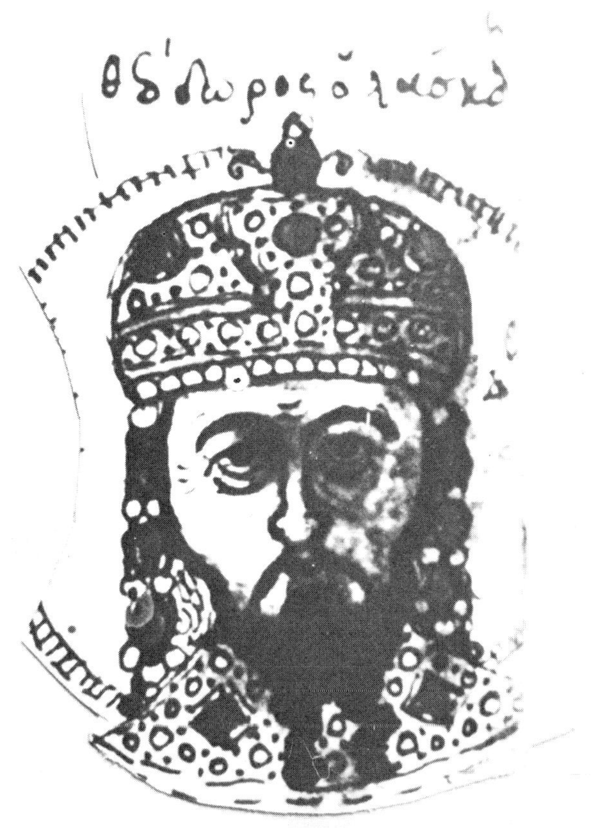

Theodore I Laskaris, pen and wash drawing. Cod. Gr. 122. Biblioteca Estense, Modena.

Nicaea was better consolidated. When it became apparent that the Crusaders had their hands full fighting the Bulgars, the Byzantines of Asia Minor under Theodore Laskaris realized they would have a much-needed breathing space in which they could establish a firm base for the empire-in-exile. Theodore at last agreed to take the title of Emperor, and was duly crowned by the Patriarch in 1208.[2]

In addition to constant watchfulness lest the Crusaders attempt something against Nicaea, Theodore Laskaris also had a full slate of problems with the Seljuk Turks. His father-in-law, Alexios III, found refuge with them and thereby provided the Seljuks with an excellent tool for aggression against the Nicaean empire. In a great pitched battle, Theodore and the sultan came into direct, hand-to-hand conflict. The Turk unhorsed the little Byzantine emperor, who then slashed madly at the legs of the sultan's horse. Much to Theodore's surprise the sultan fell. Loyal guards who surrounded the emperor promptly helped him to slay his great enemy, and it was thus that Theodore Laskaris, in spite of his small size and his bad eye, performed a mighty deed of war that was remembered as long as he lived and that vastly enhanced his prestige as a military leader. Significantly, after his slaying of the sultan, Theodore never again took such a great personal risk in battle.[3] It was after this encounter, incidentally, that Alexios III was taken prisoner by Theodore and placed in a monastery.

The Nicaean empire flourished under Theodore's rule. After the death of his first empress, Anna, and a brief second marriage to Philippa of Armenia that ended in divorce, Theodore sought to end hostilities with the Latin empire of Constantinople. The ruler there by this time was a woman, the empress Yolande de Courtenay, Baldwin's sister, and she agreed to send her young daughter Marie to be Theodore's bride. Had they had sons, the breach between the rival imperial lines might have been healed, but, as it turned out, Marie and Theodore had no children. At his death, the throne went to his daughter by Anna, Irene Laskaris, and her husband John Doukas Vatatzes.

The portrait of Theodore in the Modena manuscript is unfortunately marred by water stains. It is nevertheless interesting for its faithful depiction of the emperor's thin, pinched face and curly, black forked beard. True to the ideal that the emperor's image must be perfect even if the emperor was not, the artist has conscientiously avoided depicting any flaw in Theodore's eye.

---

[1]George Akropolites (Bonn), p. 34.

[2]Ostrogorsky, *History of the Byzantine State*, p. 428.

[3]Gardner, *The Lascarids of Nicaea*, pp. 82-83.

JOHN III DOUKAS VATATZES

1222-1254

The greatest of the Nicaean emperors was John Doukas Vatatzes, during whose long reign the empire-in-exile recovered much of its previous strength and prestige, even though Constantinople still remained in the hands of the Courtenays. Vatatzes claimed to be a remote relative of the Doukas dynasty and placed great emphasis on his middle name;[1] actually he gained the throne by marriage to the emperor Theodore's daughter, Irene Laskaris, a young widow. The marriage was reputedly a very happy one. Although Irene was

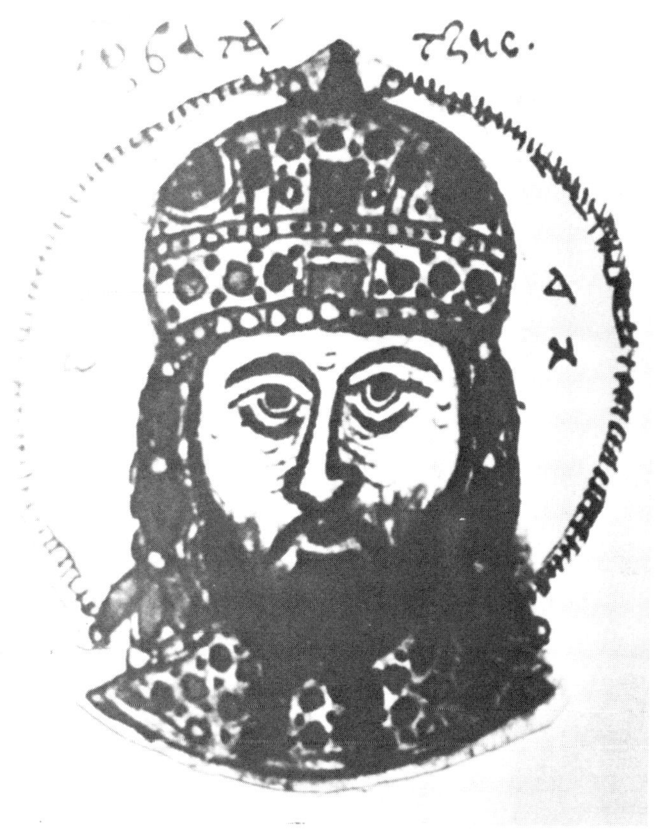

John Doukas Vatatzes, pen and wash drawing. Cod. Gr. 122. Biblioteca Estense, Modena.

injured in a horseback riding accident not long after the birth of their only child, Theodore II, and remained an invalid for the rest of her life, she was interested in scholarly activity and writing. Thanks to her, the Byzantine court became a center of learning and culture.

Diplomat, warrior, and humanitarian, John Doukas Vatatzes won the admiration and love of his subjects to a far greater extent than most of his predecessors. He was particularly concerned with establishing charitable institutions: schools, hospitals, and even libraries received imperial support. His determination that the empire maintain itself so far as possible without imports (especially those from Venice) led him to undertake a vast program to encourage home industry. Practicing what he preached, he saw to it that his imperial estates were carefully managed to increase productivity. From his profits on the sale of eggs, he once had a special 'Egg Crown' made for Irene, its egg-shaped jewels a symbol of his economic program.[2]

Although he was an epileptic, Vatatzes usually felt well enough to lead his forces in person. Allied with the Bulgars through most of his reign, his long-range goal was the reconquest of Constantinople and permanent ouster of the Courtenays. Though they won many smaller victories, Vatatzes and his ally, Tsar Ivan Asen of Bulgaria, had to lift their one attempted siege of the capital city; the old walls were simply too thick to be penetrated.

Some years after Irene's death, John Doukas Vatatzes sought an alliance with the brilliant and controversial Holy Roman Emperor and King of Sicily, Frederick II. As part of their contract, John, who was in his fifties, married Frederick's twelve-year-old daughter, Constance-Anna Hohenstauffen.

As John grew older, his attacks of epilepsy grew more frequent. One day when he was walking in his imperial garden he suffered a severe seizure. His attendants carried him to a nearby tent where he died.

Although he was never officially canonized, Vatatzes was remembered for centuries as St. John the Merciful, and as long as there were Orthodox Greeks in the area that had once been the Nicaean state, his feast day was celebrated on November 4.[3]

If the Modena manuscript is a reliable guide, John Doukas Vatatzes wore a curly forked beard in imitation of his father-in-law and predecessor. Comparison of the two portraits reveals that behind the superficial similarity, Laskaris and Vatatzes are distinctively different types: Vatatzes has a fuller face and heavier beard, and a generally more robust appearance.

---

[1]Polemis, *The Doukai*, pp. 106-107.

[2]Ostrogorsky, *History of the Byzantine State*, p. 443.

[3]Gardner, *The Lascarids of Nicaea*, pp. 195-196.

THEODORE II LASKARIS
1254-1258

Moody, suspicious, ill-tempered, and nervous, Theodore II Laskaris inherited his father's epilepsy but very little of his father's charismatic charm. It is unclear why Theodore chose his mother's surname, Laskaris, rather than his father's; perhaps he thought Vatatzes (which derived from a word meaning bramble bush) lacked imperial dignity. John Vatatzes and Theodore apparently did not get along too well. As long as he lived, Vatatzes deprived his son of the usual honors accorded a co-emperor, alleging that too much flattery would spoil the young man.[1]

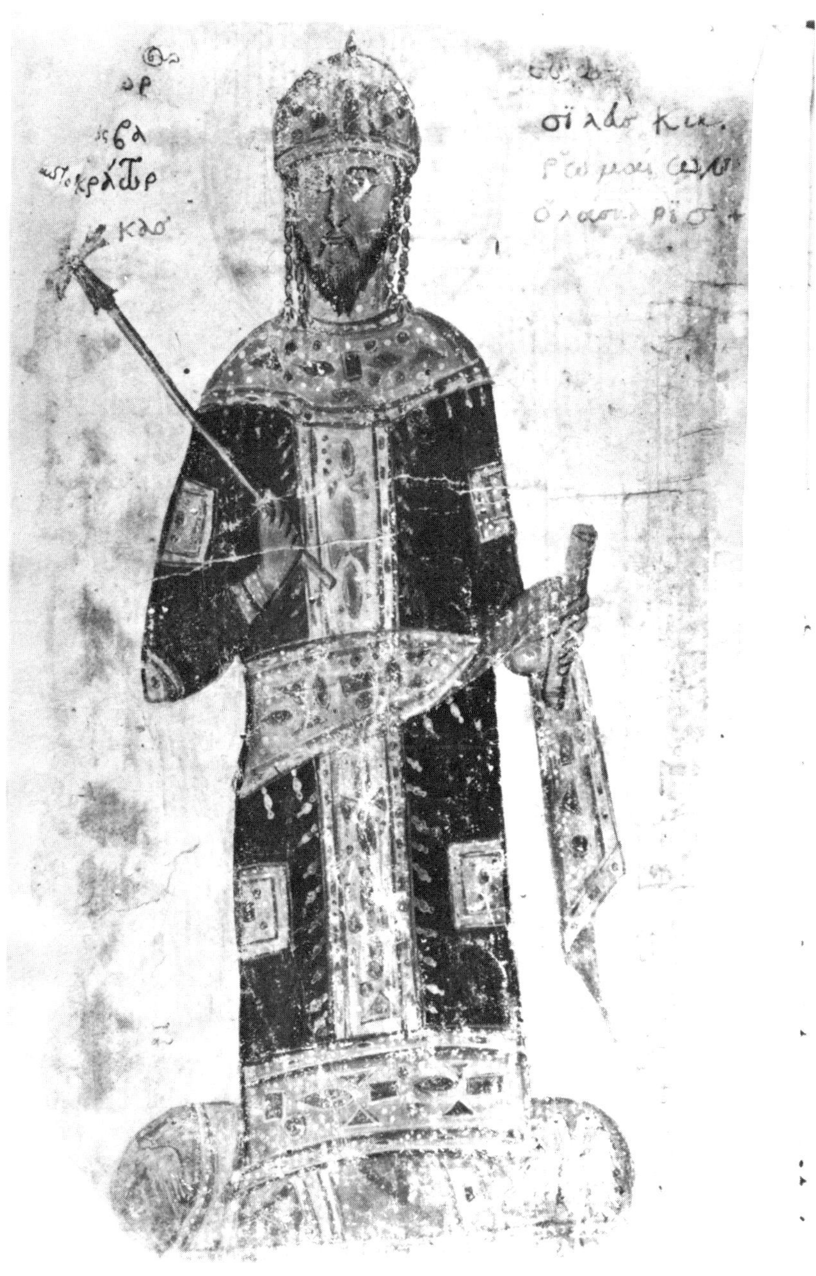

Theodore II Laskaris, manuscript miniature: Cod. Monacensis Ms. Gr. 442. Staatsbibliothek, Munich.

Like his mother, Theodore was scholarly. He received an excellent education and considered himself a great writer, though present-day scholars consider his literary style atrocious—too full of rhetoric to possess much clarity of meaning. It is no surprise that his works remain largely untranslated from the original Greek.

Theodore's ill health caused him to believe that enemies were working magic against him, and those who aroused his suspicions sometimes suffered devastating consequences.[2] In spite of his many ills, he was a military leader of considerable ability. As if determined to defy the limitations of his frail body, he seemed to take a perverse delight in rigorous campaigning and forced marches through the bitterest winter weather.

Theodore's wife was the princess Helen Asen of Bulgaria, who had been brought to the Nicaean court as a little girl and grown up there as Theodore's intended bride. They had several daughters and one son, John Laskaris, before Helen's early death. Theodore did not remarry.

As his health grew progressively worse and he realized he would not live much longer, Theodore designated his best friend, George Muzalon, to serve as regent for his son, John IV. The leading nobles were required to swear to respect this arrangement. Most of them disliked George, since he was not of noble birth himself, and, in the difficult days soon to come, their oaths would prove meaningless.

A full-length portrait of Theodore is found in a fourteenth-century manuscript of the historian Pachymeres, now in Munich.

---

[1]Gardner, *The Lascarids of Nicaea*, p. 197.

[2]Deno J. Geanakoplos, *Emperor Michael Palaeologus and the West* (Cambridge, Mass., 1959),p. 31.

John IV Laskaris, pen and wash drawing. Cod. Gr. 122. Biblioteca Estense, Modena.

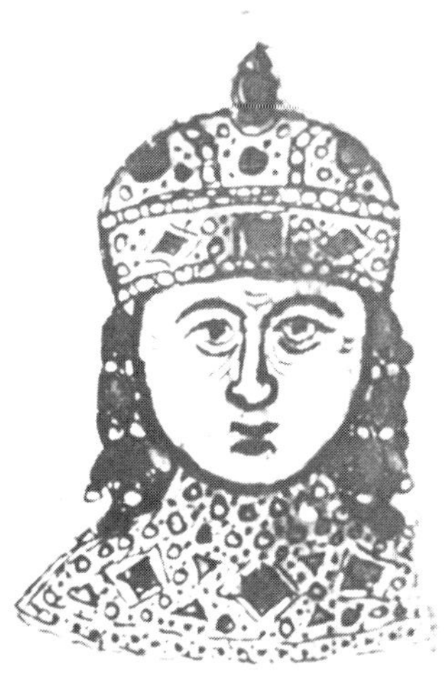

JOHN IV LASKARIS
1258-1261

John was about seven when his father Theodore II died; his mother, Helen Asen, was already dead, and the orphaned emperor was certain to be the victim of a power struggle among the ambitious men of the court. George Muzalon assumed his role as regent, but he had so many enemies that his position was far from secure.

Nine days after Theodore's death, Muzalon was assassinated in church while attending a memorial service for the late emperor. The instigator of this atrocity was in all likelihood the ambitious young aristocrat, Michael Palaiologos. In the weeks that followed, Michael, who claimed to be little John's protector and friend, began planning for his own coronation as co-emperor. The patriarch Arsenios was powerless to defend John's sole right to the throne and reluctantly performed the ceremony.

For three years, official statements were issued in the names of Michael and John. Outwardly the arrangement seemed to be working well, but Michael and his wife Theodora Doukaina had a little son of their own, and the scheming father was no doubt dreaming of the day when the Palaiologoi would replace the Laskarids for good.

In the summer of 1261, Michael's forces almost by accident seized Constantinople. The Latin emperor, Baldwin II de Courtenay, fled for his life and, not long thereafter, Michael the conquering hero entered the restored capital in triumph. In all these victory ceremonies, John Laskaris was conspicuously among the missing. A few months later, it was learned that the ruthless Michael had ordered John's eyes put out. The boy was then incarcerated in a wretched fortress in Asia Minor. He was about ten years old.[1]

The subsequent fate of this most unfortunate emperor has been the subject of some uncertainty. The best attested reports come from Pachymeres and Gregoras, who tell how Michael VIII's son, Andronikos II, paid a visit to the blind prisoner John Laskaris many years later.[2] A variant rumor has it that the damage to John's eyesight was not permanent, and that he eventually escaped and went to Sicily.[3] While one might hope the latter report is true, the former is much more likely. It is also reported that John devoted himself to a life of prayer and meditation. For this he is honored as a saint in the Russian Orthodox Church.[4]

---

[1]Nikephoros Gregoras, *Bizantina historia* (Bonn), I.93.

[2]For additional details, see Geanakoplos, *Michael VIII*, pp. 217-218.

[3]Ibid.

[4]Polemis, *The Doukai*, p. 111.

MICHAEL VIII PALAIOLOGOS

1259-1282

Michael Doukas Angelos Komnenos Palaiologos, the crafty and often cruel nobleman who seized the throne of young John Laskaris, was destined to become the founder of the last and longest-lived imperial dynasty in Byzantine history. Although the almost accidental reconquest of Constantinople in 1261 was the work of one of his generals and not of Michael personally, the accomplishment of this long-range goal augured well for the start of Michael's reign. His ruthless treatment of John Laskaris, however, following soon thereafter, cost Michael a great deal of his early popularity. The patriarch Arsenios excommunicated him. Michael in turn deposed Arsenios, but it was not until many months later that the emperor found an obliging churchman who agreed to accept the patriarchate and to lift his excommunication.

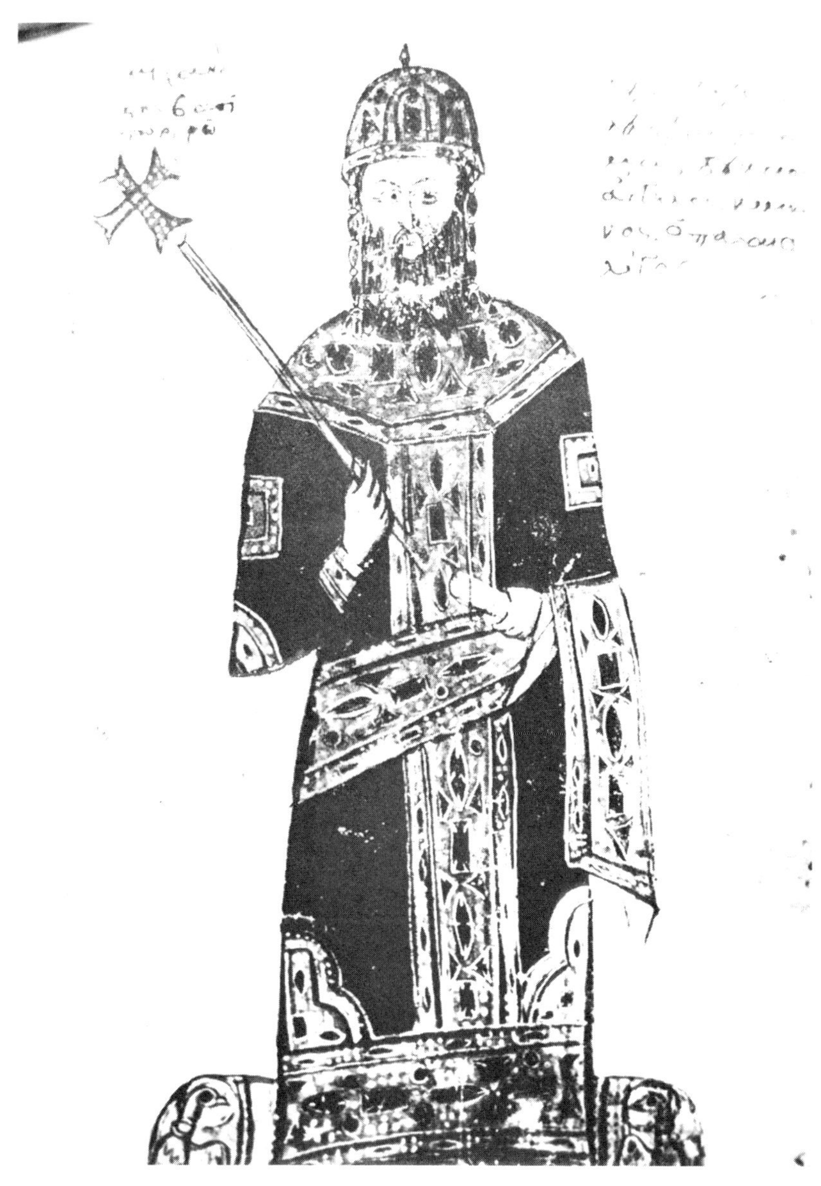

Michael VIII Palaiologos, manuscript miniature: Cod. Monacensis Ms. Gr. 442. Staatsbibliothek, Munich.

If Michael was unpopular, he was nonetheless an exceptionally able ruler, especially in the realm of foreign relations.[1] Through a series of political marriages for his children, he built up a strong network of alliances to help protect Byzantium from its current deadly enemy, Charles of Anjou, King of Sicily. Michael also realized that a most effective way to stall off Charles' frequently threatened Crusade against the empire was to express interest in a reunion of the Orthodox and Roman Catholic churches. While such a possibility for reunion existed, Michael felt confident that the Papacy would refuse to bless Charles' crusading invasion.

Negotations dragged on for several years before Michael actually sent envoys to the Pope's Council of Lyons in France, where they signed an official statement of reunion. Michael would soon realize that consenting to such an arrangement was one thing, while enforcing it was another. The vast majority of Orthodox Byzantines wanted nothing to do with western Catholicism; the atrocities of successive waves of Latin Crusaders were too deeply imprinted in popular memory. Though Michael tried to institute the union by force, and even resorted to fierce cruelties to compel its acceptance, he made little real progress. When a new pope, Martin IV, who was a close friend of Charles of Anjou, succeeded to the papal throne, Michael found himself excommunicated from the Catholic Church for failure to "implement the Union." Charles of Anjou's crusade received papal blessing and it seemed only a matter of time before the great invasion.

Faced by this crisis, Michael secretly intrigued with the Kingdom of Aragon, and a plot was hatched to launch a revolution in Sicily—an uprising that would prohibit Charles' leaving his kingdom. This intrigue worked perfectly, and Michael felt that he had indeed saved his empire.

Few Byzantines appreciated Michael's efforts. When the much-despised emperor died in 1282, his son Andronikos, fearing demonstrations of violence, had him buried secretly, with none of the amenities that usually surrounded an Orthodox emperor's funeral. Unloved and unmourned, the first of the Palaiologoi had passed from the scene.

From the fourteenth century Munich manuscript of Pachymeres comes a noted portrait of the shifty-eyed emperor Michael, robed in imperial splendor, a likeness which, while not drawn from life, seems to present a vivid glimpse of the founder of the house of Palaiologos.[3]

---

[1]The definitive work on this subject is Geanakoplos, *Emperor Michael Palaeologus and the West*. On the Palaiologoi in general see also Constance Head, *Imperial Twilight* (Chicago, 1977).

[2]For details see Sir Steven Runciman, *The Sicilian Vespers* (Cambridge, England, 1958).

[3]For additional portraits of Michael VIII see Spatharakis, *Portrait*, plates 19 and 59.

ANDRONIKOS II PALAIOLOGOS
1282-1328

The long reign of Andronikos II marks a period of steady decline for the Byzantine Empire. The emperor was a far more humane man than his father, Michael. Devoutly Orthodox, scholarly, and conscientious, he seemed likely to be a capable ruler; but, as it turned out, he was unable to cope successfully with the disasters of his time. Before his reign ended, the Ottoman Turks had succeeded in conquering practically all of Byzantine Asia Minor.

Byzantium's failure to halt the spread of Ottoman power was largely caused by the unwise military policies of the emperor and his advisors. In the early years of his reign, Andronikos ordered a sharp reduction of Byzantine troops and (in order to save money) disbanded the navy completely. Later on, when the folly of such unpreparedness became amply clear, the Byzantines tried to rebuild their former military strength, but it was too late to undo the consequences of the Ottoman conquest.

Andronikos II made another very serious mistake when he contracted for the services of the Catalan Grand Company, Spanish mercenaries headed by a German adventurer, Roger de Flor.[1] The Catalans refused to conform to what was expected of them. Though they occasionally fought the Turks, they seemed more often to be the enemies of the Byzantines, plundering imperial lands and terrorizing the inhabitants. It was several years before Andronikos was able to rid himself of these undesirable "allies," and then only because the Catalans decided to direct their military efforts elsewhere.

Unfortunate in his statesmanship, Andronikos seemed equally unlucky in his private life. His first wife, Anna of Hungary, died very young. Andronikos then married Yolande-Irene of Montferrat, a fiery Italian princess. Though in the early years of their marriage they seemed happy enough, Yolande was deeply resentful of the fact that Anna's son, Michael IX, was Andronikos' heir and eventual co-emperor, while her own three sons were merely private citizens. When Andronikos continually refused Yolande's pleas to divide the imperial territories and give each of her children a share, the empress gradually turned against her husband. Finally they separated permanently, and Yolande moved to Thessaloniki.

In 1320, a tragedy of far-reaching consequences faced Andronikos—the sudden death of his son, the co-emperor Michael IX. The fact that Michael's son, the future Andronikos III, was indirectly to blame for this sad happening caused grandfather and grandson to turn against each other, and eventually civil war broke out between them.[2]

The ultimate victory of young Andronikos III meant that Andronikos II was forced to abdicate after a forty-six year reign. Some months later, he became a monk under the name of Brother Anthony. He died in 1332.

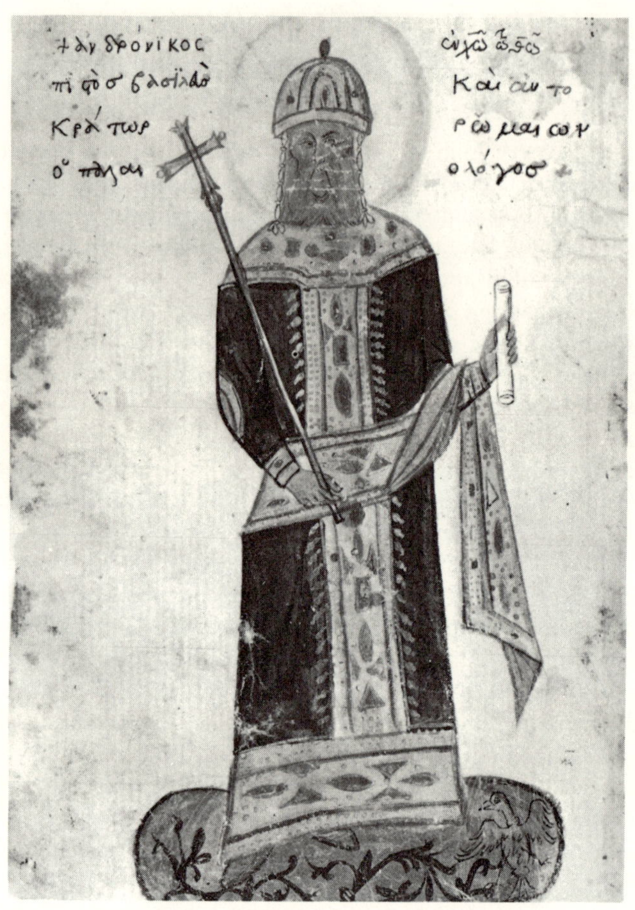

Andronikos II Palaiologos, manuscript miniature: Cod. Monacensis Ms. Gr. 442. Staatsbibliothek, Munich.

The manuscript illustration on this page is one of several existing portraits of Andronikos II, all of which emphasize his long beard, cut straight across in a peculiar square-shaped fashion. Nikephoros Gregoras, who was a close associate of Andronikos, adds these details: "He was tall of stature, handsome of face, and above all, venerable, as if possessing rulership and formidability by nature."[3]

---

[1]For details see Alfonso Lowe, *The Catalan Vengeance* (London, 1972).

[2]A detailed study of the civil war of the Andronikoi may be found in Angeliki E. Laiou, *Constantinople and the Latins: The Foreign Policy of Andronicus II* (Cambridge, Mass., 1972), pp. 284 ff.

[3]Nikephoros Gregoras, *Bizantina historia*, X,1 (Bonn), I, 472-473.

ANDRONIKOS III PALAIOLOGOS
1328-1341

Andronikos' troubles began when, as a young man, he was accidentally responsible for the death of his brother. When this bad news was carried to their father, the co-emperor Michael IX, he was so shocked that he died of heart failure. This led Andronikos II, the grandfather, to turn bitterly against young Andronikos and to seek means to eliminate his claim to the throne.[1]

Young Andronikos was a likeable person, carefree and easy-going, but surrounded by powerful friends who urged him to fight for his rights. His best friend, John Kantakouzenos, was particularly insistent that the old emperor must not be allowed to deprive the rightful heir of the succession. War broke out; young Andronikos attracted widespread support and proved to be a capable military leader, though there is little doubt that the mastermind behind the uprising was that of Kantakouzenos.

The war of the two Andronikoi continued off and on for several years. Though old Andronikos II agreed to recognize his grandson as co-emperor, the two continued on bad terms. Finally old Andronikos was forced to abdicate. Andronikos III offered to let him remain in the palace, but the ex-emperor was so unhappy there that he moved to a private residence. He became a monk, but did not enter a cloister.

Meanwhile Andronikos III reigned, with John Kantakouzenos the undoubted power behind the throne. Andronikos even granted his dear friend the right to sign his name in red ink (a privilege usually reserved for the emperor alone). Kantakouzenos was also often seen wearing garments from the emperor's wardrobe and generally behaving imperially. Andronikos longed to make him co-emperor and would have done so had not Kantakouzenos refused to accept this honor.

Though there were some who resented Kantakouzenos' influence, Andronikos was a generally popular emperor. He was never one to insist on elaborate ceremony; he loved riding and hunting and the festivities of tournaments, in which he took part personally.[2] Many western adventurers clustered around his court, and both of his wives were western princesses. The first of these, Adelheid of Brunswick, died during the civil war, but the second, the intriguing Anne of Savoy, lived to enjoy the position of empress throughout her husband's reign and then to cause trouble for many years to come.

Though Andronikos III surely realized that he ruled over a declining state, his reign was not without military successes, and he also instituted certain widely praised judicial reforms.

In 1341, the still-young emperor became ill at a church council meeting and died four days later. He left a nine-year-old son, John V (named for John Kantakouzenos), and no clear plans for a regency. Obviously, the boy's

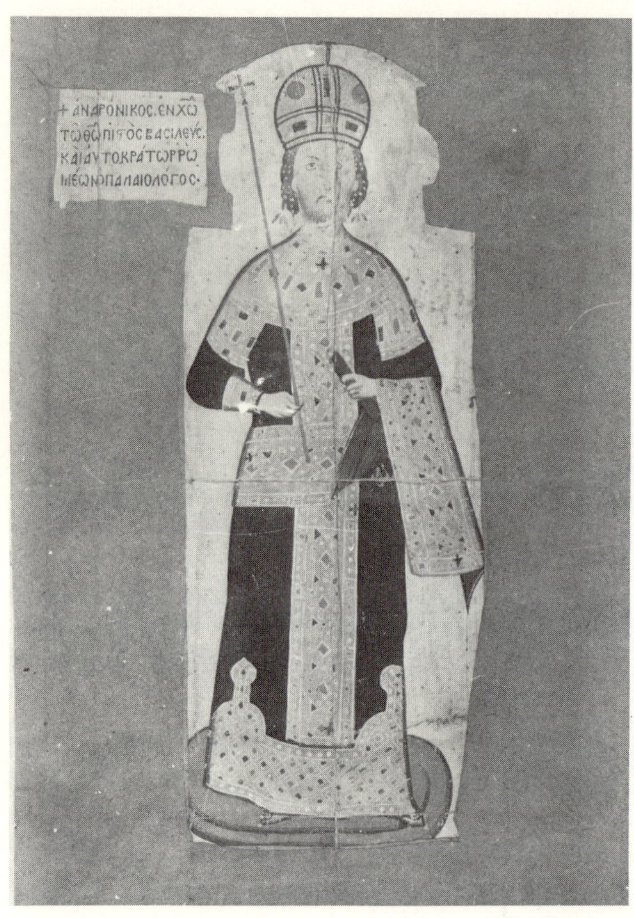

Andronikos III Palaiologos, manuscript miniature: Cod. Hist. F. 601, Landesbibliothek, Stuttgart.

mother, Anne of Savoy, would attempt to govern on his behalf. In the years that followed, it became amply clear that Andronikos' early death was a major tragedy for Byzantium.

A fourteenth-century manuscript now in Stuttgart is the source for a portrait of Andronikos III.

---

[1]An important monograph presenting a detailed study of Andronikos III is Ursula V. Bosch, *Andronikos III Palaiologos, Versuch einer Darstellung der byzantinischen Geschichte in den Jahren 1321-1341* (Amsterdam, 1965).

[2]John VI Kantakouzenos, *Historiarum libri VI (Bonn), I.205.*

JOHN VI KANTAKOUZENOS
1347-1354

Technically, Andronikos III's little son John V belongs on the emperor-list before John VI Kantakouzenos. Yet it was Kantakouzenos who dominated the Byzantine scene all through John V's growing-up years and who eventually reigned with him as senior co-emperor.

Kantakouzenos, who was a distant cousin of the Palaiologoi, is a complex personality, a strange mixture of ambition and patriotism. Much of the source material about him comes from his own writings, and he naturally tried to present himself to his readers in the best possible light. He was undoubtedly a brilliant man, and it is not hard to see how he was repelled by the stupidity and lack of statesmanship of Anne of Savoy. Anne, who could have used his help, instead was determined to despise him. In the months following Andronikos' death, Kantakouzenos was subjected to numerous humiliations by Anne's henchmen. His city house was plundered and his old mother thrown into prison.[2] Kantakouzenos and his wife, Irene Asen, took refuge in the town of Didymoteichos, and, from that stronghold, late in 1341, Kantakouzenos proclaimed himself a candidate for the imperial throne.

For six years a devastating civil war was carried on between Anne and Kantakouzenos. Both sides employed foreign mercenaries, especially Turks and Serbs who robbed and slew sundry Byzantines with little regard for which side they supported. To win more Turkish aid, Kantakouzenos even sent one of his daughters to join the sultan's harem. Anne, equally desperate for resources, pawned the crown jewels and plate to the republic of Venice.

In 1347, Kantakouzenos' forces gained entry into Constantinople. The victorious claimant proved exceptionally generous toward Anne; his quarrel had never been with her or her son John V, he alleged, but with their unscrupulous advisors. Kantakouzenos was crowned as senior co-emperor, though his imperial diadem was made of gilded leather and bits of colored glass, and the dishes at his coronation banquet were earthenware and pewter.[3] To cement their imperial partnership, fourteen-year-old John V married Helena Kantakouzene, also fourteen, the new emperor's daughter.

As emperor, John Kantakouzenos made sincere efforts to rebuild Byzantine military and naval strength, and to cope with the worsening economic situation. The onset of the Black Death (bubonic plague) which killed well over half of the inhabitants of Constantinople, added vastly to the difficulties Kantakouzenos faced.

Nor was John V satisfied to remain a junior partner in the emperorship as he grew into his late teens. The civil war was renewed, and finally, in 1354, John V's forces took Constantinople by a clever ruse.

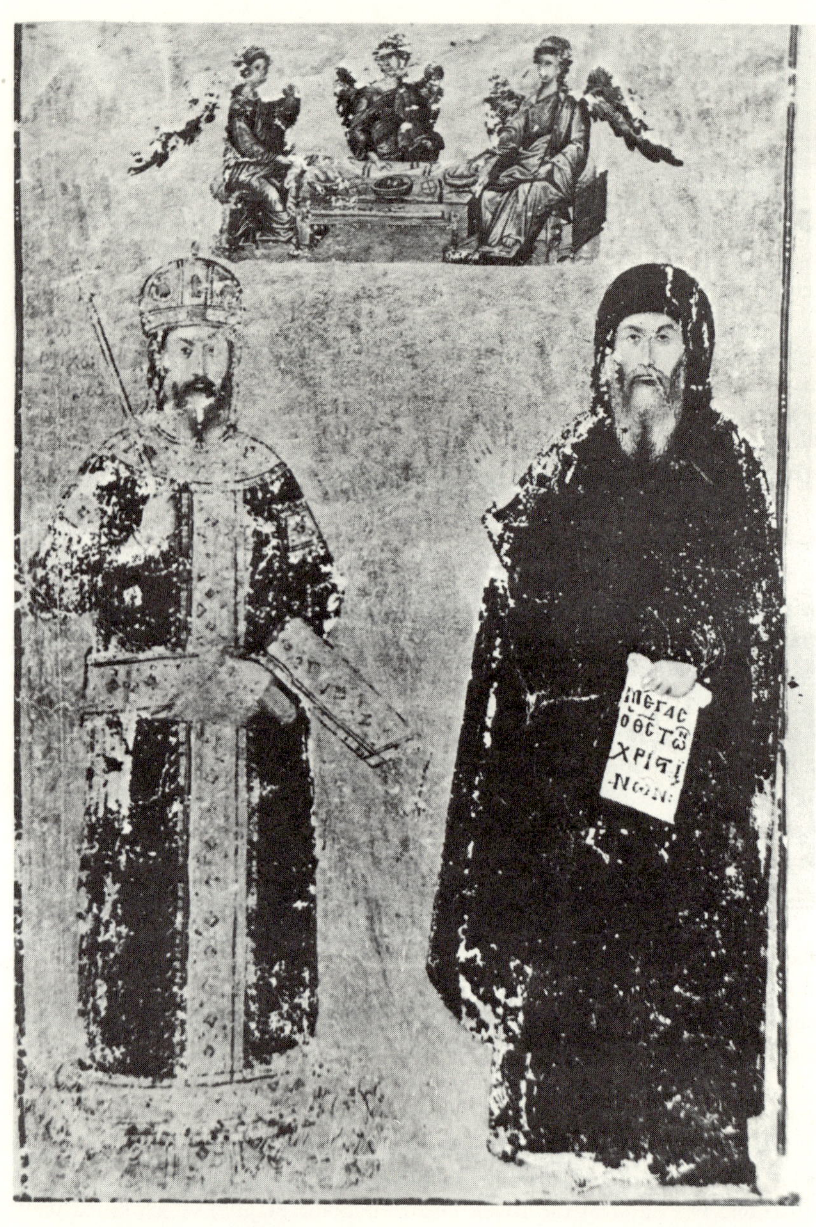

John VI Kantakouzenos, as Emperor and as Brother Joasaph, manuscript miniature: Cod. Gr. 1242. Bibliothèque Nationale, Paris.

John Kantakouzenos agreed to abdicate. He became a monk, Brother Joasaph, while his wife Irene entered a convent as Sister Eugenia. In his monastic retreat, the fallen emperor devoted himself to study and writing. It is pleasant to record that he was eventually reconciled to his son-in-law John V, and though he remained a monk for the rest of his long life, he again played a vital role in the governing of the empire and served as one of John V's closest advisors for long periods of time. Only when he was well up into the eighties did he leave the capital for Mistra where one of his sons was provincial governor, and there he died in 1383, at the age of eighty-eight.

A famous dual portrait of Kantakouzenos depicts him both as Emperor John VI and as Brother Joasaph. It is an illustration in a manuscript copy of his historical writings.

---

[1]For in-depth background on John VI see Valentin Parisot, *Cantacuzène, homme d'état et historien* (Paris, 1845); Donald M. Nicol, *The Byzantine Family of Kantakouzenos* (Washington, 1968).

[2]Nicol, *The Byzantine Family of Kantakouzenos*, p. 47.

[3]N. Gregoras, *Byzantina historia* (Bonn), II, 788.

JOHN V PALAIOLOGOS
1341-1391

The son of Andronikos III and Anne of Savoy, John V had his mother's blond handsomeness as well as her craving for power and inability to use it wisely. Born in June, 1332, he was just a few days short of nine years old when he inherited the throne.[1] His adolescence was spent in the midst of the struggle with Kantakouzenos. At fourteen, young John married Helena Kantakouzene; the young people were apparently happy with each other, for Helena firmly rejected her father's attempts to dissolve the marriage a few years later, declaring, "Rather than live with my parents, I would die with John." Clearly the matrimonial alliance did not, as Kantakouzenos originally hoped, put an end to their rivalries for the throne.

John was in his early twenties when he finally pressured his father-in-law into becoming a monk. As sole emperor after so many years of war and uncertainty, John was a conspicuous failure. Though apparently well-intentioned, he was distinctly lacking in statesmanlike qualities. The recent civil wars had weakened the Byzantine state beyond repair. Ottoman Turks controlled most of the territory surrounding the shrinking empire. If the state were to survive at all, John knew he must have help from western Europe.

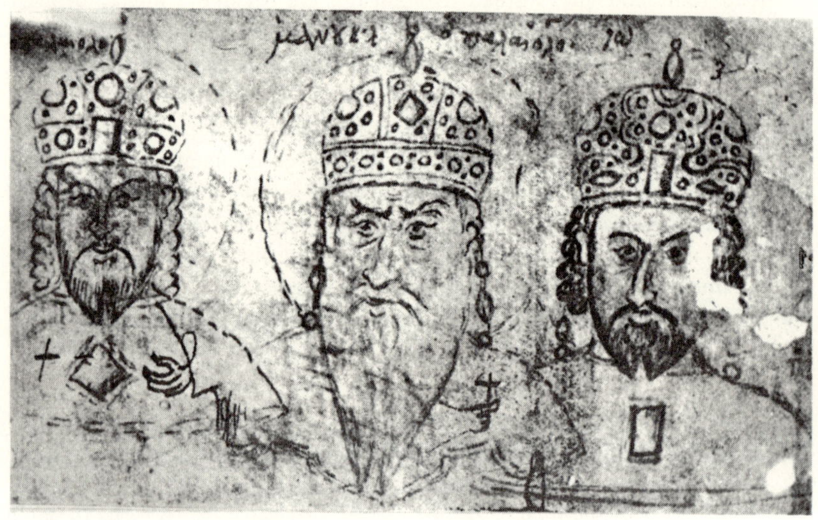

Pen drawing of John V Palaiologos (left), with son Manuel II (center) and grandson John VIII (right), Cod. Gr. 1783. Bibliothèque Nationale, Paris.

On a journey to the court of Hungary in search of such aid, John was told that he could expect nothing from the West unless he would work for the union of the churches.[2] From then on, he began to give deep consideration to the idea of his own personal conversion to Roman Catholicism; after all, his mother Anne had been at Catholic. Byzantium's need for outside help, moreover, in his opinion, justified the change. For several years he contemplated the decision before taking any definite action, for his devoutly Orthodox father-in-law Kantakouzenos urged strongly against it.[3]

Finally in 1370, John V went to Rome and, in a lavish ceremony, officially joined the Catholic Church. From Rome he went on to Venice, hoping to solicit aid from his old allies, the Venetians. Unfortunately, he had not even enough ready money to finance the homeward journey to Constantinople for himself and his entourage, and for months he was detained in Venice, until his teen-aged son, Manuel, arrived to help him smooth out his difficulties.[4]

Nor did John's conversion to Catholicism have the hoped-for results. Most of his Orthodox subjects detested him for it, while the help he thought to gain from western Europe simply did not materialize. John was so hard pressed that he had to agree to become a vassal of the Ottoman sultan.

Then in 1376, John's eldest son, Andronikos, after an earlier abortive attempt, launched a coup against him. For the three years that Andronikos IV reigned, John V languished in Constantinople's Tower of Anemas along with his younger sons, Manuel and Theodore.

With Venetian aid, John regained his throne in 1379. Andronikos was demoted but forgiven, only to continue his plotting, a habit inherited by his son, the future John VII. In 1390, this young prince with the support of the Genoese and the Turks, entered Constantinople, deposed his grandfather, and proclaimed himself emperor. His reign was very short; with Manuel's help, John V was restored to the throne he had three times lost and three times regained. Manuel volunteered himself to serve as a hostage of the Turks as a pledge of his father's loyalty.

In the last year of his life, John V, with a new burst of energy, suddenly determined to repair the crumbling fortifications of his capital city. The work was ordered to begin and was underway when word came from the sultan: either destroy what you have built up or Manuel's eyes will be put out. John commanded the demolition of his new fortifications and died, a prematurely aged and broken man.[5]

Except for its three interruptions, John V would have had the longest reign in Byzantine history. Certainly it was one of the most futile.

A sketch from a Greek manuscript now in Paris is probably a portrait of this ill-fated emperor.[6] He is depicted with his son Manuel II and his grandson John VIII, and all are clad in the bejewelled collars and crowns that were almost surely cheap replicas of the genuine crown jewels of an earlier era.

---

[1]John W. Barker, *Manuel II Palaeologus* (New Brunswick, N.J., 1969), p. 18, n. 214.

[2]Oskar Halecki, *Un empereur de Byzance à Rome* (Warsaw, 1930), pp. 111 ff.

[3]Jean Meyendorf, "Projets de Concile oecumenique en 1367: Un dialogue inédit entre Jean Cantacuzene et le legat Paul," *Dumbarton Oaks Papers* 14 (1960), 151.

[4]For bibliographical details of John V in Venice, see Head, *Imperial Twilight*, pp. 178-179, n. 6.

[5]Doukas, XIII.4 (Magoulias, p. 82).

[6]Barker, *Manuel II*, p. 532, argues convincingly that this is a portrait of John V; Spatharakis, *Portrait*, p. 235, believes, however, that it is John VII.

ANDRONIKOS IV PALAIOLOGOS

1376-1379

The eldest son of John V, Andronikos was born when his father was fifteen years old.[1] In spite of this uncommon closeness in their ages, or perhaps because of it, Andronikos and his father usually got along very badly.

When John made his famous journey to Italy, Andronikos, in his early twenties, was left as regent. Apparently, he enjoyed his position of power a great deal; he was certainly not eager to facilitate his father's return from Venice and did nothing to help him resolve his financial embarrassment there.

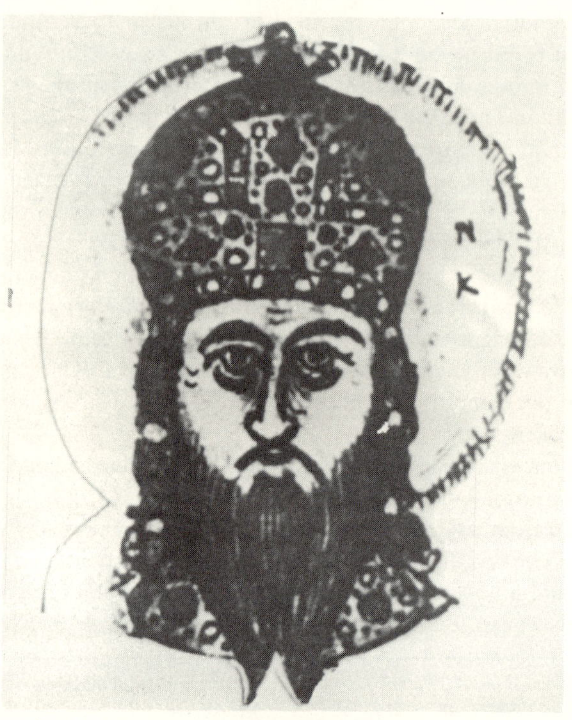

Andronikos IV Palaiologos, pen and wash drawing. Cod. Gr. 122. Biblioteca Estense, Modena.

A few years later we find Andronikos plotting with the Turkish prince Saudji for the overthrow of their respective parents, the emperor and the sultan. This attempted coup was, however, crushed. The sultan had Saudji blinded and ordered that the same be done to Andronikos. John V dared not disobey his overlord openly, but he seems to have contrived that the blinding process used on Andronikos not really destroy his sight. The young man was imprisoned along with his wife Maria-Kyratza Asen and their infant son. Later it was announced that Maria-Kyratza rubbed some wonder-working salve on her husband's eyelids, 'miraculously' restoring his sight.[2]

Another anecdote told of Andronikos' imprisonment relates how one day Maria spied a "snake of marvelous bigness" emerging from a hole in the wall of their cell. She warned Andronikos, who then strangled the snake with his bare hands and had it sent to his father. John V, grieved by this token of the grim living conditions faced by his imprisoned son, granted him his freedom—or, more likely, moved him to a more comfortable place of custody.

In any event, Andronikos finally escaped to the Genoese colony of Pera, across the Golden Horn from Constantinople. With Genoese and Turkish help, he deposed his father and tossed him into a windowless cell in the Tower of Anemas. John's younger sons, Manuel and Theodore, were also incarcerated there.

When, after a reign of three years, Andronikos lost his throne, he again fled to Pera, taking his mother and his aged grandfather, the monk Kantakouzenos, as hostages. John V had to agree to liberal peace terms in order to gain these hostages' release. Andronikos was recognized as co-emperor and heir apparent and sent off as governor to the nearby town of Selymbria.

From this new base of operations, Andronikos renewed hostilities with his father a few years later. War was still raging between them when, in 1385, Andronikos suddenly became very ill and died. Probably more than any of the other Palaiologoi, Andronikos IV undermined the empire, and his early death was no loss to the Byzantine state.

The Modena manuscript provides the only known portrait of Andronikos IV, and reveals that he wore a long flowing forked beard. The Byzantine historian Doukas reports that "Andronikos surpassed all the young men of his age in strength of body and stature, and many in beauty of form." Beyond this, we have no specific details of his appearance.

---

[1]Barker, *Manuel II*, p. 5, n. 8.

[2]Ruy Gonzâlez de Clavijo, *Embassy to Tamerlane: 1403-1406*, trans. Guy Le Strange (London, 1928), p. 86.

[3]Clavijo, *Embassy*, p. 86.

[4]Doukas, XII.1 (Magoulias, p. 79).

JOHN VII PALAIOLOGOS

1390

The future John VII was a baby when he was first imprisoned with his parents after the failure of the Andronikos-Saudji uprising. One report has it that the sultan ordered him blinded along with his father.[1] This is unlikely; but if so, he must have been treated by the same wonder-working salve as his father, for he was definitely not blind. Nonetheless, his earliest memories must have been of prison. It is no wonder that as he grew up, he apparently hated the name of John that he shared with his grandfather John V, and tried (without much success) to change it to Andronikos.[2]

After his father's loss of the throne, young John seems to have spent some time in Genoa and elsewhere outside imperial territory.[3] Little is known of his activities at this time. It was probably not until after his brief reign in 1390 that

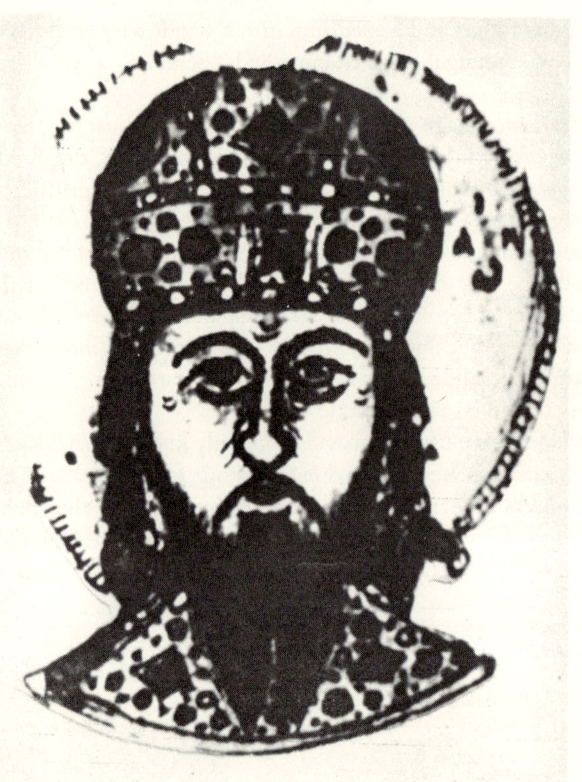

John VII Palaiologos, pen and wash drawing. Cod. Gr. 122. Biblioteca Estense, Modena.

he married Eugenia Gattilusi, his cousin, from the Greco-Italian Gattilusi family, the lords of the Isle of Lesbos. It is uncertain whether they had any children who survived infancy.[4]

In the spring of 1390, John launched the coup that placed him briefly on the throne of his grandfather. The Ottoman Turkish sultan Bayazid, who originally supported him, soon found John VII to be too independent minded to please him and was completely willing to consent to his deposition five months later.

In the years that followed, the deposed emperor continued plotting for the crown that he felt was rightly his. When his uncle Manuel II became emperor and attempted to win his friendship, John at first remained aloof. He was too busy trying to sell his imperial claim to the King of France in return for a French castle and an annual pension. Nothing resulted from this scheme, however, and in 1399, when the emperor Manuel determined to journey to the West to appeal for aid, he was able to convince John VII to reconcile with him.

John was installed as his uncle's co-emperor. Though his habits of devious intrigue continued, on the whole he did a creditable job during Manuel's three-year absence.

When Manuel returned from the West, it was arranged that John VII might keep the title of co-emperor. He moved to Thessaloniki, where he served as imperial governor until shortly before his death in 1408. When he knew that death was near, he became a monk, Brother Joasaph. He left no surviving sons, and thus, with his death, the long feud among the descendants of John V was finally ended.

The Modena manuscript portrait indicates a marked resemblance between John VII and his father Andronikos IV. This is the only definitely identified portrait of John VII.

---

[1]Raymond Loenertz, "La première insurrection d'Andronic Palaeologue [1373]," *Echos d'orient* 38 (1939), 335-336.

[2]For details see Barker, *Manuel II*, pp. 73-74, n. 106.

[3]John W. Barker, "John VII in Genoa: A Problem in Late Byzantine Source Confusion," *Orientalia Christiana Periodica* 28 (1962), 213-238.

[4]George T. Dennis, "An Unknown Byzantine Emperor: Andronikos V Palaiologos (1400-1407?)," *Jahrbuch der Österreichischen Gesselschaft* 16 (1967), 175-187.

MANUEL II PALAIOLOGOS

1391-1425

Manuel Palaiologos, second son of John V, came to the throne in his early forties after an early life of perilous adventure and hardship in the service of his father. Intelligent and scholarly, Manuel had cultivated his literary inclinations during the three years he had been a prisoner in the windowless Tower of Anemas. He was also a military man of considerable ability; against his wishes, he had been forced to serve in the Turkish army and had learned a great deal from it.

Manuel remained unmarried until he became sole emperor; he then selected as his bride a Serbian lady, Helena Dragases. Among their six sons are the last two Byzantine emperors.

Manuel was a handsome man of dignified bearing, though rather short. His hair, probably blond when he was young, turned snowy white, as did his long beard.[1] It was frequently his habit to dress in solid white—the Byzantine mourning color—in token of the sad state of his empire, and those who saw him agreed he was a most impressive sight.

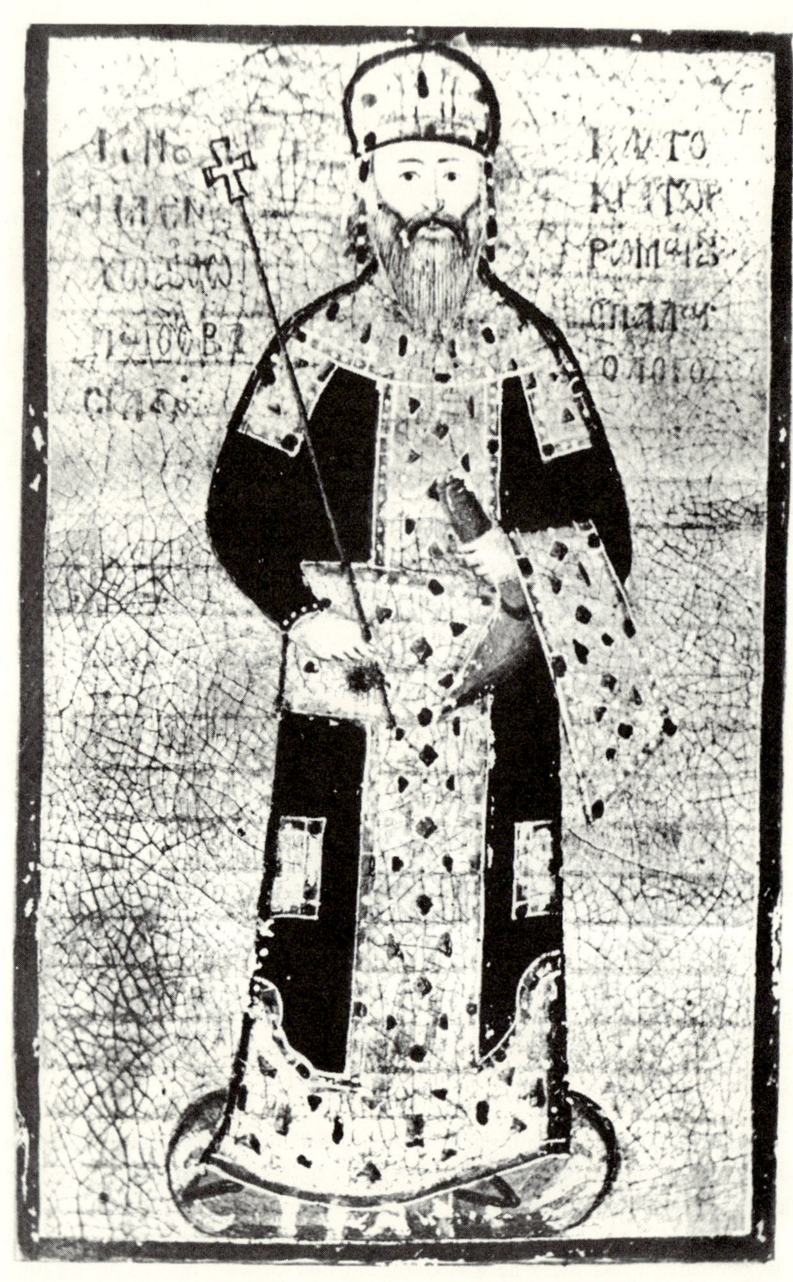

Manuel II Palaiologos, manuscript miniature: Cod. Sup. Gr. 309, f. 6. Bibliothèque Nationale, Paris.

The best of several surviving portraits of Manuel is a beautifully preserved contemporary manuscript miniature from a copy of Manuel's own "Oration on the Death of His Brother Theodore." Here, and also in another manuscript miniature of Manuel and his family, the emperor's eyes are distinctively blue.[2]

With a sense of integrity far above that of most of his contemporaries and a deep, self-sacrificing devotion to his country, Manuel was probably one of the best men ever to rule over Byzantium. In better times, his reign would have been brilliant. As it was, he came to the throne in the worst of times, and still leaves to history an unforgettable impression of dedicated commitment to his task as emperor.

After Turkish forces blockaded Constantinople for several years, Manuel, desperate for help, decided to go in person to western Europe to plead for assistance. The principal goal of his journey was France. The Orthodox Emperor of the East was a sensation in Paris, feted and entertained as visiting royalty should be. But the young French king, Charles VI, was intermittently insane, and France was in no position to send any substantial aid to Byzantium. Manuel also visited England and spent the Christmas holidays of 1400 with King Henry IV. Henry was genuinely interested in crusading, but his own throne was too insecure to permit him to give support to Manuel.[3]

The emperor remained in western Europe for three years; he then learned, much to his relief, that a Tartar attack on the Ottoman state had caused havoc among his enemies. Byzantium was to have an unhoped-for breathing space. Gratefully, Manuel returned home.

For the rest of his long reign, Manuel followed a policy of non-hostility toward the Turks. Though he and the sultan were scarcely friends, they were at least tolerant of one another. While Manuel lived, Byzantium's continued existence was assured.

He lived to the good old age of seventy-five, vigorous and capable almost to the last. Shortly before his death, his deteriorating health caused him to turn over the responsibilities of emperorship to his eldest son, John VIII. Father and son were very different; Manuel was cautious and patient, John daring and headstrong. "Do as you wish, my son," Manuel is reported to have said, "for I am old and near to death. The state and all things in it, I have given to you, so do as you wish."[4]

Old and venerable, bowed by the weight of a stormy past and an uncertain future, Manuel Palaiologos almost seems the embodiment of the dying empire. In spite of—or perhaps because of—the period when he lived, it is no exaggeration to list him among Byzantium's greatest rulers.

---

[1]Barker, *Manuel II*, pp. 396-397.

[2]Spatharakis, *Portrait*, p. 233.

[3]On Manuel's journey to the West, see in particular Barker, *Manuel II*, pp. 168 ff. See also Head, *Imperial Twilight*, pp.109-113 and p.181, n.2.

[4]George Sphrantzes, *Chronicon Minus*. Edited by J. P. Migne. *Patrologia Graeca*, vol. 156, col. 1029a-b.

JOHN VIII PALAIOLOGOS

1425-1448

One of the best-known imperial portraits is that of John VIII, in a fresco in Florence's Medici Chapel. The work of the Italian artist Gozzoli depicts John as one of the Three Wise Men, clad in a splendid Renaissance tunic of green and gold and scarlet boots with golden spurs. John's dark, handsome face is impassive beneath masses of curly brown hair and a helmet crown adorned with feathers. While Gozzoli did not paint the portrait from life, he must have had sketches of John from which to work, and there were many in Florence who no doubt remembered the emperor's famous visit to that city. Another portrait of John—this one from life—is Pisanello's medal of the emperor, on which John wears the 'Greek hat' so fashionable in the mid-fifteenth century. The profile view is most unusual, for the Byzantines themselves superstitiously disliked profiles: such a rendering suggested that the person depicted was not completely there. Pisanello, as an Italian, had no such qualms, nor apparently did John mind this break with tradition. Notes by Pisanello reveal additional interesting details about John: "He was small in stature with bent shoulders; his eyes were grey green, with dark eyebrows, hair and beard."[1]

John's ecumenical efforts at the Council of Ferrara and Florence form the most notable happening of his reign.[2] Like some of the earlier Palaiologoi (especially Michael VIII), John believed that the only way to win military support from Western Europe was by official reunion of the churches. Leaving his brother Constantine as regent, John travelled to Ferrara, Italy in 1437. With him came an entourage of about seven hundred courtiers, churchmen, scholars, and attendants. In Ferrara, John was housed in a palatial monastery while he and his seven hundred Greeks settled down to await the opening of Pope Eugenius IV's Ecumenical Council. Through the summer, John occupied himself with his favorite pastime, hunting. The council finally opened in the fall and, although it was not so well attended as John had hoped, discussions were scheduled to begin. The emperor created a minor furor when he announced that he intended to enter on horseback and ride the entire length of the council hall. This odd idea came from the fact that he was severely crippled and did not want to attempt the long walk with the eyes of the whole council upon him. The Catholic representatives balked at his suggestion, but a compromise was reached: a passage was opened and a door cut just behind the emperor's throne so that he need take only a few steps to reach his seat.[3]

Unfortunately, compromise on the theological issues at stake was not so easily reached. Lengthy debates produced practically no agreements, and when, after several months, the Council moved to Florence (to escape the rumors of plague in Ferrara) they were no closer to a settlement than they had ever been.

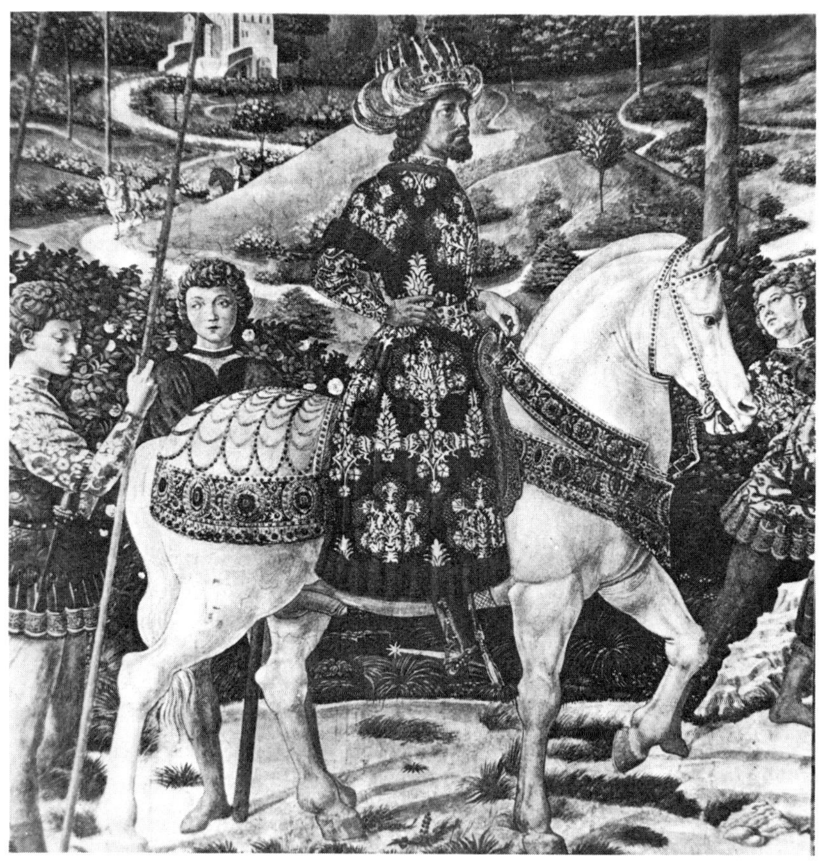

John VIII Palaiologos, detail of fresco by Benozzo Gozzoli. Medici Chapel, Florence.

John sincerely wanted a satisfactory union, and many of those who followed him shared his views, especially the learned Bessarion, who was later to become a cardinal. On the other hand, there was a hard core of opposition from the Orthodox conservatives led by Bishop Mark of Ephesus. Finally, in July 1439, a decree of union was signed by Pope, Emperor, and most of their respective delegates. John VIII believed he had scored a great diplomatic triumph.

When the emperor returned to Constantinople, however, he found widespread public opposition to the "unionizers." Shattered by the personal tragedy of the death of his wife Maria of Trebizond while he was away at the Council, John now lacked strength to implement the Union. Although he remained personally committed to the work of the ecumenical council as long as he lived, he made no effort to force it on his subjects. He knew that most of them opposed him and, unlike Michael VIII, he was not a persecutor.

John had no son to succeed him. His beloved Maria was his third and last wife; earlier he had been married briefly to a young Russian princess, Anna of Moscow, who died of the plague, and an Italian cousin, Sophia Monteferrata, whom he divorced. The crown, John knew, would go to one of his brothers and he preferred Constantine, the most loyal of them, a good soldier and sympathetic to John's ecumenical ideas.

Since there was only small response from western Europe in terms of military aid, Byzantine opposition to the Union grew stronger, if anything, as John's reign wore on. It was a sadly troubled heritage he left to his brother Constantine when he died in 1448.

---

[1]Spatharakis, *Portrait*, p. 53.

[2]Joseph Gill, S.J., *The Council of Florence* (Cambridge, England, 1959), is the definitive work.

[3]Gill, *Council of Florence*, pp. 142-146.

CONSTANTINE XI PALAIOLOGOS

1448-1453

Byzantium's last hero is Constantine Dragases Palaiologos, son of Manuel II and brother of John VIII. Before he succeeded to the throne, Constantine was Despot of the Morea, the Byzantine territory in southern Greece, the only land then left to the empire outside the immediate vicinity of Constantinople. In his younger days, he had won some brilliant victories in the Morea and built it up to be a prosperous and flourishing little state, but the 1440s had been marked by rapid Turkish advance. Thus Constantine had already tasted of sad defeat before he became the last of the emperors.

Though he was not a scholar like his father, there is otherwise much similarity between Constantine XI and Manuel II. Practically all who knew him were impressed by Constantine's valor and his deep sense of integrity. Though he was basically a man of peace, he had spent most of his life at war, and he was prepared to meet whatever might come courageously.

While no contemporary portrait of Constantine survives, a painting by a German artist may be a copy of an earlier work, portraying John VIII.

When the new emperor Constantine arrived in the capital city in 1449, there seemed no immediate threat to the existence of the small Byzantine state, for the old Ottoman sultan Murad II had for years lived on fairly peaceable terms with John VIII. Seemingly there was no reason why this situation should not continue.

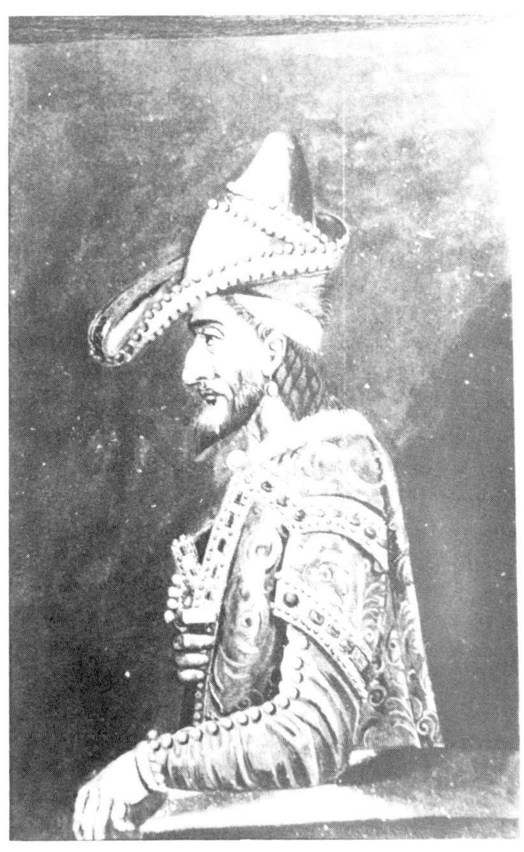

Constantine XI Dragases Palaiologos.

Meanwhile, Constantine XI concerned himself with the search for a bride.[1] He had already been married twice—each time to a Greco-Italian lady who lived only about a year after their marriage—first Magdalena-Theodora Tocco and then his cousin, Caterina Gattilusi. Neither had borne him a son, and now as emperor he sought a third marriage with the hope of providing an heir. Constantine's most trusted friend, George Sphrantzes, set out on a mission to locate a bride. The search would prove fruitless, however, for the princess of Russian Georgia who accepted Constantine's proposal learned before sailing to meet him of the radically altered situation in Constantinople, and thus never left at all.

The new crisis in the making began in 1451 when Sultan Murad died and his teenaged son, Mehmet II, succeeded to the Ottoman throne. The highly intelligent, crafty new sultan was obsessed with the idea of conquering Constantinople, and it was clear that it would be only a matter of time until siege operations began. Constantine sent desperate appeals for help to western Europe, especially to the various Italian states. Although Venice and Genoa each sent some volunteers to aid in the defense of the city, the overall response was discouragingly small. If Constantinople were to survive Mehmet's siege, it would be largely thanks to the ancient walls which had kept out so many foes in the past.[2]

The Ottoman Turks began their formal siege of the ancient city in April, 1453. For seven weeks the Byzantines and their allies heroically repulsed the Turkish attacks, in spite of the fact that the Turks had the advantage of several very large cannons that did extensive damage to the walls. Through the weeks of the siege, the emperor strove bravely to keep up the defenses of the city, to encourage the defenders, and to keep peace among the sundry volunteers who often quarreled among themselves. He had ample opportunity to escape with his life, and even received a promise from the sultan that he would be granted land elsewhere if he would surrender himself. Constantine refused to leave his city; he made it clear that he had no desire to live if Constantinople fell. Consequently he was among the defenders who died fighting for his country on the morning of May 29, 1453, when the Turks finally scaled the walls. With him died the empire that had endured for over a thousand years.

---

[1]Joannis A. Papadrianos, "The Marriage Arrangement between Constantine XI Palaeologus and the Serbian Mara (1451)," *Balkan Studies* 6 (1965), 131-138.

[2]On the siege and fall of Constantinople see Edwin Pears, *The Destruction of the Greek Empire and the Story of the Capture of Constantinople by the Turks* (1903, reprint New York, 1968); Sir Steven Runciman, *The Fall of Constantinople, 1453* (Cambridge, England, 1969).

Selected Bibliography

Section I:
Major Primary Sources Consulted

Akropolites, George. *Annales*. Edited by Immanuel Bekker. Bonn, 1837.

Ammianus Marcellinus. *Res gestae*. Edited with English translation by J.C. Rolfe. 3 vols. Cambridge, Mass., Loeb Classical Library, 1935-1940.

Cedrenus, George. *Compendium historiarum*. Edited by Immanuel Bekker. 2 vols. Bonn, 1838-1839.

Choniates, Niketas. *Historia*. Edited by Immanuel Bekker. Bonn, 1835.

Constantine VII Porphyrogenitus, Emperor. *De Administrando Imperio*. Edited by Gy. Moravcsik with English translation by R.J.H. Jenkins. Washington, 1976.

Doukas of Phokaia. *Istoria turco-bizantina: 1341-1462*. Edited by V. Grecu. Bucharest, 1958. English translation by Harry J. Magoulias, *The Decline and Fall of Byzantium to the Ottoman Turks*. Detroit, 1975.

Eusebius Pamphilus of Caesarea. *Vita Constantini*. English translation anon., *The Life of the Blessed Emperor Constantine*. London, 1845.

Evagrius Scholasticus. *Historia Ecclesiastica*. Edited by J. Bidez and L. Parmentier. London, 1898. English translation E. Walford, *A History of the Church*. London, 1864.

Gregoras, Nikephoros. *Bizantina historia*. Edited by L. Schopen and I. Bekker. 3 vols. Bonn, 1829-1855.

Julian, Flavius Claudius, Emperor. *The Works of the Emperor Julian*. Edited with English translation by Wilmer Cave Wright. 3 vols. Cambridge, Mass., Loeb Classical Library, 1913-1923.

Komnene, Anna. *Alexiad*. Edited by B. Leib. 3 vols. Paris, 1937-1945. English translation by Elizabeth A.S. Dawes, *The Alexiad of the Princess Anna Comnena*. London, 1928; reprint, 1967.

Leo Diaconus. *Historiae*. Edited by C.B. Hase. Bonn, 1828. German translation by Franz Loretto, *Nikephoros Phokas and Johannes Tzimiskes*. Köln, 1961.

Leo Grammaticus. *Chronographia*. Edited by Immanuel Bekker. Bonn, 1842.

Liutprand of Cremona. *Antapodosis; Relatio de legatione Constantinopolitana*. Edited by Joseph Bekker. Hanover, 1915. English translation by F.A. Wright, *The Works of Liudprand of Cremona*. London, 1930.

Malalas, John. *Chronographia*. Edited by Ludwig Dindorf. Bonn, 1831. English translation by M. Spinka and G. Downey, *The Chronicle of John Malalas* (Bks. 8-18). Chicago, 1940.

Manasses, Constantine. *Synopsis historica*. Edited by Immanuel Bekker. Bonn, 1837.

Procopius of Caesarea. *Opera Omnia*. Edited by J. Haury. 3 vols. Leipzig, 1905-06. Edited with English translation by H.B. Dewing and G. Downey. 8 vols. Cambridge, Mass., Loeb Classical Library, 1914-40.

Psellos, Michael. *Chronographia*. Edited by E. Renauld. 2 vols. Paris, 1926-28. English translation by E.R.A. Sewter, *Fourteen Byzantine Rulers*. Baltimore, 1966.

Scriptor Incertus de Leone Bardae Armenii filio. Edited by Immanuel Bekker. [In volume with Leo Grammaticus.] Bonn, 1842.

Symeon Magister (or Logothetes). *Chronicle*. Edited by Immanuel Bekker. Bonn, 1842.

Theophanes Confessor. *Chronographia*. Edited by Carolus de Boor. 2 vols. Leipzig, 1833.

Theophanes Continuatus. *Chronographia*. Edited by Immanuel Bekker. Bonn, 1838.

Section II: Selected Secondary Works on Imperial Iconography and Numismatics

Part A: Books

Catalog of the Byzantine Coins in the Dumbarton Oaks Collection and in the Whittemore Collection. 3 vols. Vol. I (491-602) edited by A.R. Bellinger. Vols. II (602-717 and III (717-1081) edited by Philip Grierson. Washington, 1966-1973. Much more than its name implies, this fascinating set of volumes contains not only the most detailed numismatic study of the period under consideration, but also extensive information on related subjects such as imperial costumes and regalia.

Delbrueck, Richard. *Spätantike Kaiserporträts*. Berlin-Leipzig, 1933. In this very thorough investigation of surviving imperial likenesses, particularly sculptures, from the Late Roman-Early Byzantine centuries, Delbrueck tentatively identified the emperors depicted by many unnamed statues. Though some of his theories have been questioned, his book remains a treasure-trove of data, and contains numerous excellent photographic plates.

Goodacre, Hugh. *A Handbook of the Coinage of the Byzantine Empire*. 2nd ed. London, 1957. A short but significant study of Byzantine coinage, this work also includes entertaining but brief biographical vignettes of the emperors.

Grabar, André. *L'Empereur dans l'art byzantin*. Paris, 1936; reprint, 1971. This is the classic study of imperial portraiture from the standpoint of iconographic significance.

Hendy, Michael F. *Coinage and Money in the Byzantine Empire, 1081-1261*. Washington, 1969. A very helpful work with considerable detail on imperial iconography and costume as well as numismatics.

Houston, Mary Galway. *Ancient Greek, Roman and Byzantine Costume*. 2nd ed. London, 1947; reprint New York, 1963. Contains detailed and helpful descriptions of the ceremonial garments customarily worn by Byzantine rulers.

Lampros, Sp. *Leukoma ton Byzantinon Autokratoron*. Athens, 1930. A classic (but very rare) volume in the study of imperial portraiture, Lampros' *Leukoma* (Album) contains numerous photographic reproductions, particularly of manuscript miniatures and mosaics. Major omissions are largely due to the fact that some of the most important portraits (e.g., the Hagia Sophia mosaics) were unknown at the time of this compilation. Lampros also avoided any consideration of numismatic representations of the emperors or of the Skylitzes manuscript miniatures. On the other hand, he gave a great deal of space to a set of German woodcuts of the Byzantine emperors that could not be called likenesses in the wildest stretches of imagination. In spite of these shortcomings, the *Leukoma* remains an indispensable volume for the study of imperial iconography.

Spatharakis, Iohannis. *The Portrait in Byzantine Illuminated Manuscripts*. Leiden, 1976. An interesting and important recent monograph. Not only emperors and empresses, but other distinguished Byzantines whose likenesses have survived are presented in this study. Numerous black-and-white plates and an excellent bibliography are included.

Whitting, Philip D. *Byzantine Coins*. London, 1973. Probably the best one-volume survey of the complex subject of Byzantine numismatics, this work contains many enlarged photographs of coins, including some excellent color plates. An additional helpful feature is an appendix of descriptive definitions of important items of the Byzantine imperial wardrobe and accessories, while an introductory essay on "Books and Background" provides excellent bibliographic guidance.

Wroth, W. *Catalogue of Imperial Byzantine Coins in the British Museum*. 2 vols. London, 1908; reprint as one vol., 1966. This important publication was the first to use coin photographs rather than sketches. In spite of its age, it remains one of the most important reference works in the field of Byzantine numismatics.

Part B: Shorter Monographs

Bellinger, Alfred R. "The Coins and Byzantine Imperial Policy." *Speculum* 31 (1955), 70-81.

Condurachi, E. "Sur l'origine et l'évolution du loros impérial. *Arta şi Arheologia* 11-12 (1935-36), 37-45.

Galavaris, G.P. "The Symbolism of the Imperial Costume as Displayed on Byzantine Coins." *American Numismatic Society Museum Notes* 8 (1958), 99-117.

Head, Constance. "Physical Descriptions of the Emperors in Byzantine Historical Writing." *Byzantion* 50 (1980), 226-240.

Kondakov, N.P. "Les costumes orientaux à la cour byzantine." *Byzantion* 1 (1924), 7-49.

Lampros. "H. en Rome Ektesis ton Eikonon Autokratoron tou Byzantiou." *Neos Ellenomnemom* 7 (1911), 399-434. Also exists in a French version, *Empereurs byzantines. Catalogue illustré de la collection de portraits des empereurs de Byzance*. Athens, 1911. A very important list of all imperial likenesses known to Lampros.

Section III: Important General Histories

Angold, M. *A Byzantine Government in Exile: Government and Society under the Laskarids of Nicaea, 1204-1261*. London, 1975. An important new study on an often-neglected period of Byzantine history. Cited in Section IV as Angold, *BGE*.

Barker, John W. *Justinian and the Later Roman Empire*. Madison, Wis., 1966. In addition to a very good survey of the reign of Justinian I, this volume contains valuable details on the reigns of his immediate and far less well-known successors. Includes helpful bibliography. Cited in Section IV as Barker, *Justinian*.

Brand, Charles M. *Byzantium Confronts the West: 1180-1204*. Cambridge, Mass., 1968. A detailed examination of the reigns of the later Komnenoi, the Angelos dynasty, and the Fourth Crusade. Emphasis is on Byzantine foreign policy. Cited in Section IV as Brand, *BCW*.

Bury, J.B. *A History of the Later Roman Empire from Arcadius to Irene (395-800)*. 2 vols. London, 1889. For the period 395-565, this early work of the pioneer Byzantinist J.B. Bury is superseded by his later revision, cited below; it remains, however, one of the best available detailed narratives for the years 565-800, and is closely based on Byzantine chronicle sources. Cited in Section IV as Bury, *LRE*[2].

Bury, J.B. *A History of the Later Roman Empire from the Death of Theodosius I to the Death of Justinian (395-565)*. 2 vols. London, 1923; reprint New York, 1958. Bury's detailed knowledge of source materials and his meticulous scholarship make this work one of the best general narratives of the period under consideration. Cited in Section IV as Bury *LRE*[1].

Cambridge Mediaeval History, Vol. IV. *The Byzantine Empire*. Cambridge, England, 1923. Although a newer edition has appeared (see below), the older volume of the *CMH* dealing with Byzantine history has in no way lost its value as an independent work. Edited by J.B. Bury, it contains chapters by Charles Diehl, Albert Vogt, E.W. Brooks, A.A. Vasiliev, and Ferdinand Chalandon, among others, and adheres more closely to the chronological narrative approach than does its successor volume. Cited in the notes and suggested readings as *CMH* (old).

Cambridge Mediaeval History, Vol. IV, pts. 1 and 2. *The Byzantine Empire*. Cambridge, England, 1966-67. The new edition of the Byzantine volume of *CMH* is actually a completely different work, utilizing a somewhat different approach than the older edition. Among the writers of the narrative chapters are such noted modern Byzantinists as M.V. Anastos, Henri Gregoire, Joan M. Hussey, Donald M. Nicol and George Ostrogorsky. Editor is Joan M. Hussey. Cited in Section IV as *CMH* (new).

Diehl, Charles. *Byzantine Empresses*. Translated by Harold Bell and Theresa de Kerpely. New York, 1963. Well-researched biographical essays on thirteen of Byzantium's most famous women by a pioneer of Byzantine scholarship.

Gardner, Alice. *The Lascarids of Nicaea*. London, 1912; reprint Chicago, 1967. Although old, this volume remains an immensely valuable detailed study of the reigns of the emperors of the Laskaris-Vatatzes dynasty, 1204-1261. Cited in Section IV as Gardner, *Lascarids*.

Jenkins, Romilly. *Byzantium: The Imperial Centuries, A.D. 610-1071*. New York, 1966. Jenkins presents an exceptionally well-written chronological history of the Empire from the reign of Herakleios I to the defeat and deposition of Romanos Diogenes. Based on a thorough acquaintance with the primary sources. Jenkins' work also offers many interesting (and sometimes controversial) evaluations of the accomplishments of the various emperors. Cited in Section IV as Jenkins, *B:IC*.

Jones, A.H.M. *The Later Roman Empire, 284-602*. 2 vols. Norman, Okla., 1964. An important study, concentrating on economic history. Cited in Section IV as Jones, *LRE*.

Nicol, Donald M. *The Last Centuries of Byzantium, 1261-1453*. New York, 1972. Nicol details the reigns of the Palaiologos emperors, with special emphasis on political and military events. Good details. Particularly useful is the excellent bibliography. Cited in Section IV as Nicol, *LCB*.

Ostrogorsky, George. *History of the Byzantine State*, 2nd English ed. Translated by Joan Hussey. London, 1968. The best one-volume survey of the entire history of the Empire. Vast bibliographic detail. Cited in Section IV as Ostrogorsky, *HBS*.

Stein, Ernst. *Histoire du Bas-Empire*. Vol. I (in 2 vols. 284-476). Paris, 1959. Vol. II (476-565). Paris-Brussels-Amsterdam, 1949. Vol. I is the French translation with much expansion of Stein's earlier work, *Geschichte des spätrömischen Reiches*. Vienna, 1928. Vol. II was composed in French at the outset. A well researched and very detailed narrative history of the early Byzantine centuries. Cited in Section IV as Stein, *HB-E*.

Stratos, Andreas N. *Byzantium in the Seventh Century*. 4 vols. Translated by Marc Ogilvie-Grant (vol. I) and Harry T. Hionides (Vols. II-IV). Amsterdam, 1968-1978. Stratos' extremely detailed and well-researched volumes begin with the reign of Phokas and are designed to continue through the end of the Herakleian dynasty. (English translation of the concluding volume V has not yet appeared.) Cited in Section IV as Stratos, *B in SC*.

Vasiliev, Alexander. *A History of the Byzantine Empire: 324-1453*. Madison, Wis., 1958. A classic work by one of the most important pioneers of modern Byzantine studies. Somewhat outdated, but still useful. Excellent bibliography.

Section IV:
Selected Reading on Individual Reigns

Constantine I

Alföldi, Andreas. *The Conversion of Constantine and Pagan Rome*. Trans. Harold Mattingly. Oxford, 1948.

Baker, G.P. *Constantine the Great and the Christian Revolution*. London, 1931; reprint New York, 1967.

Baynes, Norman H. *Constantine the Great and the Christian Church*. London, 1929; reprint, 1972.

Burch, Vacher. *Myth and Constantine the Great*. London, 1927.

Eadie, John W., ed. *The Conversion of Constantine*. New York, 1971. [A "problems" book with essays by a number of scholars.]

Firth, John B. *Constantine the Great: The Reorganization of the Empire and the Triumph of the Church*. 1904; reprint Freeport, N.Y., 1971.

Haendler, G. "Das neue Bild des Kaisers Konstantin und der sogennante Konstantinismus," *Theol. Versuche* 4B (1972), 71-81.

Harrison, Evelyn B. "The Constantinian Portrait." *Dumbarton Oaks Papers* 21 (1967), 81-96.

Jones, A.H.M. *Constantine and the Conversion of Europe*. London, 1948.

MacMullen, Ramsay. *Constantine*. New York, 1969.

See also: Jones, *LRE*, 77-111.

Constantius II

Blum, W. "Die Jugend des Constantius II bis zu seinem Regierungsantritt: Eine chronologische Untersuchung," *Classica et Mediaevalia* 30 (1969), 389-402.

Bruns, Gerda. "Zwei bildnisse eines spätrömischen kaisers." *Archäologisches des Deutschen reichs. Jahrbuch* 47 (1932), 135-138; 49 (1934), 61.

Duval, Y.-M. "La venue à Rome de l'empereur Constance II en 357 d'après Ammien Marcellin," *Caesarodunum* 5 (1970), 299-305.

Edbrook Robert Owen Jr. "The Visit of Constantius II to Rome in 357 and its Effect on the Pagan Senatorial Aristocracy." *American Journal of Philology* 97 (1976), 40-61.

Klein, Richard. *Constantius II und die christliche Kirche*. Darmstadt, 1977.

Michaels-Mudd, Mary. "The Arian Policy of Constantius II and its Impact on Church-State Relations in the Fourth-Century Roman Empire." *Byzantine Studies* 6 (1979), 95-111.

See also: Jones, *LRE*, I, 112-119.

Julian

As the last effective pagan emperor of Rome and the only worshipper of the old gods in the long line of Byzantine emperors, Julian remains one of the most

fascinating personalities of late antiquity. For insight into his character, there is no substitute for his own writings, available in English translation by W.C. Wright in the Loeb Library series (3 vols., Cambridge, Mass., 1913-23). Also revealing are the writings of his contemporaries, Ammianus Marcellinus (see Bibliography) and Libanius of Antioch, *Selected Works*, Vol. I, "The Julianic Orations," Trans. A.F. Norman. Cambridge, Mass., 1969.
Worthwhile modern studies of Julian include:

Alföldi, A. "Some Portraits of Julianus Apostate." *American Journal of Archaeology* 66 (1962), 403-405.

Bidez, Joseph. *La Vie de l'empereur Julien*. Paris, 1930; reprint, 1965.

Bowersock, G.W. *Julian the Apostate*. Cambridge, Mass., 1978.

Browning, Robert. *The Emperor Julian*. Berkeley, Cal., 1976.

Head, Constance. *The Emperor Julian*. Boston, 1976.

Kaegi, Walter Emil. "Research on Julian the Apostate, 1945-1964." *Classical World* 58 (1965), 229-238. [Very helpful for bibliography.]

Jovian

Jones, *LRE*, I, 138-139.

Valens

Jones, *LRE*, I, 139-154.

Theodosius I

Downey, Glanville. *Antioch in the Age of Theodosius the Great*.

Duckett, Eleanor. "Theodosius the Great," in *Medieval Portraits from East and West*. Ann Arbor, 1972, pp. 1-13.

Ensslin, Wilhelm. *Die Religionspolitik des Kaisers Theodosius d. Gr.* Munich, 1953.

Hodgkin, Thomas. *The Dynasty of Theodosius*. 1889; reprint New York, 1971.

Jones, D. "The Emperor Theodosius," *History Today* 21 (1971), 669-672.

King, Noel Q. *The Emperor Theodosius and the Establishment of Christianity*. Philadelphia, 1960.

Lippold, Adolf. *Theodosius der Grosse und seine Zeit*. Stuttgart, 1968.

Jones, *LRE*, I, 154-169.

Arcadius

Duckett, Eleanor. "The Empress Eudoxia and Saint John Chrysostom," in *Medieval Portraits from East and West*. Ann Arbor, 1972, pp. 14-57.

Geffroy, Auguste. "La collone d'Arcadius à Constantinople d'après un dessin inédit." *Académie des inscriptions et belles-lettres*. Paris. *Monuments et mémoires* 2 (1895), 99-130.

Strzygowski, Josef. "Die säule des Arkadius in Konstantinopel." *Archäologisches institut des Deutschen reichs. Jahrbuch* 8 (1893), 230-249.

See also: Bury, *LRE*[1], Vol. I, pp. 106-109.
Jones, *LRE*, I, 177-179.

Theodosius II

Diehl, Charles. "Athenais," in *Byzantine Empresses*. New York, 1963, pp. 22-43.

Duckett, Eleanor. "Pulcheria and Theodosius II," in *Medieval Portraits from East and West*. Ann Arbor, 1972, pp. 1972, pp. 121-166.

See also: Bury, *LRE*[1], Vol. I, pp. 212-235.
Jones, *LRE*, I, 173-182.

Marcian

Bury, *LRE*[1], Vol. I, pp. 235-239.

Jones, *LRE*, I, 217-221.

Leo I

Poulson, Vagn. "Le premier byzantin." *Byzantion* 25-27 (1955-57), 509-512.

See also: Bury, *LRE*[1], Vol. I, pp. 314-323.
Jones, *LRE*, I, 221-224.

Leo II

This unfortunate child's reign is too short to merit much if any mention in historical studies. For pertinent details, see the suggested reading for the reign of his father and successor, Zeno the Isaurian.

Zeno

Brooks, E.W. "The EmperorZenon and the Isaurians," *English Historical Review* 8 (1893), 209-238.

See also: Bury, *LRE*[1], Vol. I, pp. 389-404.
Jones, *LRE*, I, 224-230.
Stein, *HB-E*, II, 7-76.

Anastasius I

Capizzi, C. *L'Imperatore Anastasio I (491-518): Studio sulla sua vita, la sua opera e la sua personalita*. (Orientalia Christiana Analecta, 184). Rome,. 1969.

Charanis, Peter, *The Religious Policy of Anastasius I.* Madison, Wis., 1939. Second edition reprinted as *Church and State in the Later Roman Empire*. Thessaloniki, 1974.

See also: Bury, *LRE*[1], Vol. I, pp. 429-452.
Jones, *LRE*, I, 230-237.
Stein, *HB-E*, II, 77-106, 157-217.

Justin I

Most of the works dealing with his far more famous successor Justinian I also contain background on the life and reign of old Justin. See also: Vasiliev, Alexander A. *Justin the First*. Cambridge, Mass., 1950.

See also: Bury, *LRE*[1], Vol. II, pp. 16-23.
Jones, *LRE*, I, 266-269.
Stein, *HB-E*, II, 219-273.

Justinian I

Justinian and his empress Theodora have probably attracted more scholarly attention than any other Byzantine rulers. Among the most outstanding modern studies are:

Baker, G.P. *Justinian*. New York, 1931.

Barker, John W. *Justinian and the Later Roman Empire*. Madison, Wis., 1966.

Bridge, Antony C. *Theodora: Portrait in a Byzantine Landscape*. London, 1978.

Browning, Robert. *Justinian and Theodora*. New York, 1971.

Diehl, Charles. "Theodora," in *Byzantine Empresses*, pp. 44-64.

Diehl, Charles. *Justinien et la civilisation byzantine au VIe siècle. 2 vols. Paris, 1901.*

Downey, Glanville. *Constantinople in the Age of Justinian*. Norman, Okla., 1960.

Holmes, W.G. *The Age of Justinian and Theodora*. 2 vols., 2nd ed. London, 1912.

Ure, Percy Neville. *Justinian and His Age*. Harmondsworth, 1951.

See also: Bury, *LRE*[1], Vol. II, pp. 23-436.
Jones, *LRE*, I, 269-302.
Ostrogorsky, *HBS*, pp. 68-79.
Stein, *HB-E*, II, pp. 275-780.

Justin II

Cameron, Averil. "The Empress Sophia." *Byzantion* 45 (1975), 5-21.

See also: Barker, *Justinian*, pp. 211-219.

Bury, *LRE*[2], Vol. II, pp. 70 ff.
Jones, *LRE*, I, 303-306
Ostrogorsky, *HBS*, p. 79.

Tiberius Constantine

Barker, *Justinian*, pp. 219-221.

Jones, *LRE*, I, 307-309

Ostrogorsky, *HBS*, p. 79.

Maurice Tiberius

Goubert, P. *Byzance avant l'Islam: Byzance et l'Orient sous les successeurs de Justinien: L'Empereur Maurice*. Paris, 1951.

Higgins, M.J. *The Persian War of the Emperor Maurice*. Washington, 1939.

Stratos, A.N. *Byzantium in the Seventh Century*, Vol. I. Amsterdam, 1968, pp. 40-56.

See also: Barker, *Justinian*, pp. 221-229.
Jones, *LRE*, I, 309-315
Ostrogorsky, *HBS*, pp. 79-83.

Phokas

Stratos, *B in SC*, I, 57-91.

Stratos, A.N. "An Unknown Brother of the Emperor Phocas." *Jahrbuch der Österreichischen Byzantinistik* 27 (1978), 11-17.

Veh, Otto. "Zur Geschichte des Kaisers Phokas." *Wissenschaftliche Beilage zum Jahresbericht 1953/54 des Hum. Gymn. Fürth i Bayer.*

See also: Ostrogorsky, *HBS*, pp. 83-86.

Herakleios

Baynes, Norman H. "The Military Operations of the Emperor Heraclius." *The United Services Magazine* 46 (1913), 526 ff. and 47 (1913), 30 ff.

Kaegi, W.E., Jr., "Two Notes on Heraclius." *Revue des Études Byzantines* 37 (1979), 221-227.

Lemerle, Paul. "Quelques remarques sur le règne d'Heraclius." *Centro italiano di studi sull'alto medioevo. Estr. dagli Studi mediaevali.* 3a serie, I, 2 (1960), 347-361.

Pernice, Angelo. *L'Imperatore Eraclio, Saggio di storia bizantina*. Florence, 1905.

Stratos, A.N. *Byzantium in the Seventh Century*, Vol. I, pp. 92-353; Vol. II (Trans. Harry T. Hionides. Amsterdam, 1972), pp. 1-174.

Van Grunsven-Eygenraam, Mariette. "Heraclius and the David Plates." *Bull. ant. Besch*. 48 (1973), 158-174.

See also: Barker, *Justinian*, pp. 231-247.
Jenkins, *B:IC*, 15-35
Ostrogorsky, *HBS*, pp. 92-112.

Herakleios-Constantine

Stratos, *B in SC*, II, pp. 175-185.

See also. Ostrogorsky, *HBS*, pp. 112-114.

Constantine III (also known as Constans II)

Brooks, E.W. "Who Was Constantine Pogonatus?" *Byzantinische Zeitschrift* 17 (1908), 460-462.

Kaestner, Johannes. *De imperio Constantini III (641-668): Dissertatio philologica*. Leipzig, 1907.

Stratos, A.N. *Byzantium in the Seventh Century*, Vol. III. Trans. Harry T. Hionides. Amsterdam, 1975. [Entire volume is devoted to this emperor's reign.]

Westholm, Alfred. "A Hoard of Bronze Coins of Constans II." *Nordisk numismatik aarsskrift*. 1940, pp. 135-147.

See also: Bury, *LRE*², Vol. II, pp. 287 ff.
Jenkins, *B:IC*, pp. 36-42
Ostrogorsky, *HBS*, pp. 114-123.

Constantine IV

Brooks, E.W. "The Brothers of the Emperor Constantine IV." *English Historical Review* 30 (1915), 42-51.

Stratos, A.N. *Byzantium in the Seventh Century*, Vol. IV. Trans. Harry T. Hionides. Amsterdam, 1978. [Constantine IV's reign is the subject of this entire volume.]

See also: Bury, *LRE*², Vol. II, pp. 308 ff.
Jenkins, *B:IC*, pp. 42-50
Ostrogorsky, *HBS*, pp. 123-129.

Justinian II

Breckenridge, James D. *The Numismatic Iconography of Justinian II*. New York, 1959.

Head, Constance. *Justinian II of Byzantium*. Madison, Wis., 1972.

Head, Constance. "On the Date of Justinian II's Restoration." *Byzantion* 39 (1969), 104-107.

Head, Constance. "Towards a Reinterpretation of the Second Reign of Justinian II." *Byzantion* 40 (1970), 14-32.

See also: Jenkins, *B:IC*, pp. 50-59
Ostrogorsky, *HBS*, pp. 129-146.

Leontios

Head, Constance. "Who Was the Real 'Leo the Isaurian'?" *Byzantion* 41 (1971), 105-108.

Kent, J.C.P. "The Mystery of Leontios II." *Numismatic Chronicle* 6th Series, 14 (1954), 217-218.

See also: Jenkins, *B:IC,* pp. 58-59
Ostrogorsky, *HBS*, pp. 140-141.

Tiberius Apsimar

Bury, *LRE*², Vol. II, pp. 354 ff.

Jenkins, *B:IC*, pp. 58-59.

Ostrogorsky, *HBS*, p. 141.

Philippikos Vardan

Bury, *LRE*², Vol. II, pp. 367 ff.

Jenkins, *B:IC*, pp. 59-60.

Ostrogorsky, *HBS*, pp. 152-154.

Anastasios II Artemios

Bury, *LRE*², Vol. II, pp. 370 ff.

Jenkins, *B:IC*, pp. 60-61.

Ostrogorsky, *HBS*, pp. 154-15Q.

Theodosios III

Bury, *LRE*², Vol. II, pp. 372 ff.

Jenkins, *B:IC*, p. 61.

Ostrogorsky, *HBS*, pp. 155-156.

Leo III

Gero, Stephen. *Byzantine Iconoclasm during the Reign of Leo III, with Particular Attention to the Oriental Sources*. Louvain, 1973.

Schenk, Karl. *Kaiser Leo III.* Halle, 1880.

Schenk, Karl. "Kaiser Leons III Waltern im Innern." *Byzantinische Zeitschrift* 5 (1896), 257-301.

See also: *CMH* (old), pp. 1-11.
CMH (new), pp. 61-72.
Jenkins, *B:IC*, pp. 61-68.
Ostrogorsky, *HBS*, pp. 156-165.

Constantine V

Gero, Stephen. *Byzantine Iconoclasm during the Reign of Constantine V, with Particular Attention to the Oriental Sources*. Louvain, 1977.

Lombard, Alfred. *Etudes d'histoire byzantine: Constantin V, empereur des Romaines*. Paris, 1902.

See also: Bury, *LRE*², Vol. II, pp. 450 ff.
CMH (old), pp. 11-19.
CMH (new), pp. 72-81.
Jenkins, *B:IC*, pp. 68-73
Ostrogorsky, *HBS*, pp. 165-175.

Leo IV

CMH (old), p. 19.

CMH (new), pp. 81-82.

Jenkins, *B:IC*, pp. 90-91.

Ostrogorsky, *HBS*, pp. 175-177.

Constantine VI

Bury, *LRE*², Vol. II, pp. 480 ff.

CMH (old), pp. 19-24.

CMH (new), pp. 82-89.

Jenkins, *B:IC*, pp. 92-103.

Ostrogorsky, *HBS*, pp. 177-181.

Irene

Diehl, Charles. "Irene" in *Byzantine Empresses*, pp. 65-93.

Tsirpanlis, Constantine N. "Byzantine Reactions to the Coronation of Charlemagne." *Byzantina* 6 (1974), 347-360.

See also: *CMH* (old), pp. 19-26.
CMH (new), pp. 82-91.
Jenkins, *B:IC*, pp. 92-104.
Ostrogorsky, *HBS*, pp. 177-186.

Nikephoros I

Charanis, Peter. "Nicephorus I, the Saviour of Greece from the Slavs." *Byzantina-Metabyzantina* 1 (1946), 76 ff.

CMH (old), pp. 27-29.

CMH (new), pp. 91-96.

Jenkins, *B:IC*, pp. 117-127.

Ostrogorsky, *HBS*, pp. 186-200.

Stavrakios

This tragic emperor's reign is so short as to merit scarcely a mention in most survey works. See the suggested reading for the reign of his father and predecessor, Nikephoros I.

Michael I Rhangabé

CMH (old), p. 29.

CMH (new), pp. 96-98.

Jenkins, *B:IC*, pp. 127-129.

Ostrogorsky, *HBS*, pp. 197-200.

Leo V Gnuni

CMH (old), pp. 29-32.

CMH (new), pp. 98-100.

Jenkins, *B:IC*, pp. 130-139.

Ostrogorsky, *HBS*, pp. 200-203.

Michael II

CMH (old), pp. 32-34.

CMH (new), pp. 100-102.

Jenkins, *B:IC*, pp. 140-146.

Ostrogorsky, *HBS*, pp. 203-206.

Theophilos

Diehl, Charles. "The Blessed Theodora," in *Byzantine Empresses*, pp. 94-113.

Ciehl, Charles. "La Légende de l'empereur Théophile," *Sem. Kond.* 4 (1931), pp. 31 ff.

Rosser, J. "Theophilus' Khurramite Policy and its Finale: The Revolt of Theophobus' Persian Troops in 838." *Byzantina* 6 (1974), 263-271.

See also: *CMH* (old), pp. 34-40.
CMH (new), pp. 102-104
Jenkins, *B:IC*, pp. 146-152.
Ostrogorsky, *HBS*, pp. 206-209.

Michael III

Grégoire, Henri. "Michel III et Basile le Macedonien dans les inscriptions d'Ancyre." *Byzantion* 5 (1929/30), 327-346.

Jenkins, Romilly J.H. "Constantine VII's Portrait of Michael III." *Bulletin de l'Académie de Belgique* 34 (1948), 71-77.

Karlin-Hayter, Patricia. "Études sur les deux histoires du regne de Michel III." *Byzantion* 41 (1971), 452-496.

Mango, Cyril. "When Was Michael III Born?" *Dumbarton Oaks Papers* 21 (1967), 253-258.

Vasiliev, Alexander. "The Emperor Michael III in Apocryphal Literature." *Byzantina-Metabyzantina* 1 (1946), 237-248.

See also: *CMH* (old), pp. 40-48.
CMH (new), pp. 105-116.
Jenkins, *B:IC*, pp. 153-167.
Ostrogorsky, *HBS*, pp. 217-232.

Basil I

Adontz, N. "L'age et l'origine de l'empereur Basile I." *Byzantion* 8 (1933), 475-500 and 9 (1934), 223-260.

Jenkins, Romilly J.H. "The Classical Background of the *Scriptores post Theophanem*." *Dumbarton Oaks Papers* 8 (1954), 11-30.

Moravcsik, Gyula. "Sagen und Legenden über Kaiser Basileos I." *Dumbarton Oaks Papers* 15 (1961), 59-126.

Spatharakis, I. "The Portraits and Date of the Codex Par. Gr. 510." *Cah. Archeol.* 23 (1974), 97-105.

Tobias, Norman. "Basil I and Byzantine Strategy." *Byzantine Studies* 3 (1976), 30-55.

Tobias, Norman. *Basil I (867-886): The Founder of the Macedonian Dynasty*. Ann Arbor, 1969. [Microfilm.]

Vogt, Albert. *Basil 1er, Empereur de Byzance a la fin du IXe siècle*. Paris, 1908.

See also: *CMH* (old), pp. 49-54.
CMH (new), pp. 114-125.
Jenkins, *B:IC*, pp. 183-197.
Ostrogorsky, *HBS*, pp. 233-241.

Leo VI

Grumel, V. "La Chronologie des événments du règne de Léon VI." *Echos d'Orient* 35 (1936), 5-42.

Jenkins, Romilly J.H. "Three Documents Concerning the Tetragamy." *Dumbarton Oaks Papers* 16 (1962), 229-241.

Mango, Cyril. "The Legend of Leo the Wise." *Zbornik Radova Vizantološkog Instituta* 6 (1950), 59-93.

Stiernon, D. "Léon VI, le Sage, empereur de Constantinople." *Diction. de Spirit.* 9 (1976), 615-623.

Vogt, Albert. "La jeunesse de Léon VI le Sage." *Revue kistorique* 174 (1934), 389-428.

Wood, Dorothy. *Leo VI's Concept of Divine Monarchy Illustrated in a Cave Chapel*. London, 1964.

See also: *CMH* (old), pp. 54-59.
CMH (new), pp. 125-134.
Jenkins, *B:IC*, pp. 198-227.
Ostrogorsky, *HBS*, pp. 241-261.

Alexander

Jenkins, R.J.H. "The Emperor Alexander and the Saracen Prisoners." *Atti dello VIII Congresso Inernazionale di Studi Bizantini* 1 (Rome, 1953), 389-393.

Karlin-Hayter, Patricia. "The Emperor Alexander's Bad Name." *Speculum* 44 (1969), 585-596.

Underwood, P.A. and Ernest J.W. Hawkins. "The Mosaics of Hagia Sophia at Istanbul: The Portrait of the Emperor Alexander." *Dumbarton Oaks Papers* 15 (1961), 189-217.

See also: *CMH* (old), pp. 59-60.
CMH (new), p. 134.
Jenkins, *B:IC*, pp. 227-230.
Ostrogorsky, *HBS*, p. 261.

Constantine VII Porphyrogenitos

Because Constantine VII is one of the few emperors who was also a significant man of letters, his own writings are of considerable importance. These include:

De Administrando Imperio. Edited by Gy. Moravcsik with English translation by R.J.H. Jenkins. Washington, 1967.

Le Livre des Cérémonies, 2nd ed. Edited with French translation by A. Vogt. 2 vols. in 4. Paris, 1967.

Modern works of interest include:

Head, Constance. "Imperial Partners: Constantine VII and Romanus Lecapenus." *History Today* 22 (1972), 624-634.

Rambaud, Alfred N. *L'Empire grec au Xe siècle: Constantin Porphyrogenete*. Paris, 1870; reprint, New York, 1963.

Toynbee, Arnold. *Constantine Porphyrogenitus and his World*. London, 1973.

See also: *CMH* (old), pp. 59-67.
CMH (new), pp. 134-146
Jenkins, *B:IC*, pp. 230-268.
Ostrogorsky, *HBS*, pp. 261-283.

Romanos I Lekapenos

In addition to materials listed below, see selected readings for Romanos' co-emperor, Constantine VII.

Runciman, Sir Steven. *The Emperor Romanus Lecapenus and his Reign*. Cambridge, 1929; reprint, 1969.

See also: *CMH* (old), pp. 61-63.
CMH (new), pp. 137-144.
Jenkins, *B:IC*, pp. 234-255.
Ostrogorsky, *HBS*, pp. 265-279

Romanos II

Diehl, Charles. "Theophano," in *Byzantine Empresses*, pp. 114-135.

See also: *CMH* (old), pp. 67-69.
CMH (new), p. 147.
Jenkins, *B:IC*, pp. 269-276.
Ostrogorsky, *HBS*, pp. 283-284.

Nikephoros II Phokas

Head, Constance. "Nikephoros Phokas, The Morning Star." *Mankind* 3, no. 1 (June, 1971), 8 ff.

Lampsidis, O. "Ein unbekannter Kunstgrift des Nikephoros Phokas bei der Landung auf Chandax (Kreta) (960)." *Byzantinische Zeitschrift* 69 (1976), 9-12.

Schlumberger, Gustave. *Un empereur byzantin au dixieme siècle: Nicéphore Phocas.* Paris, 1890; reprint, 1923.

See also: *CMH* (old), pp. 69-77.
CMH (new), pp. 147-156.
Jenkins, *B:IC*, pp. 270-291.
Ostrogorsky, *HBS*, pp. 284-293.

John I Tzimiskes

Schlumberger, Gustave. *L'Epopée byzantine à la fin du dixième siècle.* 3 vols. Paris, 1896-1905. [Vol. I deals with the reign of John Tzimiskes and the early years of Basil II.]

See also: *CMH* (old), pp. 78-82.
CMH (new), pp. 156-175.
Jenkins, *B:IC*, pp. 290-300.
Ostrogorsky, *HBS*, pp. 293-298.

Basil II

Arbagi, Martin. "The Celibacy of Basil II." *Byzantine Studies* 2 (1975), 41-45.

Schlumberger, G. *L'Epopée byzantine.* [Latter part of Vol. I and all of Vol. II.]

See also: *CMH* (old), pp. 83-96.
CMH (new), pp. 175-192.
Jenkins, *B:IC*, pp. 301-332.
Ostrogorsky, *HBS*, pp. 298-315.

Constantine VIII

CMH (old), pp. 96-98.

CMH (new), pp. 193-195.

Jenkins, *B:IC*, pp. 333-339.

Ostrogorsky, *HBS*, p. 321.

Zoe Porphyrogenita

Diehl, Charles. "Zoe the Porphyrogenita," in *Byzantine Empresses*, pp. 136-173.

Oikonomides, Nicholas. "The Mosaic Panel of Constantine IX and Zoe in Saint Sophia." *Revue des Études Byzantines* 36 (1978), 219-232.

Schlumberger, G. *L'Epopée byzantine*. Vol. III.

Whittemore, Thomas. "A Portrait of the Empress Zoe and of Constantine IX." *Byzantion* 18 (1948), 223-227.

See also: *CMH* (old), pp. 98-115.
CMH (new), pp. 193-200.
Jenkins, *B:IC*, pp. 339-346.
Ostrogorsky, *HBS*, pp. 321 ff.

Romanos III Argyros

Jeanselme, Edouard. "La maladie et la mort de Romaine III Argyre, empereur de Byzance." *Communication à la Soc. Franç. d'hist. de la médecine* 17 (1923).

See also: Selected readings listed for Romanos' wife and co-ruler, Zoe.

Michael IV Paphlagon

See selected readings listed for Michael's wife and co-ruler, Zoe.

Michael V Kalaphates

See selected readings for Michael's adoptive mother and co-ruler, Zoe.

Constantine IX Monomachos

Baranyne, Magda. *The Crown of the Emperor Constantine Monomachos*. Budapest, 1937.

See also: selected readings for Constantine's wife and co-ruler, Zoe.

Theodora Porphyrogenita

Mädler, Heinrich. *Theodora, Michael Stratiotikos, Isaak Komnenos: Ein Stück byzantinischer Kaisergeschichte*. Lepzig, 1894.

See also: *CMH* (old), pp. 115-116.
CMH (new), pp. 204-205.
Jenkins, *B:IC*, pp. 361-363.
Ostrogorsky, *HBS*, pp. 337-338.
Selected readings for Theodora's sister and sometime co-ruler, Zoe.

Michael VI Bringas

CMH (old), pp. 116-118.

CMH (new), p. 205.

Jenkins, *B:IC*, pp. 363-366.

Ostrogorsky, *HBS*, p. 338.

Isaac I Komnenos

Shepard, J. "Isaac Comnenus' Coronation Day." *Byzantinoslavica* 38 (1977), 22-30.

See also: *CMH* (old), pp. 318-324.
CMH (new), pp. 205-207.
Jenkins, *B:IC*, pp. 366-367.
Ostrogorsky, *HBS*, pp. 338-341.

Constantine X Doukas

Polemis, Demetrios I. *The Doukai: A Contribution to Byzantine Prosopography*. London, 1968.

See also: *CMH* (old), pp. 324-325
CMH (new), pp. 207-208.
Jenkins, *B:IC*, p. 367.
Ostrogorsky, *HBS*, pp. 341-344.

Eudokia Makrembolitissa

Flach, Johannes Louis. "Die Kaiserin Eudocia Macrembolitissa: eine Skizze aus dem byzantinischen Gelehrtenleben des elften Jahrhunderts." Tübingen, 1876.

Oikonomides, N. "Le serment de l'impératrice Eudocie." *Revue des Études Byzantines* 21 (1963), 101-128.

See also selected readings for Eudokia's two husbands, Constantine Doukas and Romanos Diogenes.

Romanos IV Diogenes

CMH (old), pp. 325-326

CMH (new), pp. 209-210.

Jenkins, *B:IC*, pp. 369-374.

Ostrogorsky, *HBS*, pp. 344-345.

Michael VII Doukas

CMH (old), pp. 326-327.

CMH (new), p.211.

Ostrogorsky, *HBS*, pp. 345-348.

Nikephoros III Botaneiates

Lieb, B. "Nicéphore III Botaniatès (1078-81) et Marie d'Alanie." *Actes du VIe Congres Intern. d'Études byzantines* 1 (1950), 129-140.

Mely, Fernand de. "Le camée de Nicéphore Botoniate, à l'Heiligenkreuts (Austriche)." *Académie des inscriptions et belles-lettres*. Paris. *Commission de la Fondation Piot: Monuments et Mémoires* 6 (1899), 195-200.

See also: *CMH* (old), pp. 326-327.
CMH (new), pp. 211-212.
Ostrogorsky, *HBS*, pp. 348-349.

Alexios I Komnenos

For the reign of Alexios Komnenos, there is no substitute for the remarkable work written by his own daughter. A good English translation is *The Alexiad of The Princess Anna Comnena*, trans. Elizabeth A.S. Dawes. London, 1928; reprint, 1967.

Significant modern studies include:

Alexandrides, K. "Über die Krankheiten des Kaisers Alexios I. Komnenos." *Byzantinische Zeitschrift* 55 (1962), 69-75.

Buckler, Georgina. *Anna Comnena*. Oxford, 1929.

Chalandon, Ferdinand. *Essai sur le règne d'Alexis Ier Comnène*. Paris, 1900.

Dalven, Rae. *Anna Comnena*. New York, 1972.

De Wald, E.T. "The Comnenian Portraits in the Barberini Psalter." *Hesperia* 13 (1944), 78-86.

Diehl, Charles. "Anna Comnena" and "Irene Ducas" in *Byzantine Empresses*, pp. 174-225.

Ganshof, F.L. "Robert le Frison et Alexis Comnène." *Byzantion* 31 (1961), 57 ff.

Gautier, P. "L'édit d'Alexis Ier Comnène sur la réforme du clergé." *Revue des Études Byzantines* 31 (1973), 166-201.

Head, Constance. "Alexios Komnenos and the English." *Byzantion* 47 (1977), 186-198.

Munro, D.C. "Did the Emperor Alexius I ask for aid at the Council of Piacenza, 1095?" *American Historical Review* 27 (1922), 731 ff.

See also: *CMH* (old), pp. 327-350.
CMH (new), pp. 212-219.
Ostrogorsky, *HBS*, pp. 349-350; 356-375.

John II Komnenos

Browning, Robert. "The Death of John II Comnenus." *Byzantion* 31 (1961), 229-235.

Chalandon, Ferdinand. *Les Comnènes: Jean II Comnène et Manuel I Comnène*. Paris, 1912.

See also: *CMH* (old), pp. 351-361.
CMH (new), pp. 219-226.
Ostrogorsky, *HBS*, pp. 376-380.

Manuel I Komnenos

Brand, Charles M. *Byzantium Confronts the West: 1180-1204*. Cambridge, Mass., 1968, pp. 14-30.

Chalandon, Ferdinand. *Les Comnènes: Jean II Comnène et Manuel I Comnène*. Paris, 1912.

Darrouzes, J. "Decret inédit de Manuel Comnène." *Revue des Études Byzantines* 31 (1973), 307-317.

Diehl, Charles. "Bertha of Sulzbach," in *Byzantine Empresses*, pp. 226-243.

Urbansky, Andrew B. *Byzantium and the Danube Frontier*. New York, 1968.

Vasiliev, Alexander A. "Manuel Comnenus and Henry Plantagenet." *Byzantinische Zeitschrift* 29 (1929-30), 233-244.

Wirth, P. "Kaiser Manuel Komnenos und die Ostgrenze, Rückeroberung und Wiederaufbau der Festung Dorylaion." *Byzantinische Zeitschrift* 55 (1962), 22 ff.

See also: *CMH* (old), pp. 362-379.
CMH (new), pp. 226-243.
Ostrogorsky, *HBS*, pp. 380-394.

Alexios II Komnenos

Brand, Charles. *BCW*, pp. 31-50.

Diehl, Charles. "Agnes of France," in *Byzantine Empresses*, pp. 244-248.

Wirth, Peter. "Wann wurde Kaiser Alexios II Komnenos geboren?" *Byzantinische Zeitschrift* 49 (1956), 65-67.

See also: *CMH* (old), pp. 379-382.
CMH (new), pp. 243-244.
Ostrogorsky, *HBS*, pp. 394-397.

Andronikos I Komnenos

Brand, Charles. *BCW*, pp. 38-75.

Danstrup, John. "Recherches critiques sur Andronicos Ier." *Yearbook of the New Society of Letters at Lund*. Lund, 1944. pp. 71-101.

Diehl, "Agnes of France," in *Byzantine Empresses*, pp. 248-258.

Diehl, Charles. "Les romanesques aventures d'Andronic Comnène." *Figures byzantines*, 2nd ser. Paris, 1908.

Jurewicz, Oktawiusz. *Andronikos I Komnenos*. Amsterdam, 1970.

Minorskii, Vladimir F. "Khaquani and Andronicus Comnenus." *Bulletin of the School of Oriental and African Studies* 11, pt. 3 (London).

Tivčev, P. "Le règne de l'empereur de Byzance Andronic Ier Comnène (1183-1185)." *Byzantinoslavica* 23 (1962), 19-40.

See also: *CMH* (old), pp. 381-384.
CMH (new), pp. 244-245.
Ostrogorsky, *HBS*, pp. 395-400.

Isaac II Angelos

Brand, Charles. *BCW*, pp. 76-116.

Cognasso, F. "Un imperatore bizantino della decadenza: Isacco II Angelo." *Bessarione* 31 (1915), 29-60 and 247-289.

McNeal, Edgar H. "The Story of Isaac and Andronikos." *Speculum* 9 (1934), 324-329.

See also: *CMH* (old), p. 384.
CMH (new), pp. 245-247.
Ostrogorsky, *HBS*, pp. 401-408.

Alexios III Angelos

Brand, Charles. *BCW*, pp. 117-157.

See also: *CMH* (old), p. 384.
CMH (new), pp. 247-249.
Ostrogorsky, *HBS*, pp. 408-415.

Alexios IV Angelos

Works having to do with the Fourth Crusade are appropriate not only for the short and unfortunate reign of Alexios IV, but also for his immediate predecessor and successor.

Bradford, Ernie. *The Great Betrayal: Constantinople, 1204*. London, 1967.

Brand, Charles. *BCW*, pp. 236-251.

Queller, Donald E. *The Fourth Crusade: The Conquest of Constantinople, 1201-1204*. Philadelphia, 1977.

Queller, Donald E., ed. *The Latin Conquest of Constantinople*. New York, 1971.

See also: *CMH* (old), pp. 415-419.
CMH (new), pp. 275-284.
Ostrogorsky, *HBS*, pp. 415-416.

Alexios V Doukas Mourtzouphlos

Brand, Charles. *BCW*, pp. 248-257.

See also: *CMH* (old), p. 419.
CMH (new), pp. 284-286.
Ostrogorsky, *HBS*, p. 416.

Theodore I Laskaris

Angold, M. *A Byzantine Government in Exile: Government and Society under the Laskarids of Nicaea, 1204-1261*. London, 1975.

Gardner, Alice. *The Lascarids of Nicaea*. London, 1912; reprint Chicago, 1967. pp. 52-115.

See also: *CMH* (old), pp. 478-486.
CMH (new), pp. 295-296.
Ostrogorsky, *HBS*, pp. 427 ff.

John III Doukas Vatatzes

Amantos, C. "Giovanni Ducas Batatzis." *Atti dello VIII Congresso Internazionale di Studi Bizantini* 1 (Rome, 1953), 313-314.

Angold, *BGE*.

Diehl, "Constance of Hohenstaufen," in *Byzantine Empresses*, pp. 259-275.

Gardner, *Lascarids*, pp. 116-196.

Heisenberg, A. "Kaiser Johannes Batatzes der Barmherzige." *Byzantinische Zeitschrift* 14 (1905), 160 ff.

Merendino, E. "Federico II e Giovanni III Vatatzes." *Byzantino Sicula II-Quad. dell'Istit. di Studi Bizant. e Neoell.* 8 (1975), 371-383.

See also: *CMH* (old), pp. 486-500.
CMH (new), pp. 307-321.
Ostrogorsky, *HBS*, pp. 434 ff.

Theodore II Laskaris

Angold, *BGE*.

Draseke, J. "Theodore Laskaris." *Byzantinische Zeitschrift* 3 (1894), 498-515.

Gardner, *Lascarids*, pp. 197-232.

Pappadopoulos, J.B. *Theodore II Lascaris, empereur de Nicée*. Paris, 1908.

See also: *CMH* (old), pp. 500-506.
CMH (new), pp. 321-324.
Ostrogorsky, *HBS*, pp. 444-446.

John IV Laskaris

Angold, *BGE*.

Gardner, *Lascarids*, pp. 231-240.

See also: *CMH* (old), pp. 506-508.
CMH (new), p. 324.
Ostrogorsky, *HBS*, pp. 446-450.

Michael VIII Palaiologos

Chapman, Conrad. *Michel Paléologue, restaurateur de l'Empire byzantin*. Paris, 1926.

Geanakoplos, D. J. *Emperor Michael Palaeologus and the West*. Cambridge, 1959.

Gill, Joseph. "Notes on the *De Michaele et Andronica Palaeologis* of George Pachymeres." *Byzantinische Zeitschrift* 68 (1975), 295-303.

Nicol, Donald M. *The Last Centuries of Byzantium*. New York, 1972. pp. 45-96.

See also: *CMH* (old), pp. 507-513.
CMH (new), pp. 324-340.
Ostrogorsky, *HBS*, pp. 446-465.

Andronikos II Palaiologos

Alexander, Paul J. "A Chrysobull of the Emperor Andronicus II Palaeologus in Favor of the See of Kanina in Albania." *Byzantion* 15 (1940-41), 167-207.

Bănescu, N. "Le patriarche Athanase Ier et Andronic II Palaeologue: État religieux, politique et social de l'Empire." *Académie Roumaine: Bulletin de la section historique* 23 (1942), 28-56.

Diehl, Charles. "Yolande of Montferrat," in *Byzantine Empresses*, pp. 276-286.

Gill, Joseph. "Emperor Andronicus II and Patriarch Athanasius I." *Byzantina* 2 (1970), 13-19.

Laiou, Angeliki E. *Constantinople and the Latins: The Foreign Policy of Andronicus II*. Cambridge, Mass. 1972.

Lowe, Alfonso. *The Catalan Vengeance*. Boston, 1972.

Marinesco, C. "Tentatives de mariage de deux fils d'Andronic Paléologue avec des princesses latines." *Revue historique du sud-est Européen* 1(1924), 139-143.

Nicol, *LCB*, pp. 99-171.

Spatharakis, I. "The Proskynesis in Byzantine Art: A Study in Connection with a Nomisma of Andronicus II Palaeologus." *Bulletin ant. Beschav.* 49 (1974), 190-215.

See also: *CMH* (new), pp. 340-354.
Ostrogorsky, *HBS*, pp. 480-498.

Andronikos III Palaiologos

Bosch, Ursula V. *Kaiser Andronikos III Palaiologos: Versuch einer Darstellung der Byzantinischen Geschichte in den Jahren 1321-1341*. Amsterdam, 1965.

Diehl, Charles. "Anna of Savoy," in *Byzantine Empresses*, pp. 287-308.

Nicol, *LCB*, pp. 159-190.

See also: *CMH* (new), pp. 350-356.
Ostrogorsky, *HBS*, pp. 499-510.

John VI Kantakouzenos

Charanis, Peter. "Internal Strife in Byzantium During the Fourteenth Century." *Byzantion* 15 (1940-41), 208-230.

Meyendorf, Jean. "Projets de Concile oecuménique en 1367: Un dialogue inedit entre Jean Cantacuzène et le legat Paul." *Dumbarton Oaks Papers* 14 (1960), 149-177.

Nicol, Donald M. "The Abdication of John Cantacuzene." *Byzantinische Forschungen* 2 (Amsterdam, 1967), 269-283.

Nicol, Donald M. *The Byzantine Family of Kantakouzenos (Cantacuzenus), ca. 1100-1460*. Washington, 1968.

Nicol, *LCB*, pp. 191-261.

Parisot, Valentin. *Cantacuzène, homme d'état et historien*. Paris, 1845.

Weiss, Günter. *Joannes Kantakouzenos: Aristokrat, Staatsman, Kaiser und Mönch*. Wiesbaden, 1969.

See also: *CMH* (new), pp. 356-367.
Ostrogorsky, *HBS*, pp. 514-531.

John V Palaiologos

Charanis, Peter. "The Strife Among the Palaeologi and the Ottoman Turks, 1370-1402." *Byzantion* 16 (1942-43), 286-315.

Charanis, Peter. "An Additional Note to the Article, 'The Strife Among the Palaeologi and the Ottoman Turks, 1370-1402.' " *Byzantion* 17 (1944-45), 330.

Chrysostomides, Julian. "John V Palaeologus in Venice (1370-71) and the Chronicle of Caroldo: a Reinterpretation." *Orientalia Christiana Periodica* 31 (1965), 76-84.

Gill, Joseph. "John V Palaeologus at the Court of Louis I of Hungary (1366)." *Byzantinoslavica* 38 (1977), 31-38.

Halecki, Oscar. "Two Palaeologi in Venice, 1320-1371." *Byzantion* 17 (1944-45), 331-335.

Halecki, Oscar. *Un Empereur de Byzance à Rome: Vingt ans de travail pour l'Union des églises et pour la defence de l'empire d'orient*. Warsaw, 1930.

Loenertz, Raymond-J. "Jean V Paléologue à Venise (1370-1371)." *Revue des Études Byzantines* 16 (1958), 217-232.

Loenertz, Raymond-J. "Une Erreur Singulière de Laonic Chalcocandyle: Le prétendu second mariage de Jean V Paléologue." *Revue des Études Byzantines* 15 (1957) 176-181.

Nicol, *LCB*, pp. 265-309.

See also: *CMH* (new), pp. 356-374.
Ostrogorsky, *HBS*, pp. 534-549.

Andronikos IV Palaiologos

Loenertz, Raymond-J. "La Première insurrection d'Andronic Paléologue." *Echos d'Orient* 38 (1939), 334-345.

Nicol, *LCB*, pp. 288-296.

See also: *CMH* (new), pp. 372-373.
Ostrogorsky, *HBS*, pp. 539 ff.

John VII Palaiologos

Barker, John W. "John VII in Genoa: A Problem in Late Byzantine Source Confusion." *Orientalia Christiana Periodica* 28 (1962), 213-238.

Dennis, George T. "An Unknown Byzantine Emperor, Andronicus V Palaeologus (1400-1407?)" *Jahrbuch der Österreichischen Byzantinischen Gesselschaft* 16 (1967), 175-187.

Dölger, Franz. "Johannes VII, Kaiser der Rhomäer, 1390--1408." *Byzantinische Zeitschrift* 31 (1931), 21-36.

Nicol, *LCB*, pp. 302-303.

Wirth, P. "Manuel II Palaiologos und der Johanniterorden: Zur Genesis der Allianz gegen Johannes VII." *Byzantina* 6 (1974), 385-389.

Wirth, P. "Zum Geschichtesbild Kaiser Johannes' VII Palaiologos." *Byzantion* 35 (1965), 592-600.

See also: *CMH* (new), p. 374.
Ostrogorsky, *HBS*, pp. 547 ff.

Manuel II Palaiologos

Barker, John W. *Manuel II Palaeologus*. New Brunswick, N.J., 1969.

Barker, John W. "On the Chronology of the Activities of Manuel II Palaeologus in the Morea in 1415." *Byzantinische Zeitschrift* 55 (1962), 39-55.

Dennis, George T., ed. and trans. *The Letters of Manuel II Palaeologus*. Washington, 1967.

Dennis, George T. "Official Documents of Manuel II Palaeologus." *Byzantion* 41 (1971), 45-58.

Dennis, George T. *The Reign of Manuel II Palaeologus in Thessalonica, 1382-1387*. Rome, 1960.

Jugie, M. "Le Voyage de l'empereur Manuel Paléologue en Occident (1399-1403)." *Echos d'Orient* 15 (1912), 322-332.

Marinesco, C. "Deux empereurs byzantins: Manuel II et Jean VIII Paléologue, vus par des artistes occidentaux." *Le Flambeau* 40 (Nov.-Dec., 1957), 759-762.

Nicol, Donald M. "A Byzantine Emperor in England: Manuel II's Visit to London in 1400-1401." *University of Birmingham Historical Journal* 12, 2 (1971), 204-225.

Schlumberger, Gustave. *Un Empereur de Byzance à Paris et à Londres*. Paris, 1916.

Wessel, K. "Manuel II und seine Familie. Zur Miniatur des Cod. Ivoires A 53 des Louvre." *Festschrift H. Wentzel*. Berlin, 1975. pp. 219-229.

See also: *CMH* (new), pp. 375-380.
Ostrogorsky, *HBS*, pp. 542-560.

John VIII Palaiologos

Gill, Joseph. *The Council of Florence*. Cambridge, 1959.

Gill, Joseph. *Personalities of the Council of Florence*. New York, 1964.

Nicol, *LCB*, pp. 357-389.

Vasiliev, Alexander A. "Pero Tafur, A Spanish Traveler of the Fifteenth

Century and his Visit to Constantinople, Trebizond, and Italy." *Byzantion* 7 (1932), 75-122.

See also: *CMH* (new), pp. 380-385.
Ostrogorsky, *HBS*, pp. 560-567.

Constantine XI Palaiologos

Amantos, Constantine. "La Prise de Constantinople." *Le Cinq Centième Anniversaire de la Prise de Constantinople: L'Hellénisme Contemporain*. Athens, 1953, pp. 9-22.

Carroll, Margaret. "Notes on the Authorship of the 'Siege' Section of the *Chronicon Maius* of Pseudo-Phrantzes, Book III." *Byzantion* 41 (1971), 28-44.

Kolias, G. "Constantin Paléologue. Le dernier defenseur de Constantinople." *L'Hellénisme Contemporain*. Athens, 1953, pp. 41-54.

Mijatovich, Chedomil. *Constantine Palaeologus*. 1892; reprint Chicago, 1968.

Nicol, *LCB*, pp. 390-417.

Papadrianos, Ioannis A. "The Marriage Arrangement Between Constantine XI Palaeologus and the Serbian Mara (1451)." *Balkan Studies* 6 (1965), 131-138.

Pears, Edwin. *The Destruction of the Greek Empire and the Story of the Capture of Constantinople by the Turks*. 1903; reprint New York, 1968.

Runciman, Sir Steven. *The Fall of Constantinople, 1453*. Cambridge, 1965.

See also: *CMH* (new), pp. 385-387.
Ostrogorsky, *HBS*, pp. 567-571.

Appendix I

Emperors and Empresses of Byzantium

Emperor	Empress
Constantine I	Fausta
Constantius	Galla
	Eusebia of Macedonia
	Faustina of Antioch
Julian	Helena, daughter of Constantine I
Jovian	Charito
Valens	Albia Domnica
Theodosius I	Aelia Flaccilla
	Galla, daughter of Valentian I
Arcadius	Eudoxia the Frank
Theodosius II	Athenaïs-Eudokia of Athens
Marcian	Pulcheria, daughter of Arcadius
Leo I	Verina
Leo II	(unmarried, died in childhood)
Zeno	Ariadne, daughter of Leo I
Anastasios I	Ariadne, daughter of Leo I
Justin I	Lupicinia-Euphemia
Justinian I	Theodora
Justin II	Sophia, niece of Theodora
Tiberius Constantine	Ino-Anastasia
Maurice Tiberius	Constantina, daughter of Tiberius Constantine
Phokas	Leontia
Herakleios I	Fabia-Eudokia
	Martina
Herakleios-Constantine	Gregoria-Anastasia
Herakleios II (Heraklonas)	(unmarried)
Constantine III (Constans)	Fausta
Constantine IV	Anastasia
Justinian II	Eudokia
	Theodora of the Khazars
Leontios	unknown

Tiberius Apsimar	unknown
Philippikos Vardan	unknown
Anastasios II Artemios	Irene
Theodosios III	unknown
Leo III	Maria
Constantine V	Irene of the Khazars Maria Eudokia
Leo IV	**Irene of Athens**
Constantine VI	Maria of Amnia Theodote
Nikephoros I	unknown
Stavrakios	Theophano of Athens
Michael I Rhangabé	Prokopia, daughter of Nikephoros I
Leo V	Barca-Theodosia
Michael II	Thekla Euphrosyne, daughter of Constantine VI
Theophilos	Theodora the Blessed
Michael III	Eudokia Dekapolitissa
Basil I	Eudokia Ingerina
Leo VI	Theophano Zoe Zautzina Eudokia Baiane Zoe Carbopsina
Alexander	unknown
Constantine VII	Helena Lekapena, daughter of Romanos I
Romanos I Lekapenos	Theodora
Romanos II	Bertha-Eudokia the Frank Theophano
Nikephoros II Phokas	Theophano, widow of Romanos II
John I Tzimiskes	Theodora, daughter of Constantine VII
Basil II	(unmarried)
Constantine VIII	Helena Alypia
Romanos III Argyros	**Zoe Porphyrogenita**
Michael IV Paphlagon	**Zoe Porphyrogenita**
Michael V Kalaphates	unknown (probably unmarried)
Constantine IX Monomachos	**Zoe Porphyrogenita**
(unmarried)	**Theodora Porphyrogenita**
Michael VI Bringas	unknown

Isaac I Komnenos	Aikaterini of Bulgaria
Constantine X Doukas	**Eudokia Makrembolitissa**
Romanos IV Diogenes	**Eudokia Makrembolitissa**
Michael VII Doukas	Maria of Alania
Nikephoros III Botaneiates	Verdenia
	Maria of Alania
Alexios I Komnenos	Irene Doukaina
John II Komnenos	Priska-Irene of Hungary
Manuel I Komnenos	Bertha-Irene of Sulzbach
	Marie of Antioch
Alexios II Komnenos	Agnes-Anne of France
Andronikos I Komnenos	Agnes-Anne of France
Isaac II Angelos	Margaret-Mary of Hungary
Alexios III Angelos	Euphrosyne Doukaina Kamatera
Alexios IV Angelos	(unmarried)
Alexios V Doukas Mourtzouphlos	Eudokia Angelina, daughter of Alexios III
Theodore I Laskaris	Anna Angelina, daughter of Alexios III
	Philippa of Armenia
	Marie de Courtenay
John III Doukas Vatatzes	Irene Laskaris, daughter of Theodore I
	Constance-Anna Hohenstauffen
Theodore II Laskaris	Helen Asen of Bulgaria
John IV Laskaris	(unmarried)
Michael VIII Palaiologos	Theodora Doukaina
Andronikos II Palaiologos	Anna of Hungary
	Yolande-Irene of Montferrat
Andronikos III Palaiologos	Adelheid-Irene of Brunswick
	Anne of Savoy
John VI Kantakouzenos	Irene Asen
John V Palaiologos	Helena Kantakouzene, daughter of John VI
Andronikos IV Palaiologos	Maria-Kyratza Asen
John VII Palaiologos	Eugenia Gattilusi
Manuel II Palaiologos	Helena Dragases
John VIII Palaiologos	Anna of Moscow
	Sophia Monteferrata
	Maria Komnene of Trebizond
Constantine XI Palaiologos	Magdalena-Theodora Tocco
	Caterina Gattilusi

Index